Editorial Project Manager
Karen J. Goldfluss, M.S. Ed.

Editor-in-Chief
Sharon Coan, M.S. Ed.

Art Coordinator
Cheri Macoubrie Wilson

Creative Director
Elayne Roberts

Cover Artists
Denise Bauer

Imaging
James Edward Grace

Production Manager
Phil Garcia

Acknowledgements
ClarisWorks screen shots and clip art courtesy of Apple Computer, Inc. Used with permission.

Publishers
Rachelle Cracchiolo, M.S. Ed.
Mary Dupuy Smith, M.S. Ed.

P9-BZF-059

The Best of Multiple Intelligences Activities

from

Teacher Created Materials

Compilation By

Tiffany Alvis, Gannon Burks, Susan Hasegawa, Lisa Huntsman, Sheila Kopka, Nicole Krause, Stephanie Larson, Cara Laughlin, Linda Madrid, Naoko Mizuta, Susan Nybida, Nicole Nichols, Shelby Olmstead, Leigh Ann Romero, Jennifer Rungo, Jason Safranek, Colette Seu, Allison Smith, Emily Stacks, Erika Svedeman, Karen Tompkins, and Ben Dillow (Professor, The University of Redlands, CA).

Updates to the Web sites featured in our books
are available at:

www.teachercreated.com

Teacher Created Materials, Inc.
6421 Industry Way
Westminster, CA 92683
www.teachercreated.com

©1999 Teacher Created Materials, Inc.
Reprinted, 2004

Made in U.S.A.
ISBN-1-57690-464-4

Table of Contents

Table of Contents *(cont.)*

Introduction

The educational community has been clamoring for change for many years. Journal headlines suggest solutions. Politicians offer advice. Parents have their ideas of what should be done. There has been a growing trend in home schooling. Teachers are frustrated. Administrations seem ineffective. All of this scurrying about has had dire effects on the very people we are trying to help—the students!

What is the solution? Many creative people have developed curricula, new approaches to learning, and new teaching techniques. Teachers often go to seminars heralding a "new, improved, and guaranteed successful" approach to classroom instruction. These presentations are often inspiring and full of great ideas. More often than not, teachers find themselves going back to their same classrooms, full of intent to implement these ideas, only to find the same textbooks, the same students, and the same old attitude about new ideas taking too much energy.

Teachers do not give up their quests for solutions, however. They keep searching, and once in awhile they find a theory, technique, or idea that really works for them, and they embrace it. Teachers adopted the theory of multiple intelligences because it did not require the discarding of previous ideas. Instead of starting over with some brand new plan, they could just supplement the good things they were already doing with ideas that would reach even more of their students.

The theory of multiple intelligences makes sense. It involves taking what teachers already do in the classroom and expanding that to enable them to be more successful with all of their students. We have all heard quotes about the fraction of our brains that we use. Studies have shown that only 10%–25% of the human brain is actually used. The theory of multiple intelligences ensures whole-brain learning. The use of different parts of the brain guarantees that teachers and students alike will use larger portions of their brains. The theory is encouraging and does not limit anyone to a preconceived notion of how smart they are. It stresses real-life learning, not the memorization of artificial, irrelevant snatches of information.

Celebrate learning with your students. Let them know that their potential is limitless. Help them develop into successful, self-confident, well-rounded citizens by incorporating multiple intelligences into their lives. Putting this theory in practice has improved the personal and professional lives of teachers in amazing ways.

What Are the Multiple Intelligences?

Although he reminds us there could be many more, the eight intelligences identified by Howard Gardner, author of *Frames of Mind*: *The Theory of Multiple Intelligences* (Basic Books, 1983), are the following:

☞ **Verbal/Linguistic**	☞ **Logical/Mathematical**
☞ **Visual/Spatial**	☞ **Musical/Rhythmic**
☞ **Bodily/Kinesthetic**	☞ **Interpersonal**
☞ **Intrapersonal**	☞ **Naturalist**

(Verbal/Linguistic and Logical/Mathematical intelligences are the most recognized, appreciated, and taught. They are the intelligences that assure success in school.)

Verbal/Linguistic

Verbal/linguistic intelligence is also called verbal intelligence. It is different from the other intelligences because everyone who speaks can be said to possess it at some level, although it is clear that some people are more linguistically talented than others. Verbal/linguistic intelligence expresses itself in words, both written and oral, and in auditory skills. People who have this kind of intelligence can learn by listening. They like to read, write, and speak, and they like to play with words. They are often seen as possessing high levels of the other intelligences simply because standard testing tools usually rely on verbal responses, no matter which type of intelligence is being assessed.

Logical/Mathematical

Logical/mathematical intelligence includes scientific ability. It is the kind of intelligence that is often called "critical thinking." People with this kind of intelligence like to do things with data; they see patterns and relationships. They like to solve mathematical problems and play strategy games, such as checkers and chess. They tend to use graphic organizers both to please themselves and to present their information to others. This kind of intelligence is highly valued in our technological society.

Visual/Spatial

Visual/spatial intelligence is sometimes called visual intelligence. People with this kind of intelligence tend to think in pictures and learn best from visual presentations such as movies, pictures, videos, and demonstrations using models and props. They like to draw, paint, or sculpt their ideas and often represent moods and feelings through art. They are good at reading maps and diagrams and they enjoy solving mazes and putting together jigsaw puzzles. Visual/spatial intelligence is often experienced and expressed through daydreaming, imagining, and pretending.

What Are the Multiple Intelligences? *(cont.)*

Musical/Rhythmic

Musical/rhythmic intelligence is sometimes called rhythmic or musical intelligence. People with this kind of intelligence are sensitive to sounds, environmental as well as musical. They often sing, whistle, or hum while engaging in other activities. They love to listen to music; they may collect CDs and tapes, and they often play an instrument. They sing on key and can remember and vocally reproduce melodies. They may move rhythmically in time to music (or in time to an activity) or make up rhythms and songs to help them remember facts and other information. If musical/rhythmic intelligence is not recognized as a talent, it is often treated as a behavior problem.

Bodily/Kinesthetic

Bodily/kinesthetic intelligence is sometimes called kinesthetic intelligence. People with this kind of intelligence process information through the sensations they feel in their bodies. They like to move around, act things out, and touch the people they are talking to. They are good at both small and large muscle skills and enjoy physical activities and sports of all kinds. They prefer to communicate information by demonstration or modeling. They can express emotion and mood through dance.

Interpersonal

Interpersonal intelligence is evident in the individual who enjoys friends and social activities of all kinds and is reluctant to be alone. People with this kind of intelligence enjoy working in groups, learn while interacting and cooperating, and often serve as mediators in case of disputes, both in a school situation and at home. Cooperative learning methods could have been designed just for them, and probably the designers of cooperative learning activities as an instructional method have this kind of intelligence also.

Intrapersonal

Intrapersonal intelligence is shown through a deep awareness of inner feelings. This is the intelligence that allows people to understand themselves, their abilities, and their options. People with intrapersonal intelligence tend to be independent and self-directed and have strong opinions on controversial subjects. They have a great sense of self-confidence and enjoy working on their own projects and just being alone.

Naturalist

Naturalist intelligence is the eighth intelligence to meet Howard Gardner's criteria. According to Gardner, this intelligence focuses on the individual's ability "to recognize and discriminate among flora and fauna, and other things in the world like clouds and rocks."

Eight Criteria for Defining the Intelligences

- **Each of the intelligences can potentially be isolated by brain damage.** Gardner worked with people who had suffered brain damage, through accidents or illness, at the Boston Veterans Administration. He found that in some instances, brain damage could destroy a person's ability in one intelligence area and leave the other intelligences intact.

- **Each of the intelligences exists in exceptional people (savants or prodigies).** This means that there might be people who are exceptionally musically talented but who cannot get along well with others, have difficulty communicating, and have a hard time functioning in regular life experiences.

- **Each of the intelligences has a process of developing during normal child development and has a peak end-state performance.** For example, the verbal/linguistic intelligence presents itself in early childhood, while logical/mathematical intelligence peaks in adolescence and early adulthood.

- **Each of the intelligences is evidenced in species other than human beings.** We hear music and rhythm in bird songs. We find the visual/spatial intelligence in a bat's ability to navigate without eyesight.

- **Each of the intelligences has been tested using various measures not necessarily associated with intelligence.** For example, interpersonal and intrapersonal intelligences have been tested with the Coopersmith Self-Esteem Inventory. The Wechsler Intelligence Scale has been used to test logical/mathematical and linguistic/verbal abilities, as well as visual/spatial intelligence through picture arrangements in a subtest.

- **Each of the intelligences can work without the others being present.** For instance, a student who reads well, with good comprehension, might have trouble building a model using written directions because he or she cannot make a transfer between the two intelligences (verbal/linguistic and visual/spatial).

- **Each of the intelligences has a set of identifiable operations.** Gardner compares this to a computer needing a set of operations in order to function (like DOS). He suggests that each of the intelligences will one day be able to manifest itself in computer form because we can specify the steps necessary to do what each intelligence enables us to do.

- **Each of the intelligences can be symbolized or has its own unique symbol or set of symbols.** For example, bodily/kinesthetic intelligence uses sign language. Logical/mathematical intelligence uses computer languages. Interpersonal intelligence uses gestures and facial expressions.

Why Should the Intelligences Be Taught?

Many Reasons

There are many reasons for addressing multiple intelligences in your classroom. Once you have determined the intelligences of the students in your class, you can enrich and cultivate each individual's dominant intelligences, remediate and strengthen the weaker ones, or just allow everyone to experience all of them.

There is some controversy about these choices. Some people feel that students will develop spontaneously in their areas of strength and should, therefore, be helped to develop their weaker areas. Other people stress the importance of facilitating the flowering of the dominant intelligences. Still others feel that all areas should be cultivated in everyone, no matter what the natural strengths and weaknesses.

Aren't They Natural Talents?

An argument can be made that the less well-recognized intelligences, those other than the verbal/linguistic and logical/mathematical, are really talents that will eventually appear naturally in those students lucky enough to be born with them. To a certain extent this is probably true, but many times these talents may remain latent, never discovered or discovered much later in life because they were not triggered by experiences.

However, if an individual is placed in an environment that is rich in all kinds of intellectual and sensory stimuli, he or she may have what Howard Gardner calls a "crystallizing" experience. This can be a life-changing event. Gardner discusses Menuhin, the violinist, who first heard the violin played at the age of three and never lost his passion for it. Although not everyone will have such a dramatic experience, many students will discover interests and capabilities that will last throughout their lives.

The kind of rich environment that nurtures crystallizing experiences is particularly important for very young children because it gives them such an early start. Nevertheless, older children, as well as adults, can benefit from this kind of environment too. Think of someone like Grandma Moses who was exposed to painting very late in life and became famous for her work in that medium.

What About the Real World?

It is a fact that our society demands competence in the first two intelligences, verbal/linguistic and logical/mathematical. We would be cheating our students if we did not help them to get ready for life in the real world of tests and academic achievement, but this emphasis does not need to preclude the other intelligences. Many schools are meeting all of these needs.

Why Should the Intelligences Be Taught? *(cont.)*

You are already teaching with the multiple intelligences. The purpose of this section is to enable you to take a look at the students in your classroom in a new light. Are you reaching all of your students all of the time? How about some of your students all of the time? Would you like to reach all of your students most of the time?

Consider Your Teaching and Learning Styles

Now that you know what the multiple intelligences are, take a survey of your teaching style. Refer to the chart on page 10 for information on the effects a teacher's learning style may have on his or her teaching. Every time you do an activity, analyze it for which intelligences it targets. Think about the past week and do a mental checklist of all of the intelligences you have used. Chances are you will have used each of them to a degree, but, depending on your grade level, 75% or more of your activities will be verbal/linguistic, logical/mathematical, and, maybe, some interpersonal. (Lower grade teachers do use more of the intelligences due to the nature of your curriculum.) Your goal should be to use the intelligences equally, or as close to equally as you can comfortably get. Use the multiple intelligences (MI) calendar to keep a realistic record of your activities.

Using the range of intelligences will also help you to find out what intelligence strengths your students have. Watch how their eyes shine when you hit their strong intelligences! Make a note of their strengths so you can target their weaknesses through their strong intelligences.

Why Should the Intelligences Be Taught? *(cont.)*

Use this calendar to keep track of the teaching strategies you use in your weekly classroom planning.

Monday	Tuesday	Wednesday	Thursday	Friday	MI
					Verbal/Linguistic
					Logical/Mathematical
					Visual/Spatial
					Bodily/Kinesthetic
					Musical/Rhythmic
					Interpersonal
					Intrapersonal
					Naturalist

© Teacher Created Materials, Inc.   9   # 2464 The Best of Multiple Intelligences

Include the Multiple Intelligences in Your Lessons

The remaining sections of this book provide lesson plan ideas that will help you have a wide range of activities in each of the intelligences. They are by no means the only activities to be used. It is hoped that these activities will get your creativity flowing and that you will come up with many more ideas on your own.

Teaching students about their intelligence strengths helps them to be self-advocates in their learning. They can internalize how they learn which will help them cope with the teaching styles of teachers who might not be aware of the multiple intelligences. However, teaching students about the intelligences might not be viable, depending on the specific group you are dealing with, their age, or the point at which you are during the school year.

You already teach with the intelligences. These activities can help to broaden your teaching strategies palette and help you reach all of your students more of the time. In each category you will find activities to help develop the students' weak intelligences through the use of their strong intelligences.

Why Should the Intelligences Be Taught? *(cont.)*

Use this calendar to keep track of the teaching strategies you use in your weekly classroom planning.

Monday	Tuesday	Wednesday	Thursday	Friday	MI
					Verbal/Linguistic
					Logical/Mathematical
					Visual/Spatial
					Bodily/Kinesthetic
					Musical/Rhythmic
					Interpersonal
					Intrapersonal
					Naturalist

How Can the Intelligences Be Taught Through the Curriculum?

There are two ways to teach the intelligences through the curriculum: they can be taught "straight," or they can be infused into the regular curriculum. A different strategy is employed for each method.

Strategy #1: Begin with the type of intelligence and think of assignments that incorporate various areas of the curriculum. The example below moves from the Interpersonal Intelligence out into the curriculum.

Intelligence: Interpersonal

Curricular Activities/Assignments:

- Make up a "friendship dance" and perform it for a group or for the class.

- Paint a picture of friendship or love or anger.

- Make up 10 math problems about the people in your class.

- Write a play for your group to perform. Assign roles and direct rehearsals.

- Try to meet one new person a day for a week.

Strategy #2: Begin with an area of the curriculum and devise an approach that would involve each of the intelligences. The following example begins with an area of the curriculum and suggests an activity for each of the intelligences.

Curriculum Area: Math

Intrapersonal
- Ask the children to reflect on and write about their progress in math.

Interpersonal
- Start cross-age tutoring with another class.

Verbal/Linguistic
- Ask children to write a story from the point of view of a number.

Logical/Mathematical
- Teach children how to play "Othello" as an exercise in logic.

Visual/Spatial
- Create a city/picture using only rectangles, triangles, and circles.

Bodily/Kinesthetic
- Stand like a number. Have children approximate numbers with their bodies.

Musical/Rhythmic
- Show a videotape explaining the relationship of math to music or play "musical chairs" emphasizing math concepts of subtraction or "one less."

How Can the Intelligences Be Taught Through the Curriculum? *(cont.)*

Teaching the Intelligences "Straight"

Most teachers do not welcome the idea of adding another area to their already crowded curriculum. Nevertheless, there are real benefits to teaching by starting from the intelligences and moving out into the curriculum. First, the material involving the intelligences will not be forced, artificial, or insignificant. Second, dealing with the intelligences in an open and above-board manner will automatically involve the processes of meta-intelligence (metacognition applied to the intelligences) with all of its benefits.

There are many ways of moving out into the curriculum from a given intelligence.

Linguistic intelligence, for example, can be discussed and then illustrated with activities involving the alphabet, phonics, spelling, reading, writing, listening, presenting oral reports, and playing word games. Logical/mathematical intelligence can be discussed and then illustrated with activities involving numbers, patterns, computation, measurement, geometry, statistics, probability, problem solving, logic, games of strategy, and graphic organizers.

Infusing the Intelligences into the Curriculum

If you want to keep teaching your regular curriculum without adding another area to your lesson plans, you can endeavor to make sure that all, or as many as possible, of the intelligences are infused into every lesson. Since the infusion should be meaningful, this is not as easy to do as it may appear at first glance. However, some of the intelligences are easier to infuse than others and some curricular areas are easier than others to manipulate. Most social studies lessons lend themselves nicely to the infusion approach. Using an objective from United States history, your lesson plan might look something like this:

Infusion Lesson Plan

Objective: Students will be able to list sequentially and differentiate among the wars in which the United States has been involved.

Synopsis of lesson: Over the period of a week (or longer, if necessary) students will review material and complete the following:

- meet together in cooperative groups to develop strategies for remembering the sequence of wars in which the United States has been involved *(Interpersonal)*

- design and create a mural showing distinguishing features of the periods in which the wars occurred *(Visual/Spatial)*

- learn a song representative of the period in which a given war occurred *(Musical/Rhythmic)*

- learn a dance representative of the period in which a given war occurred *(Bodily/Kinesthetic)*

- gather data about some aspect of the wars (e.g., countries involved, casualties, length, etc.) and then organize the data in a graph *(Logical/Mathematical)*

- reflect on the values represented by the opposing sides in the conflicts *(Intrapersonal)*

- write a piece in which the student portrays the values represented by the opposing sides in one or more of the conflicts; any genre may be used *(Linguistic)*

How Can the Intelligences Be Taught Through the Curriculum? *(cont.)*

Infusing the Intelligences Into the Curriculum *(cont.)*

Thematic units provide an excellent opportunity for infusion of the intelligences through the curriculum. If you use a thematic approach in your classroom, most of the activities relate to and reinforce the chosen topic. As you connect the theme to areas of the curriculum, plan activities that will meet the intelligences of your students. (Create an organizer like the one below for planning such activities.) A sample literature-based thematic unit using a variety of multiple intelligences is provided on page 14.

Planning Activities to Meet Learning Styles

Learning Style	Students With This Style	Activities Reinforcing This Style
Verbal/Linguistic		
Logical/Mathematical		
Visual/Spatial		
Musical/Rhythmic		
Bodily/Kinesthetic		
Interpersonal		
Intrapersonal		
Naturalist		

How Can the Intelligences Be Taught Through the Curriculum? *(cont.)*

Infusing the Intelligences Into the Curriculum *(cont.)*

Sample Thematic Unit

Theme: Importance of the Sun

Level: Challenging

Literature: "All Summer in a Day" by Ray Bradbury, from *The Stories of Ray Bradbury,* (Knopf, 1980)

Literature Summary: Nine-year-old Margot, born on Earth, remembers the sun, while the children born on Venus do not. They know only the constant rain; however, the sun is slated to shine for one full hour this day, and everyone waits expectantly. Margot yearns for the sun most of all, but a cruel prank from her classmates brings about a tragic conclusion for Margot—and for themselves.

Getting Started: Brainstorm as a class about what the world would be like with constant rain for seven years. How would it look, feel, smell, and sound? How would life be different? Dim the lights and play a recording of rain showers and storms. Have the students write in any way they feel comfortable the experience of the rain and lack of sunshine.

Enjoying the Literature: Read the story aloud, taking care to express the various moods of the story in your vocal intonations. Express the monotony of the constant rain, the excitement of the children, the tension of their conflict with Margot, and their fervor in the sunshine.

Curriculum Connections:

Language Arts: Have students write descriptive poems about the sun, using the couplet written by Margot as a model. Have students describe their feelings when they got something they really wanted for a long time. Ask them to write about losing something very special that they perhaps had been taken for granted. Discuss the places in the story where the reader can see Margot's reactions to the loss of the sun in her life.

Science: In groups of four or five, have students plan ways to create a scientific model of the world described in Bradbury's story. As a class choose the method easiest or best to recreate it, and then do so. This can be as simple or as elaborate as you choose.

Social Studies: In small groups plan and design an underground city. List all special needs (fresh air access, food production, sewage, etc.) and foreseeable problems (transportation, housing, etc.). Encourage students to suggest a solution for each of these needs and problems in the design of the city.

Math: Have students create word problems dealing with the sun shining for one hour every seven years. For example, a child was born on February 27, 1990, two days before the sun came. On May 6, 2004, how many times has that child seen the sun?

Art: Have the students close their eyes and ask them to draw a mental picture as you read the sequence where the children experience the sun for the first time. Provide the students with several mediums (watercolors, pastels, crayons, colored pencils), and tell them to color what they saw in their minds' eyes.

Music: Using whatever materials are available in the classroom, have small groups devise ways to recreate the sounds of a rainstorm. With lights dimmed, each group can perform its story for the class.

How Can the Intelligences Be Assessed?

Can the Intelligences Be Assessed?

We know for sure that the verbal/linguistic and logical/mathematical intelligences can be assessed because we do it all the time. All of the standard tests assess either through language—oral or written—or through mathematical notation combined with language. Both IQ tests and achievement tests are language based; if a student's intelligence lies elsewhere, he or she might not get into college and may never find out that he or she is very talented in some area that is not as highly valued by society.

Can the other intelligences identified by Gardner—visual/spatial, bodily/kinesthetic, musical/rhythmic, interpersonal, intrapersonal, and naturalist—be assessed? And, if so, how can this be done without filtering the assessment through language, logic, mathematics? Gardner urges the use of assessment that is "intelligence-fair." Assessment that is intelligence-fair must be such that an intelligence can be judged directly and not through the medium of another intelligence.

What Instruments Can Be Used?

What testing instruments and procedures do we have now that will lend themselves to intelligence-fair assessment? Most of the so-called "new" or alternative assessments can be adapted for this purpose. Used in this way, they will, of course, still be subject to the same criticisms they are facing now.

Critics of alternative assessment methods say they are not "reliable." Reliable assessment can be defined as assessment that is consistent, no matter who scores it. This has always been true for normed tests, tests that were tried out on a representative population and standardized to produce percentiles, grade-level equivalencies, and letter grades—all of which could be used for purposes of comparison. The people who believe that reliability, as defined above, is all-important seem to be saying that teachers need an outside authority to validate all measurements of progress. They are also saying, whether they mean to or not, that all testing must be done objectively, through the verbal/linguistic or logical/mathematical intelligences.

Alternative assessment is not objective. In fact, it is subjective. It uses instruments such as observations verified by checklists and anecdotal records and portfolios with rubrics and reflections. It is not exact. Its application may vary from place to place, school to school, teacher to teacher, and student to student. It is a tool for measuring student performance on an ongoing basis. It can be used to make recommendations about steps that should be taken both in school and at home to ensure future progress, an area of concern that Gardner feels has been long neglected in favor of norming or ranking.

Application in the Classroom

Although Gardner recommends and does research on intelligence-fair assessment, he looks at the process from the point of view of a psychologist. It is up to educators to take this information and apply it in a way that is consistent with what actually goes on in a school. Teachers are necessarily aware of their accountability both to their administrators and, increasingly, to the parent and taxpayer communities. So, what are the tools that are presently available, and how can teachers use them to assess the seven intelligences and still meet their professional responsibilities? Let's look at the instruments mentioned above—observations verified by checklists and anecdotal records and portfolios with rubrics and reflections.

How Can the Intelligences Be Assessed? *(cont.)*

Observation

We have already taken a look at observation as a method of identifying students' intelligences. Observation in a classroom for purposes of assessment sounds easier than it is. Anyone with some experience and empathy can look around a classroom and see what is going on, but in order to be used as an assessment tool, observation must be structured, documented, and repeated at regular intervals.

Observation can be structured by being linked to specific activities. For example, you might decide to formally observe your cooperative groups to determine their levels of performance in the area of interpersonal intelligence. After thinking this through, you would design an easy-to-use checklist representing the goals you want your groups to reach.

You would then document your observations by using the checklist you designed and repeat this process once a month or once a quarter or at whatever intervals work for you. This process will give you a consistent record of progress over a period of real time.

Checklists

The checklist mentioned so casually above is not as easy and self-explanatory as it may sound. It is, of course, a list of things to be checked off by the observer. But what things? We have all gotten into the habit of depending on objective, multiple-choice tests designed to measure incremental, and usually minimal, proficiency skills to tell us what our students know. For instance, many reading tests measure knowledge of phonics. A good reader—someone who can read words and comprehend their meanings—who learned to read by generalizing from sight vocabulary might easily fail a phonics test.

In order to make a meaningful checklist, you must do a task analysis. Figure out what really goes into the achievement of a particular goal. For example, what characteristics and accomplishments really represent interpersonal intelligence in a group situation? Put in the things that are important and leave out those that are irrelevant. Try out your checklist a couple of times before you decide to base your whole assessment system on it. Development of a good checklist is worth the time you will need to put into it.

Check Chart for

Marty	Ben	Maria	Gabe	Tam	Vince	Danny
?	√ –	+	?	– – –	+ +	
Julie	**Mary**	**Fran**	**Robert**	**Jenny**	**Marilyn**	**Carl**
?	+	+ + +	+ + ? + + + + + +	+ –	? ?	
Pam	**Luan**	**Betsy**				
+ +	+ +	– ?				
				David	**Tuan**	**Liz**
				+ +	+ + +	– + ?
				Roger	**Mario**	**Terri**
				+ +	– + +	? ? ?

Key

? = student has a question	√ = participation
+ = correct response	– = needs individual attention

How Can the Intelligences Be Assessed? *(cont.)*

Anecdotal Records

Observations can also be documented through the use of anecdotal records. Anecdotal records used to be lists of comments stated objectively and used to document behavior problems. The new style of anecdotal records are positive comments that document the development and growth of students. They depend on teacher interpretation and judgment and focus on the things students can do, not what they cannot do. Anecdotal records can be kept on ordinary paper, but it is convenient to have special forms that will remind you to note the names and dates of your observations.

Date	Student's Name	Comment
3/14/94	Peter Matthews	Moved to back of room so he could concentrate—new maturity?
3/14/94	Marty Myers	No homework again—she mentioned something going on at home—maybe conference later
3/15/94	José Lopez	All he can talk about is the track meet this afternoon—changed conference to tomorrow

Portfolios

Portfolios can be thought of as containers in which to gather and store all of the records generated by the new methods of assessment. They can also be thought of as an assessment method which provides a way to take a look at and compare work in order to observe progress over a period of time. Portfolio assessment is most often thought of in connection with written work (thus documenting the products of the verbal/linguistic and logical/mathematical intelligence); however, it is just as possible to collect, store, and compare video and audio tapes documenting products of the visual/spatial, bodily/kinesthetic, musical/rhythmic, and interpersonal intelligences. Art objects, athletic activities, dance and musical performances, and group activities, such as debates are all examples that come to mind.

Reflections

Reflections are a form of self-assessment. They engage the intrapersonal intelligence, the hardest intelligence to see in action. Reflections were originally developed for, and have been associated with, the writing process. They are, however, equally adaptable to any other work that has been completed by a student.

They can be removed from the written emphasis of the verbal/linguistic domain by allowing students to reflect orally using a tape recorder and documenting the oral account with photographs. If students have personal tapes stored in their portfolios, they can rewind, listen to what they previously recorded, and consider the progress they have made before making new comments.

Rubrics

Rubrics are a useful addition to the assessment toolbox. The word "rubric" literally means "rule." When used in connection with assessment, a rubric is a scoring guide based on the requirements that were established to differentiate among the degrees of competency displayed in completing a task.

Once upon a time rubrics were secret documents hidden away by the teacher or by the district testing office and brought out only to grade the writing samples that determined whether a student would pass or fail or even graduate. Today, however, rubrics are shared with and even developed by students. They are no longer developed just for writing samples but can be constructed for any task. A student who is generating a writing sample or any other product should have free access to the rubric which describes the standards by which the finished work will be judged.

Translation

The last assessment tool is sometimes called "translation." It is a technique in which information taken in through one intelligence is put out through another. Students using this technique are often delighted to find that they have knowledge they had never been able to put into words. You might ask your bodily/kinesthetic students to dance their summary of a poem or mime their understanding of a rule. You can also let your students with visual/spatial intelligence paint their impressions of a piece of music or draw what the other side of a pictured object would look like.

A checklist could undoubtedly be constructed to document the observation of this technique, but it is entirely subjective for both student and teacher and might better be left as an experience of personal growth and expression.

Accessing One Intelligence Through Another Intelligence

 **Bodily/Kinesthetic and Visual/Spatial: Sample**

Visualization:

Grades 2–4: After learning about a particular topic, have students close their eyes and lead them on an imaginary tour of a related activity they will actually be doing. Help them visualize the process they will be going through, step by step. Describe a beautiful, successful project. Give specific details of how that project was achieved. After they have visualized doing the activity, have them open their eyes and actually do it. Taking the time to go through all of the steps before beginning the activity might help students plan carefully for the steps of the actual activity. If they can see what they should do in their imaginations, they will have an easier time making the connection in real life.

Animated Colors:

Grades K–2: A connection between feelings and colors was made between the visual/spatial and intrapersonal areas. Now guide the students through a colors and actions connection. This might be less intimidating if you use color crayons as puppets. If RED were to act, what would he or she do? What would BLUE do? How about GRAY? Let students show their ideas of what the different crayons would do. Then, put the crayons away and let students each decide on actions for themselves. Pretend you are YELLOW. What would you do? Now you are PURPLE. Show what purple does.

Picture Reporting:

After going on a field trip, help visual/spatial students to access what they did and saw by having them draw a picture to report on the event. The picture, for them, will be like a camera image that will commit their learning to a deeper level. Letting them know of this activity before they leave on the field trip will enable them to take pictures throughout the day and make the same connection without having paper and crayons to actually go through the process. They can make their plans for pictures in their minds.

Edible Art:

With colored chalk draw a rainbow on the board. Discuss its many colors. Then give each student a paper plate with three blobs of colored pudding, icing, cream cheese, or yogurt—one yellow, one blue and one red. Give each student a craft stick and challenge each to make the colors of the rainbow. Later, give each student a graham cracker on which to paint a minirainbow. When it is all done—eat the art!

Accessing One Intelligence Through Another Intelligence *(cont.)*

Displays:

Visual/spatial students like to see evidence of what they can do. Create displays that include their work and encourage them to use their bodies.

See the bulletin board ideas on this page and the next for other bodily/kinesthetic displays. Use the displays from your existing resources to supplement this section.

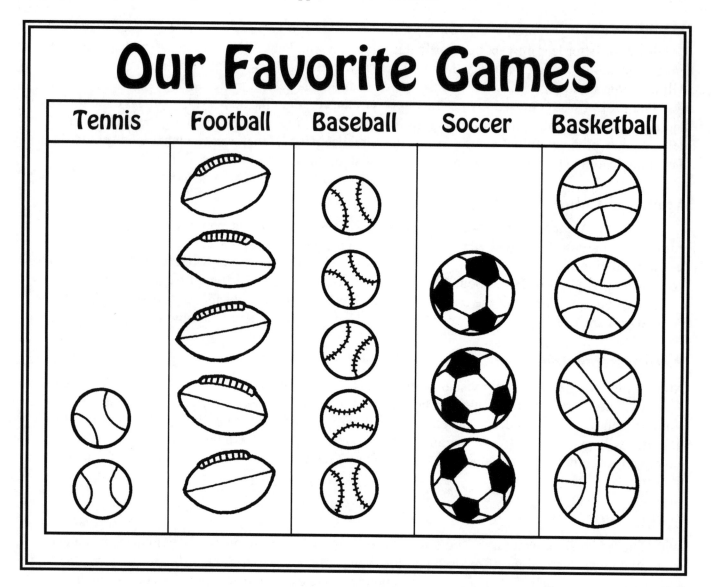

Create a pictograph for the bulletin board. Take a survey of which sport each student prefers and display the results. You might wish to add names to the tags on the graph.

This bulletin board can also be used with other surveys (favorite teams, subjects, foods, activities, etc.).

Accessing One Intelligence Through Another Intelligence *(cont.)*

Display different body smart activities on a bulletin board similar to the one above.

Use the bottom bulletin board idea to remind students to cultivate all seven intelligence areas, not just one or two.

How to Use This Book

The information on pages 4 through 21 summarizes each of the intelligences, addresses the reasons for teaching the intelligences, and provides some methods of teaching them. For further reading of Howard Gardner's work on multiple intelligences, refer to the following books:

Multiple Intelligences: The Theory in Practice (Basic Books, 1993)

The Unschooled Mind: How Children Think and How Schools Should Teach (Basic Books, 1991)

Frames of Mind: The Theory of Multiple Intelligences (Basic Books, 1983)

The activities in *The Best of Multiple Intelligences* were chosen from a variety of books published by Teacher Created Materials. (**Note:** The location of each activity page in its original Teacher Created Materials book can be found in the book reference index on pages 395 through 397.)

There are five sections in which activities for all eight intelligences have been included. The five sections are as follows:

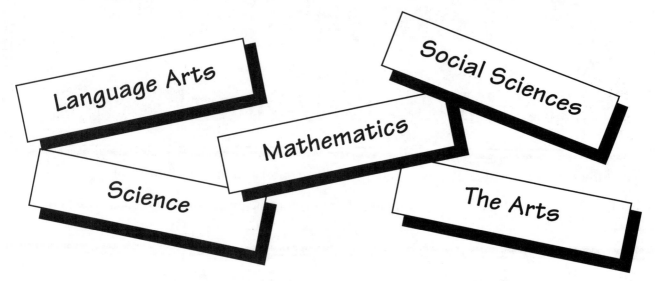

Several activities on two difficulty levels (identified as Lower Grades and Upper Grades) are included for each intelligence. For example, lower and upper grade activities for the verbal/linguistic intelligence in the Language Arts section can be found on pages 24 through 33.

To identify the grade level and the intelligence, check the information at the top of each page. The activity pages are not identified by a specific grade level. Instead, you can determine whether an activity is appropriate for your classroom needs by first choosing the general level (Lower Grades or Upper Grades) and then selecting suitable activity pages within that level.

Pages labeled "Lower Grades" generally refer to activities for grades Kindergarten through 3, while those labeled "Upper Grades" are most appropriate for grades 4 through 8.

Lower Grades = K–3
Upper Grades = 4–8

We hope you and your students enjoy the variety of activities in this book as you explore the eight intelligences and expand your understanding of each.

Teaching the Language Arts Through the Multiple Intelligences

"How to . . ." Speech

Organization

Name: _____ **Date:** _____

Directions: Speaking and listening skills are important in all parts of life. To help practice these skills, you will be developing a "How to . . . ." speech. During your "How to . . ." speech, you will be teaching us how to do something. For instance, you may choose to teach us how to tie shoelaces, brush teeth, or make a peanut butter and jelly sandwich. Pick a topic that interests you and remember to include details and props!

Brainstorm: Alone or with a partner, brainstorm a list of possible "How to . . ." topics. Write your ideas in the box below.

Brainstorm!

Action Alphabet Class Book

Activity:

The class will make an alphabet book of verbs.

Materials:

- chart paper
- large pieces of construction paper (1 per child)
- stapler, hole punch and yarn, or hole punch and binding rings

- marker
- poster board
- crayons

Preparation:

1. List the alphabet letters on the chart paper, leaving space to the right of each to list words.

2. Make a front and back cover for the class book from poster board. Title ideas include "The Action Alphabet," "First Grade's Action Alphabet," and "Room 10's Action Alphabet."

Directions:

Review verbs with the children. Have the children brainstorm a list of action words, one or more per alphabet letter. Record the verbs next to the appropriate letter on the chart paper.

Allow each child to choose a letter and a corresponding verb from the list. The children will each make a page for the class book, using construction paper. Each page should contain the following:

- the alphabet letter
- the verb
- an illustration

Depending on the developmental level of the children, a sentence which includes the verb can be written on each page.

Bind the completed pages and the cover to make a class book.

Recorded Story

Tape record a reading of your favorite short story. Afterwards, use headphones and listen to the story during your free time.

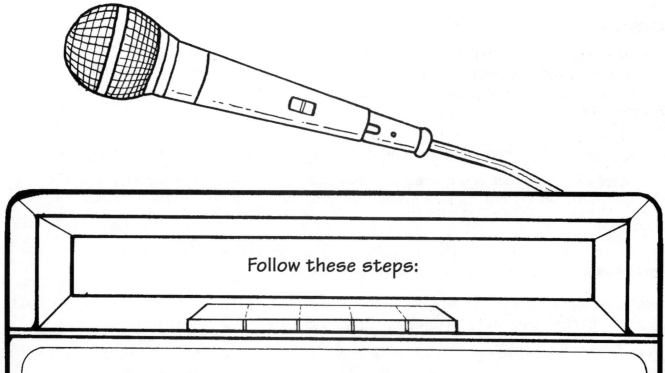

Follow these steps:

1. Choose a part of the story to read. (Your teacher may assign you a part.)

2. With a partner, practice reading with expression.

3. Sit in the order in which you will be reading your part.

4. Listen and watch as your teacher explains how to use the recorder and microphone to record your parts.

5. One at a time, you and the other readers will come up to the tape recorder and slowly read the parts you have been practicing.

6. When you have finished recording, rewind the tape. Listen to and enjoy your tape-recorded reading of the story.

Pair Them Up

Activity:

Students will match synonym pairs.

Materials:

- shoe pattern below (10 per set)
- colored pencils, markers, or crayons
- marking pen
- laminating machine (optional)

Preparation:

1. Reproduce, color, and cut out the shoe shape as many times as necessary.
2. Write one synonym on each shoe, making five pairs for each student group or each student working at a center.
3. Laminate for durability, if desired.
4. Store each set of tennis shoes in a different shoebox.

Directions:

Instruct the students to read the word on each shoe. Students can match the shoe pairs by placing the synonym shoes on top of one another.

Note: Other skills such as compound words and contractions can be reviewed in this way.

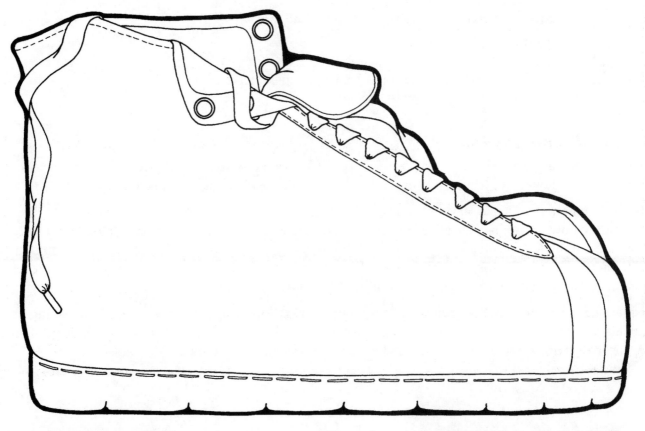

Writing a Narrative Story

Activity:

The class will write a narrative story.

Materials:

- Narrative Writing Web (page 29, enlarged on chart paper, overhead transparency, or chalkboard)
- chart paper
- marking pen

Preparation:

Create an experience for the children such as going on a field trip, raising butterflies, taking a tour of the school, completing a memorable art project, or watching an interesting nature video.

Directions:

To be narrative writers, the students are asked to tell a story or to describe a series of events in chronological order. In a personal narrative, the author tells about a personal experience, describing the event and his or her reactions or feelings toward what happened. In narrative writing as a whole, any story can be told.

The primary features of personal narrative writing are:
- a first-person point of view (I, we).
- chronological organization (events unfold as they happen).
- the significance of the events is revealed.
- the reader shares the writer's thoughts and feelings.

The primary features of narrative writing on the whole are:
- the setting (time and place) are clear.
- the characters are developed.
- a problem, conflict, or disagreement motivates the characters.
- the story progresses through a series of events.
- the problem is solved (solution).

All narrative writing should:
- state the purpose and topic.
- describe the people, places, and events.
- describe exactly what happened.
- describe what was seen, heard, and felt.

After a common experience, have the students brainstorm the various aspects of the experience. Teach the children how to use the Narrative Writing Web by recording their responses on the enlarged web. Using the completed web for ideas, have the children compose the story, telling about their common experience. Write their story on chart paper. When complete, read the story aloud. Go through each element of narrative writing to be sure that it has been included.

Display the story for future reference and reading practice. Repeat this lesson often before asking the students to write individual stories based on this model. When they are ready, offer them the guidelines for narrative writing and a writing web and have them write and share their own narratives.

Narrative Writing Web

Name: _____

topic

Word Power!

Some authors are very artistic, painting word pictures in rich detail. They leave us with powerful memories of the scenes they describe and the people whose lives they create. Among the literary devices used by such writers are *imagery, simile, personification,* and *paradox.*

Read the following excerpts from one story. Underline examples of imagery, circle all similes, draw a box around any personification, and put brackets around the paradox. Use the definitions in the box to help you with your analysis. Sometimes, more than one literary device may be used in an example.

Imagery: vivid description appealing to any or all of the five senses	Simile: comparison between two dissimilar things, using like or as
Personification: giving inanimate objects human characteristics	Paradox: self-contradictory statement that is nevertheless somehow true

1. "... the sun sank like stone into the purple sea."

2. "They began to relax, listening to the sound-filled silence."

3. "The still afternoon stood poised on tiptoe, holding its breath for the crack of thunder and following downpour."

4. "Like foam on a painted wave, the delicate blossoms dusted the surface of the low grass near the stream."

5. "... three armchairs and an old rocker stood stiffly in the room, like strangers at a party, uneasy and silent."

6. "The prairie they crossed was humming with the drone of bees, and grasshoppers jumped before them as if springs in the earth were flipping them up miniature kangaroos."

7. "The clouds spread apart, and the sky opened up its dazzling blue like an unfolding silken curtain, shimmering with light and power till she became dizzy."

8. "Like colors spilled from a paintbox, the evening sky spread out in pools of shining red and pink and orange, curling and darkening around the edges."

Challenge: Find some examples of these literary devices in your story and write them on the back of this paper or on another sheet of paper.

Book Report Activities

There are many ways to report on a book. After you have finished reading the literature selection, choose one method of reporting that interests you. It may be a way your teacher suggests, an idea of your own, or one of the ways mentioned below.

■ **See What I Read?**

This report is visual. A model of a scene from the story can be created, or a likeness of one or more of the characters from the story can be drawn or sculpted.

■ **Time Capsule**

This report provides people living in the future with the reasons your story or book is such an outstanding book. Make a time-capsule design and neatly print or write your reasons inside the capsule. You may wish to "bury" your capsule after you have shared it with your classmates. Perhaps one day someone will find it and read your selection because of what you wrote.

■ **Act It Out!**

This report lends itself to a group project. A size-appropriate group prepares a scene from the story for dramatization, acts it out, and relates the significance of the scene to the entire book. Costumes and props will add to the dramatization.

■ **Who or What?**

This report is similar to "20 Questions." The reporter gives a series of clues about a character from the story in vague-to-precise, general-to-specific order. After all clues have been given, the identity of the mystery character must be deduced. After the character has been identified, the same reporter presents another 20 clues about an event in the story.

■ **Dress 'n' Guess!**

Come to class dressed as one of the characters. Tell the class your version of the story from that character's perspective. Act like that character, and answer any questions the class may have about you and your life.

■ **Sales Talk**

This report serves as an advertisement to "sell" your selection to one or more specific groups. You decide on the group to target and the sales pitch you will use. Include some kind of graphics in your presentation.

■ **Literary Interview**

This report is done in pairs. One student will pretend to be a character in the story, steeped completely in the persona of his or her character. The other student will play the role of a television or radio interviewer, trying to provide the audience with insights into the character's personality and life. It is the responsibility of the partners to create meaningful questions and appropriate responses.

■ **Historical**

Consider one of your interests. Research the way that interest or a related one was interpreted in the year the story is set. Report to the class. Some possible topics are food, entertainment, transportation, politics, and lives of the people.

How to Read a Poem

If you want to write poems that you and others will enjoy reading, you will need to strengthen your "poetic ear." When you have a poetic ear, you can enjoy and appreciate reading and writing poetry. To strengthen your poetic ear, you need to read lots of poetry and write it, too.

Here is a very famous poem by American poet, Robert Frost. Read this poem, and other poems, by following the list of directions at the bottom of the page. After you've done this with a few poems, you will start to notice that your poetic ear is getting stronger.

Stopping by Woods on a Snowy Evening

Whose woods these are I think I know.
His house is in the village though;
He will not see me stopping here
To watch his woods fill up with snow.
My little horse must think it queer
To stop without a farmhouse near
Between the woods and frozen lake
The darkest evening of the year.
He gives his harness bells a shake
To ask if there is some mistake.
The only other sound's the sweep
Of easy wind and downy flake.
The woods are lovely, dark and deep
But I have promises to keep,
And miles to go before I sleep,
And miles to go before I sleep.

First, read the poem carefully all the way through. Next, read the poem aloud. When you read a poem, pay more attention to the punctuation than to the ends of lines. If there is no punctuation, go right to the next line as you read just as you would for a sentence in a story. Listen to it as you read.

Extension: Write this poem on a piece of art paper and illustrate it. Choose several poems you like and write them in a poetry journal where you can collect your favorites.

Interviewing Tips

Before the Interview

The following preparation activities will help make your interview a success.

❑ **Watch a good interviewer on television.** Note the manner in which the interviewer talks to his or her subject.

❑ **Read as much as you can about the subject** before you meet that person so you will know what questions to ask.

❑ **Prepare your questions ahead of time.** Don't waste the subject's time by filling it with a lot of "uh's" and "oh's."

❑ **Make an appointment in advance.**

During the Interview

The following actions and attitudes will help make your interview a success.

❑ **Be on time.**

❑ **Be polite and friendly.** Put the subject at ease. Let him or her know by your manner that you are interested in whatever the person has to say.

❑ **Try to look directly at the interviewee** (not your notes or elsewhere) when asking your questions.

❑ **Go to the interview prepared** with paper, two sharpened pencils or pens (two in case a lead breaks or a pen runs dry), and something hard (like a clipboard) on which to write.

❑ **Ask good questions**, but don't ask trick questions—ones which would deliberately embarrass the subject. Some of the best questions begin with *who*, *what*, *where*, *when*, *why*, and *how*. But don't limit yourself to these.

❑ **Do not restrict questions to factual matters alone.** Ask the interviewee his opinions and feelings about matters important in his life.

❑ **A good open-ended question begins like this:** "Can you tell us about . . . ?" or "Can you talk about . . . ?" This allows the interviewee to respond with his or her own thoughts and feelings without feeling hemmed in to a brief, specific response. This response may well suggest further questions from the interviewer.

Timely Chore

Each word in the time box refers to a specific time span. List the words in order from the shortest time span to the longest. Then, explain how long each time span is.

	Time Span	**How Long Is It?**
1.	_____	_____
2.	_____	_____
3.	_____	_____
4.	_____	_____
5.	_____	_____
6.	_____	_____
7.	_____	_____
8.	_____	_____
9.	_____	_____
10.	_____	_____
11.	_____	_____
12.	_____	_____

Time Box

second	hour	millennium
fortnight	day	month
minute	score	century
year	decade	week

"How Many?" Math Problems

Below are some word problems from the story *Too Much Noise* by Ann McGovern. Read each problem and then solve it in the space provided. Show your work.

---

1. Count how many animals are in the story. Add to that the number of men in the story. How many is that altogether?

2. Ten pigs were in a pig pen. Seven pigs got out. How many pigs were left in the pen?

---

3. Four cows, five sheep, and three goats were eating grass in a field. How many animals in all were eating grass?

4. Six donkeys and five cows were in the barn. Four cows left the barn. How many donkeys and cows are in the barn now?

---

5. Ten leaves fell to the ground by Peter's house. The wind blew five of them away. Then three more leaves fell to the ground. Now how many leaves are on the ground?

6. Peter's house has four sides. Each side has two windows. How many windows are on the whole house?

Teacher's Note: Fold this answer key under before reproducing. If students are to self-correct the problems, do not fold under so students can check answers.

1. 6+2=8
2. 10−7=3
3. 4+5+3=12

4. 6+5=11, 11−4=7
5. 10−5=5, 5+3=8
6. The answer 8 can be arrived at a number of ways.

Name_____

Math Code

After reading *The Cat in the Hat* by Dr. Suess, use the Math Code to answer the riddle by solving the equations below. Then match the number and write each letter in its own answer box.

Who do you find in a big red box?

0	9	7	6	10	2	5	8	3	4
N	H	O	E	T	D	I	G	A	W

9	4	3	5	4		8	6	9
+1	+5	+2	−5	+4		−1	−6	−3

2	0	4		8	8	4	9	9		2	9	6
+1	+0	−2		+2	+1	+1	−9	−1		+8	−5	+1

What a Hungry Little Guy!

Read *The Very Hungry Catepillar* by Eric Carle. Use the information in the story to match the food sets the hungry caterpillar ate with the correct dining day.

1. _____ four strawberries   a. Monday

2. _____ one apple
                                                            b. Tuesday
3. _____ three plums

4. _____ one piece of chocolate cake, one ice-cream   c. Wednesday

   cone, one pickle, one slice of Swiss cheese,

   one slice of salami, one lollipop, one piece   d. Thursday

   of cherry pie, one sausage, one cupcake,

   and one slice of watermelon   e. Friday

5. _____ two pears
                                                           f. Saturday
6. _____ one nice green leaf

7. _____ five oranges   g. Sunday

Circle the foods mentioned above that might be on a real caterpillar's diet. Cross out the foods that you think a caterpillar would probably never get a chance to taste in real life.

Cause and Effect

Name_____

Match each cause with its most likely effect.

1. _____ Bob stuck a pin in the balloon.

2. _____ Traci spilled her milk.

3. _____ My mom drove too fast.

4. _____ The electricity went out.

5. _____ The alarm clock did not ring.

A. _____ We could not see a thing.

B. _____ The policeman wrote out a ticket.

C. _____ We heard a big pop.

D. _____ We were late for school.

E. _____ There was a puddle on the floor.

Write possible causes for the following effects.

6. _____ so we left the circus early.

7. _____ so I bought a new one.

8. _____ so my mom picked us up.

9. _____ so we went to the mall.

10. _____ so I stayed in bed.

Write possible effects for the following causes.

11. My grandma was not feeling well _____

12. I did not do my homework_____

13. My brother got a yard job _____

14. My sister is too little_____

15. I do not like broccoli _____

Rankings

Complete this activity after reading the *Adventures of Huckleberry Finn*.

Directions: The following are problems a young person might face in growing up. These are also some of the problems Huck faces in the novel. Rank them from one to ten, according to how damaging they might be.

1—least damaging   **10—most damaging**

——————————— feeling you are not very smart

——————————— living with one parent only

——————————— being forced to leave home and live on your own

——————————— having no brothers or sisters

——————————— finding no help or comfort from religion

——————————— constantly being told that your feelings and ideas are not any good

——————————— meeting people who want to take advantage of you

——————————— not being allowed to go to school

——————————— living with a physically and mentally abusive parent

——————————— being considered by members of your town as not as worthy as they are

- Discuss your choices with another member of your class. Were your choices the same? How did they differ?

- Discuss answers with your teacher. How many of the class picked the same item for number 1? How many picked the same item for number 10? Why do you think the choices differed? Could it have to do with a person's own life experiences? How?

The Value of Words

In the value box, each letter of the alphabet has been given a dollar value. To find the value of a word, add the values of all the letters. For example, the word "school" would be worth $72 (19 + 3 + 8 + 15 + 15 + 12 = 72). Write words with appropriate values in each of the boxes below.

$10 Words	$20 Words
$50 Words	**$100 Words**
$101–$150 Words	**$151–$200 Words**

VALUE BOX		
A	=	$1
B	=	$2
C	=	$3
D	=	$4
E	=	$5
F	=	$6
G	=	$7
H	=	$8
I	=	$9
J	=	$10
K	=	$11
L	=	$12
M	=	$13
N	=	$14
O	=	$15
P	=	$16
Q	=	$17
R	=	$18
S	=	$19
T	=	$20
U	=	$21
V	=	$22
W	=	$23
X	=	$24
Y	=	$25
Z	=	$26

Education

List all the words you can make from the letters in "education." All the words in your list must have at least three letters, and each letter can be used only once in each word.

_____   _____   _____

_____   _____   _____

_____   _____   _____

_____   _____   _____

_____   _____   _____

_____   _____   _____

_____   _____   _____

_____   _____   _____

_____   _____   _____

_____   _____   _____

_____   _____   _____

_____   _____   _____

_____   _____   _____

_____   _____   _____

Daily Activity Graph

Like you, Jonas has certain things that must be done in a day's time with only so many hours to do them.

If we could see how this looks in a picture or graph form, it might give us a better idea of how to plan our daily activities, especially if unexpected events occur.

Suppose that Jonas's 24-hour day is spent in these ways: getting ready for school (1 hour), eating meals (1 hour), having morning and evening family rituals (1 hour), attending school (6 hours), volunteering (3 hours), doing homework (2 hours), having recreational time (2 hours), and sleeping (8 hours).

A pie graph of Jonas's day might look like this:

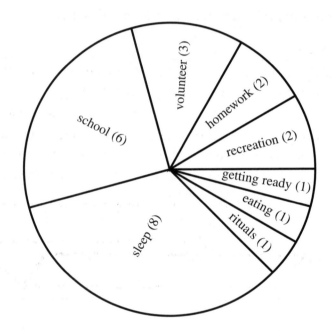

Could Jonas change his daily schedule?

_____

Make a list of things that you must do each day and the approximate amount of time it takes to do them. **For example:** If you sleep 8 hours and there are 24 hours in a day, what part of 24 hours is 8 hours? **Answer:** ¹/₃. Then ¹/₃ of your graph should be labeled sleep time.

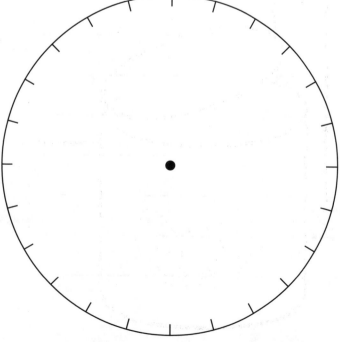

Now fill in the pie graph to the left with divided sections that will indicate your daily activities and the time allotted for each.

Are there times in your daily schedule where changes could be made to improve the day or provide fewer conflicts?

_____

_____

_____

_____

Smelling Boxes

Objective: Students will become aware of their own sense of smell in a smelling and guessing game activity.

Materials:

- a cardboard or plastic box with lid (Old prescription bottles work well for this. Be sure they are clean and have the labels removed. Sometimes a pharmacist will donate bottles to educators.)
- a sharp object to poke or cut holes in the top of the lid
- tape to secure the lid
- cotton balls
- a variety of fragrant objects (examples: perfume, baking extracts)

Directions:

- To prepare for this activity, first create "smelling boxes." Plastic works best, providing the plastic itself does not have a very definite odor.
- Place a fragrant object or cotton ball that has been soaked in a fragrance in each box.
- During circle time or another specific time of the day, ask students to smell what is in each box and guess what the fragrance is. Let students compare their ideas. At the end of the day, reveal the contents of each box. Have students discuss what they learned from the activity.

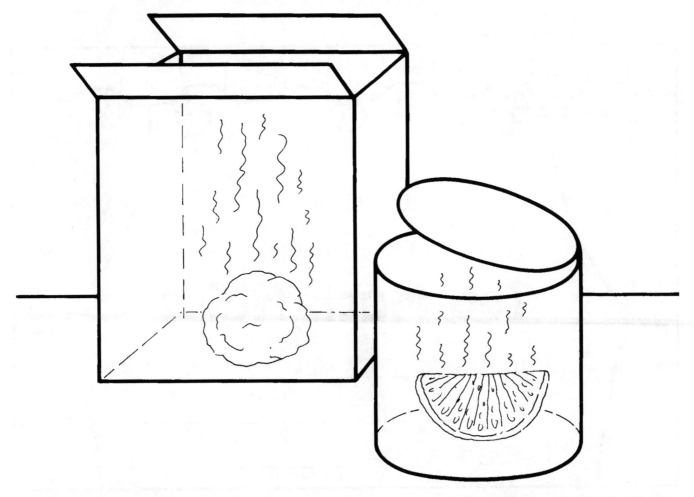

Readers' Theater

Readers' theater is an exciting and easy method of providing students with the opportunity to perform a play while minimizing the use of props, sets, costumes, and memorization. Students read the dialogue of the announcer, narrators, and characters from prepared scripts. The dialogue may be verbatim from the book, or an elaboration may be written by the performing students. Sound effects and dramatic voices can make these much like radio plays.

In a readers' theater production, everyone in the class can be involved in some way. The twelve or more speaking parts in this readers' theater combine with the construction of signs and masks to help maximize student involvement. Encourage class members to participate in off-stage activities, such as coloring and cutting out masks, making signs to be placed around speakers' necks, serving tea and cookies, delivering invitations, and greeting guests at the door.

It is not necessary to wear costumes for a readers' theater production, but the students can wear masks, hats, or signs around their necks, indicating their speaking parts.

Prepare signs by writing a reader's character (or name of the character) on a piece of construction paper or tagboard. If possible, laminate it for durability and then, staple a necklace-length piece of yarn to the top of the paper (or punch holes and tie with yarn).

Distribute copies of the following invitation to parents and other guests.

Please Join Us

for Our Presentation of

Too Much Noise

Date: _____ Time: _____

Place: _____

Presented by: _____

Drop Race

Cover this page with a sheet of wax paper. Fold the wax paper over to the back and tape it in place.

Using your finger, place a medium-size drop of water (from a faucet or a cup of water) into the starting circle.

Guide the drop of water through the maze by moving the sheet of paper around. After practicing for a few minutes, challenge a classmate to a water-drop race. Take turns seeing who can get the drop through the entire race course without going out of the lines and without dropping the drop. Have fun!

Teacher's Note: This activity also works well when the activity sheets have been laminated. If you do choose to laminate, save a class set to use year after year.

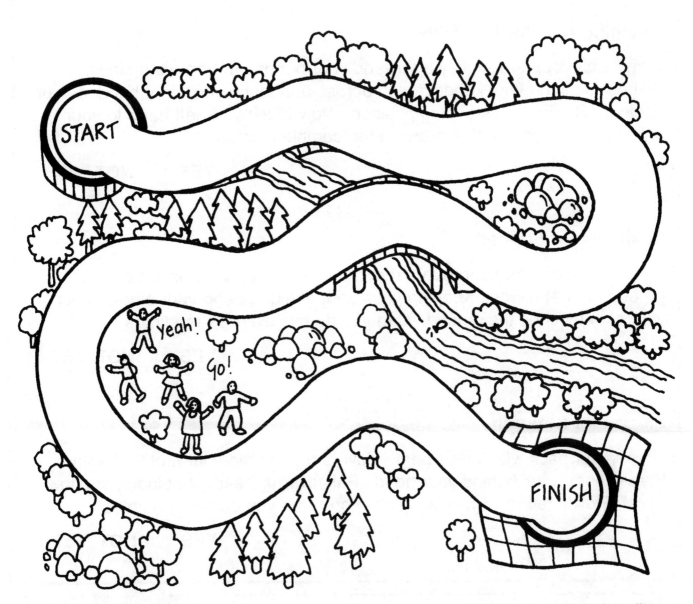

Working Out

See if you can do each of the exercises below ten times. Be sure to follow the directions carefully so that you do the exercises safely. Circle YES if you can do the exercise and NOT YET if you are not ready at this time.

Hopping for Balance

Hop on your right foot ten times and then hop on your left foot ten times. Can you do it?

YES   NOT YET

Touching Toes for Flexibility

Stand with your feet slightly apart and your hands out from your sides. Without bending your knees, reach across and touch your right hand to your left foot. Return to a standing position. Now touch your left hand to your right toe. Can you do this exercise ten complete times?

YES   NOT YET

Push-ups for Strength

With your knees on the ground, reach out and place your hands on the ground in front of you. Keeping your back straight, bend your elbows until your chin touches the ground. Can you do this exercise ten times?

YES   NOT YET

Sit-ups for Strength

Lie on your back with knees bent. Have a friend hold your feet to the floor. Place your hands behind your head. Pull up your head, shoulders, and lower back. Slowly return to your lying position. Can you do this ten times?

YES   NOT YET

Impromptu Speaking

An impromptu speech is one that has not been prepared or rehearsed. These presentations will not be polished, perfect speeches. Have fun with them and use your imagination. (Cut the following list apart and have each student draw a topic.)

Why Grass Is Green	What Makes Me Really Mad
Elephants	What I Think About Aliens
What Makes People Laugh	If I Could Invent a Candy
The Best Pet to Have	Why Dogs Are Better Than Cats (or vice versa)
My History of Bicycles	Why It's Important to Read
How I Feel About Television	The Best Way to Get Exercise
My Favorite Kind of Music	My Favorite Movie
The First Time I Ever Cooked	What I Dislike About School
What I Like About School	Which Is a Better Place to Live, the Mountains or the Beach?
My Favorite Day of the Year	How to Make Lots of Money
How to Shop for a Gift	The Best Kind of Car to Drive
Marshmallows	How to Promote World Peace
My Favorite Pair of Shoes	The Best Things About Summer
A Person I Admire	What I Don't Like About Birthdays

Finding Common Ground

Complete this activity after reading *The Outsiders* by S. E. Hinton (Bantam Doubleday Dell, 1968). The Greasers and the Socs live in two separate "worlds," unlikely to ever see the need to live harmoniously together. No one was seen as an individual by the members of the opposing gang, just "lumped" into the category of Greaser or Soc and left there. Ponyboy, Johnny, Two-Bit, Cherry, Marcia, and Randy were quite surprised to discover that members of rival groups could be individuals with hopes, fears, humor, and pain.

Suppose they had the opportunity and the desire to learn about each other sooner. Do you think the tragedies that filled *The Outsiders* could have been avoided? Perhaps, if the teachers at Ponyboy's high school had grouped their students so that people who were different could see they had similarities, tension between the gangs could have lessened.

Here is a method to group students for activities in a classroom. Duplicate a puzzle form for every four students in your classroom. (The puzzle form can be found on page 49.)

* Write a student's name on each puzzle piece. You may wish to form heterogeneous groups or simply write the names in alphabetical order.

* Laminate the puzzles for durability.

* Cut apart the puzzle pieces and mix all of them together.

* Distribute a piece to each class member.

* Ask students to move about the classroom trying to find their "puzzle mates."

Now that people have been grouped, complete an activity requiring the participation of each group member. Here are some ideas.

* Each group member has an object. The group must work together to make something whole out of the parts. (*Sample objects*: four toothpicks, a potato, yarn pieces, a plastic cup, three paper clips, a bar of soap, two rubber bands, a bell, etc.)

* Each group can develop a list of items upon which they agree. It can be a listing of things such as songs, performers, TV shows, movies, spare-time activities, foods, or sports.

Finding Common Ground *(cont.)*

Use this puzzle form for the activity suggested on page 48. You may wish to laminate the pieces for longer use. The second time you use the puzzle pieces for grouping, tell your students they may not be in the same group they were in before.

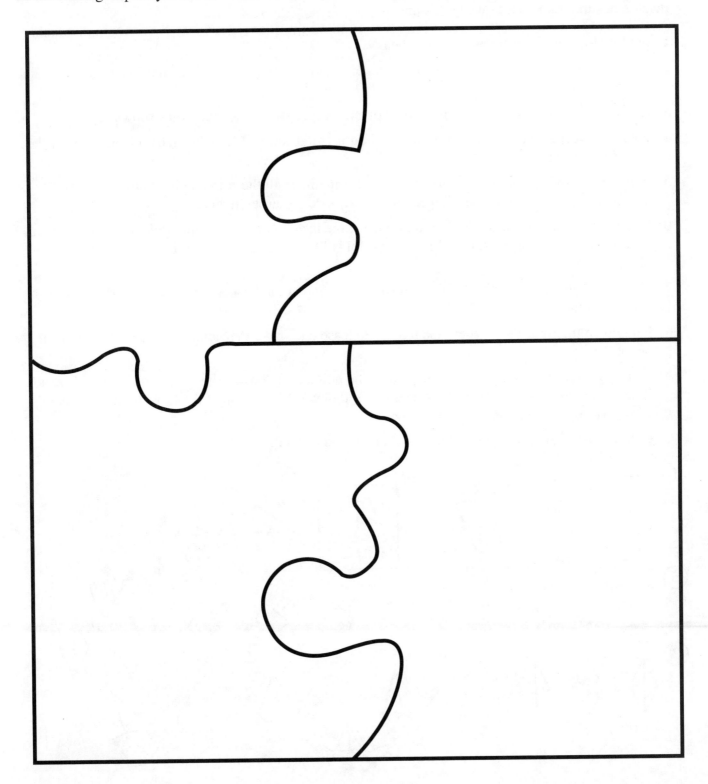

Peace Tree Art Activity

Have students research origami, the ancient art of paper folding. The directions and diagram below shows how to make origami cranes. You may wish to assemble a bulletin board with a large tree on which students can attach their origami cranes or other symbols of peace they have created as a result of discussions that took place during this unit.

1. Fold your square four times as shown below.

2. Using a diagonal fold as the center, fold the left and right edges into the center line to make a kite shape.

3. Repeat the kite fold on each corner. Your opened paper should be creased as shown.

4. Fold the paper in half to make a triangle. Hold it at the star and fold the right side up to meet the top of the triangle.

5. Release the fold and make the same fold inside out and with the fold coming between the front and back of the large triangle. Repeat on the left side. Sharpen the creases.

6. Holding the diamond shape at the star, do the same inside out, fold on the broken lines to form an upside down kite shape. You will make four folds like this: right, left, turn over, right, left. Sharpen the creases.

7. Hold the point with the star and fold down the top flap at the broken line. Turn the shape over and repeat the fold on the other side.

8. Fold down the right flap at the broken line. Release and make the same fold inside out. Repeat on the left side.

9. Turn the shape as shown and fold the end of the point at the broken line to form the crane's head. Release and make the same fold inside out. Fold down the top flap at the broken line to make a wing. Turn over and fold the other wing.

10. Roll the wings around a pencil to give them a curved shape.

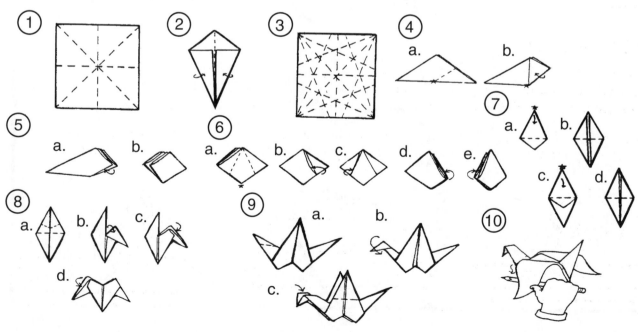

Story Scene

A shoebox can be the center of two projects the children will enjoy.

The teacher or an older child can make samples that the primary children can copy with some assistance.

DIORAMA

Materials: a shoebox (without the lid), construction paper or shelf paper, lightweight tagboard, scissors, glue, tape, crayons or markers, magazine pictures (optional), Contac® paper to cover outside of box (optional)

Directions:

1. Cut out one side out of the shoebox.

2. Cover the outside of the box, if you wish.

3. To make a pattern for the inner walls, lay the box on the construction paper and measure the size of the three outer sides. Fold the paper around the box and cut around the outline.

4. Decorate these inner walls with drawings or magazine pictures.

5. Glue the walls in place inside the box.

6. Cover the floor of the box in the same way.

7. Tagboard and construction paper may be used to make other free-standing pictures for the scene. Consider adding other materials like foil, cotton balls, fabric, yarn, clay, and twigs (for trees).

8. Label with the title, author, and artist's name.

PARADE FLOAT

Here is where the **lid** of the shoe box comes into play. Replace the **shoebox** with its **lid**, and using the same materials as for the activity above, direct the children to make a **float** for their book. They can cover the **lid** appropriately, add free-standing forms, and even add wheels if they wish!

Either of these projects may be started in class and sent home to be completed with a parent's help. They will enjoy it while the children will have the opportunity to share their reading accomplishments.

 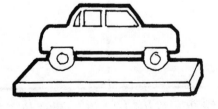 

Design A Bookmark

Look at the cover of your book. Skim through and look at the pictures. See if you can design a bookmark especially for this book.

Directions:

1. Draw your ideas on the pattern below.

2. Color your drawings in bright colors.

3. Carefully cut along the solid lines.

4. Fold on the dotted line.

5. Glue the sides together.

Enjoy your reading!

BACK   **FRONT**

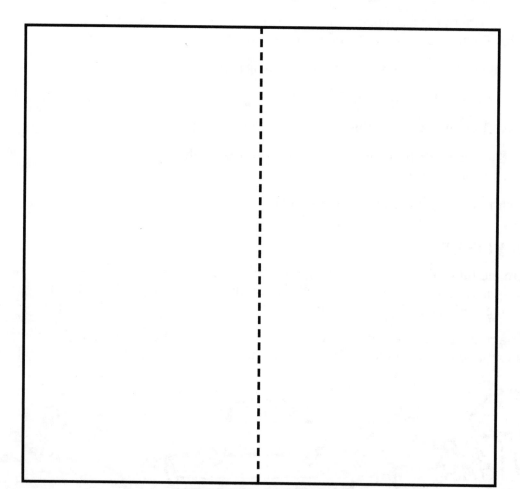

To the teacher: *In place of #4 and #5 above, the two sides may be cut apart, mounted on construction paper, and the edges fringed. (See sample above.)*

A Quilt Block for You to Color

Think back to the book, *The Keeping Quilt.* As you read each statement below, decide for yourself how true the statement is.

If the statement is always true, color the space blue.

If the statement is always false, color the space green.

If the statement is sometimes true and sometimes false, color the space yellow.

1. Great-Gramma Anna comes from a country called Russia.

2. This is a true story about the author's family, and she is now the caretaker of the quilt.

3. Families always keep the same customs and traditions through the generations and never change any of them.

4. Great-Gramma Anna learns to speak English when she comes to America.

5. The quilt, made so long ago, has been passed down through the generations, and the story of how it was made has been told.

6. Many neighborhood ladies come to help Anna's mother cut the fabric and sew the quilt.

7. The quilt shows the neighbors how wealthy Anna's family is.

8. When Anna outgrows her dress, her mama and her babushka uses it in the quilt.

9. People who came to America as immigrants always learned to speak English.

10. It is a Jewish tradition to use a gold coin, a dried flower, and salt as gifts and for special ceremonies.

11. The quilt is no different from other quilts you can buy today.

12. The quilt is used as a covering called a huppa when someone in the family gets married.

Ice Cream Monster

Directions: Use the cone and scoop shapes to make a monster like the one the animals think they see in "Ice Cream." Cut out the shapes and glue them to another paper. Add any details you want with crayons and markers.

Wild Thing Puzzle

Complete this activity after reading *Where the Wild Things Are* by Maurice Sendak (HarperCollins Child Books, 1992).

Materials:

- colored markers or crayons
- scissors
- colored construction paper
- glue

Directions:

1. Draw and color a picture of a wild thing onto the puzzle pieces.

2. Carefully cut out the puzzle pieces on the dark lines.

3. Have a partner mix up your puzzle pieces.

4. Put your puzzle back together and glue it to a piece of colored construction paper.

5. Finish the sentence below. Choose an idea from the book or create an idea of your own.

6. Cut out the sentence block and glue it under your puzzle. Read the sentence aloud in class.

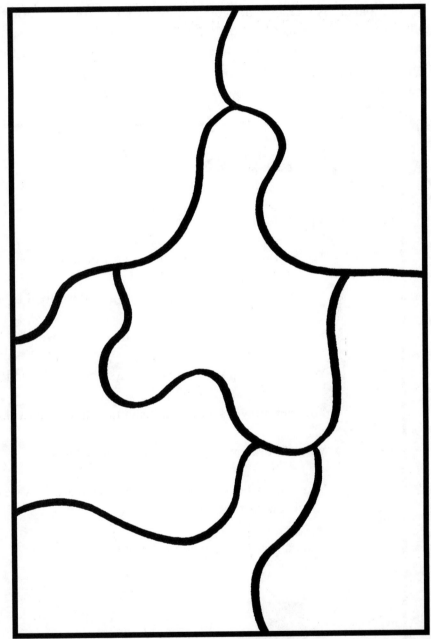

My wild thing likes to _____

_____

_____

One-Pager

Complete this activity after reading *Maniac Magee* by Jerry Spinelli (Little, 1996).

A "one-pager" is a chance for you to draw or write your reaction to *Maniac Magee*. You may do whatever you want, as long as it relates to the novel. Use a separate sheet of paper—you will need to decide whether it should have lines, have just a few lines, or be free of lines.

The only requirement is that your page has to have some color on it. If you don't want to draw, then at least put a colorful border around your writing.

Some suggestions:

✎ You can pick a favorite quote and illustrate it with your own view of the characters.

✎ You can draw a scene that the author described in words.

✎ You can draw the climactic scene of the novel.

✎ You can draw a scene that "occurs" before the action of the novel.

✎ You can draw a scene that "occurs" after the novel ends.

✎ You can draw a new book cover for the novel.

✎ You can write your feelings about the novel. For example, write about how the novel relates to the real world.

✎ You can write a review of the novel.

A Colonial Ship

Complete this activity after reading *The Witch of Blackbeard Pond* by Elizabeth G. Speare (Bantam Doubleday Dell, 1978).

Directions: Pictured below is a cross-section of the *Susan Constant*, a typical sailing ship of the seventeenth century. Label the ship with the correct parts by unscrambling the letter groups below. Write the names on the corresponding lines below the ship. Here are some reference books to which you may refer: *Stephen Biesty's Incredible Cross-Sections* by Richard Platt, (Alfred A. Knopf, 1992), *Eyewitness Visual Dictionary: The Visual Dictionary of Ships and Sailing* (Dorling Kindersley, 1991), and *Inside Story: A 16th Century Galleon* by Richard Humble (Peter Bendrick Books, 1995).

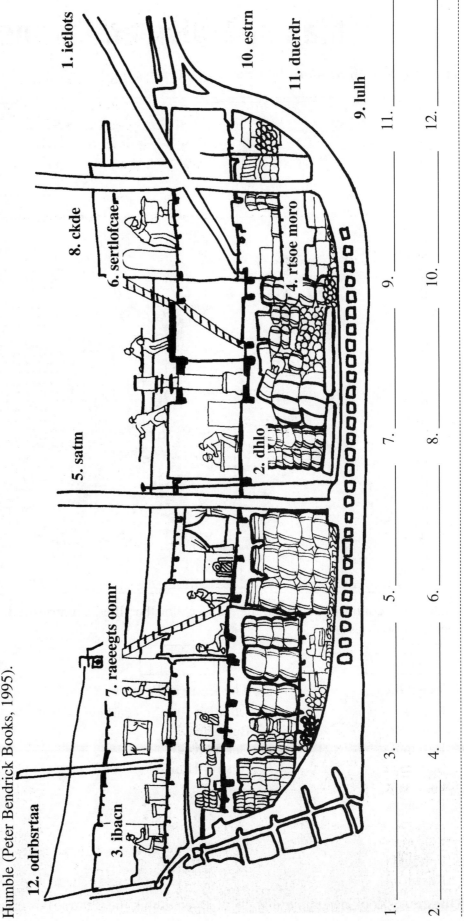

1. ietlots
10. estrn
11. duerdr
9. lulh
8. ckde
6. sertlofcae
4. rtsoe moro
5. satm
2. dhlo
7. raeeegts oomr
3. ibacn
12. odrbsrtaa

1. _____
2. _____
3. _____
4. _____
5. _____
6. _____
7. _____
8. _____
9. _____
10. _____
11. _____
12. _____

Map of a Divided Europe

Use this activity with *World War I* by Peter Bosco (Facts on File, Inc., 1991).

Locate each of the countries below on the map. Color the allied countries red, the central powers blue, and the neutral countries green.

The Allies
France
Great Britain
Belgium
Serbia
Greece
Romania
Albania
Italy
Portugal
Russia

The Central Powers
Ottoman Empire (Turkey)
Bulgaria
Germany
Austria-Hungary

Neutral Nations
Norway
Spain
Sweden
Switzerland
Denmark
Netherlands
Finland
Iceland

Quick Question! Looking at your map, how do you think the Central Powers got that name?

Significant Scenes

Every story has certain special scenes that are memorable and important to advance the action (the plot development). Which scenes do you feel are the most significant for your story?

Work with a partner to select five of those scenes and create an accordion book that presents them in order.

Directions for making an accordion book:

1. Cut six pieces of tagboard the same size and shape. You may choose any size or shape that can contain writing, illustrations, and be connected at the side edges.

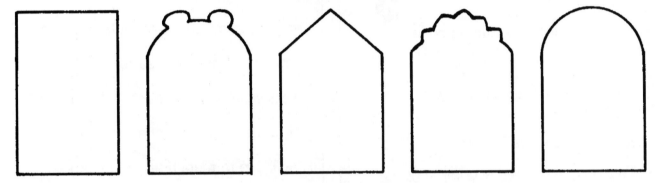

2. Tape the six pieces of tagboard together at the sides. (Put tape on both front and back.)

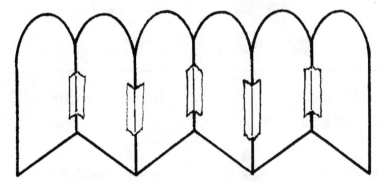

3. Design a cover for your book and illustrate the significant scenes you have selected. You may draw directly on the tagboard or on separate paper to be glued into the book.

4. Write a brief synopsis of each scene on the appropriate book page.

5. Display your accordion book for the class!

Ice Cream Songs

Read aloud *Curious George Goes to an Ice Cream Shop* by Margaret Rey and Allen J. Shalleck (Houghton Miffin, 1989). Sing the following songs written to familiar tunes and then have the class write others in the same way.

Take Me Out for Some Ice Cream

(sung to the tune of "Take Me Out to the Ball Game")

Take me out for some ice cream,

Take me out to the store.

Buy me a triple scoop jumbo cone.

I won't share; I will eat it alone!

So just scoop, scoop, scoop up the ice cream —

Give me three kinds I adore!

For it's one, two, three scoops to go

At the ice cream store!

Hot Fudge, Cherries, Toffee Crunch

(sung to the tune of "Twinkle, Twinkle, Little Star")

Hot fudge, cherries, toffee crunch,

Peanuts, whipped cream, lots to munch.

At the top of my ice cream,

So delicious, it's a dream!

Hot fudge, cherries, toffee crunch,

How I love to munch and munch!

Dip Deep the Silver Scoop

(sung to the tune of "Swing Low, Sweet Chariot")

Dip deep the silver scoop
Into the chocolate ice cream.
Dip deep the silver scoop
Into the chocolate ice cream.

I looked o'er the counter, and what did I see
Right by the chocolate ice cream?
Lots of hot fudge, caramel, and strawberry
To add to my chocolate ice cream.

Dip deep the silver scoop
And have some delicious ice cream.
Try a bite, or two, or three
Of this delicious ice cream.

The Ice Cream in the Bowl

(sung to the tune of "The Farmer in the Dell")

The ice cream in the bowl,
The ice cream in the bowl,
Hi-ho the dairy-o,
The ice cream in the bowl.

The ice cream takes a banana.
The ice cream takes a banana.
Hi-ho the dairy-o,
The ice cream takes a banana.

The banana takes some fudge (etc.).
The fudge takes some sprinkles (etc.).
The sprinkles take some nuts (etc.).
The nuts take some whipped cream (etc.).
The whipped cream takes a cherry (etc.).
The cherry takes a child (etc.).
The child eats the sundae (etc.).

Mouse Sing-Along Song

Sing to the tune of "Three Blind Mice."

If you give a mouse a cookie,
If you give a mouse a cookie,
He'll want a glass of milk,
He'll want a glass of milk,
He'll ask for a straw and a napkin too,
He'll look in the mirror and wonder who,
He'll ask and ask and ask of you,
If you give a mouse a cookie.

If you give a mouse some scissors,
If you give a mouse some scissors,
He'll give himself a trim,
He'll give himself a trim,
He'll ask for a broom and sweep and sweep,
He'll clean your house and make it neat,
He'll ask and ask and ask of you,
If you give a mouse some scissors.

If you give a mouse a blanket,
If you give a mouse a blanket,
He'll want a pillow too,
He'll want a pillow too,
He'll want a story read to him,
He'll look at the pictures again and again,
He'll ask and ask and ask of you,
If you give a mouse a blanket.

If you give a mouse a crayon,
If you give a mouse a crayon,
A picture he will draw,
A picture he will draw,
He'll sign his name with a pen,
Tape it on the fridge and then,
He'll ask and ask and ask of you,
If you give a mouse a crayon.
(Repeat the first verse.)

Grandparent Lovesongs

Use the tunes of familiar songs to create your own lovesongs for grandparents. Songs such as "Are You Sleeping?" "Mary Had a Little Lamb," "Old MacDonald Had a Farm," and "The Farmer in the Dell" provide basic melodies that can be used to create suitable lovesongs by writing your own original lines to fit the melodies.

Here is a sample to get you started. It might be performed after reading *Grandfather's Lovesong* by Reeve Lindbergh (Viking Penguin, 1993).

"I Love You"
(Sung to the tune "Are You Sleeping")

I love grandma.
I love grandma.
Yes, I do.
Yes, I do.
She is very special.
She is very special.
Yes, it's true.
Yes, it's true.

I love grandpa.
I love grandpa.
Yes, I do.
Yes, I do.
He is very special.
He is very special.
Yes, it's true.
Yes, it's true.

Create your own original Grandparent Lovesong.

_____

_____

_____

_____

_____

_____

_____

_____

(Sung to the tune of " _____ ")

Words by _____

"I Love Chocolate!" Song

Teacher Directions: Share this simple and catchy song with your students after reading *Chocolate* by Jacqueline Dineen (Carolrhoda Books, 1991). Let the students personalize the song by filling in the blank in the first verse with their favorite chocolate treats.

"I Love Chocolate!"

by C. Holzschuher

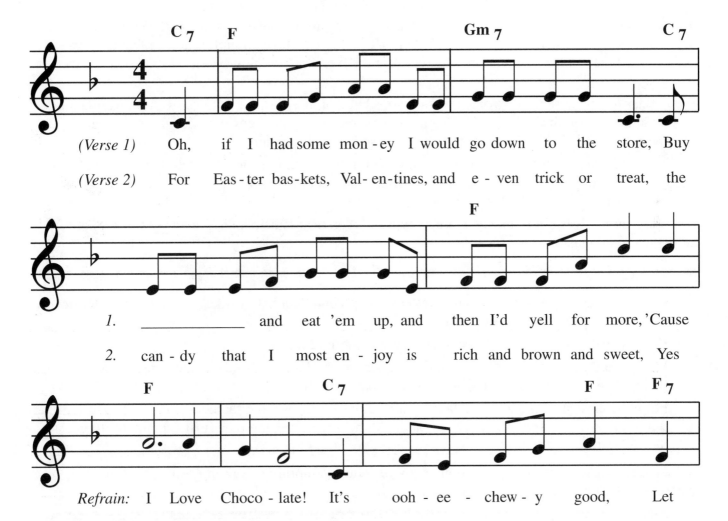

(Verse 1)   Oh,   if I had some mon-ey I would go down   to   the   store, Buy
(Verse 2)   For   Eas-ter bas-kets, Val-en-tines, and e-ven trick or   treat, the

1. _____ and eat 'em up, and   then I'd   yell   for more, 'Cause
2. can-dy   that I   most en-joy is   rich and brown and sweet, Yes

Refrain: I Love Choco-late! It's   ooh-ee-chew-y   good,   Let

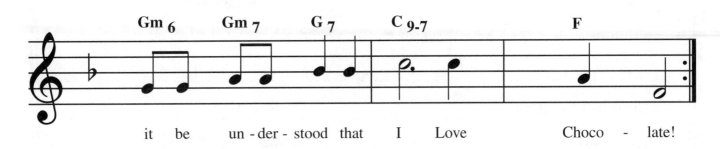

it be un-der-stood that   I   Love   Choco - late!

Toe Tappin', Knee Slappin' Music

Teacher Note: Use the following activities with *Cowboy Eyewitness Book* by David H. Murdoch (Alfred A. Knopf, 1993).

A day on the trail ended with the gathering and settling of the herd for the night. The wranglers and animals needed time to rest and recuperate after a hard day's work. Throughout the night the cowboys took turns riding around the cattle, singing melodies to sooth the restless dogies. Music was also a way to break the boredom of the quiet nights. Around the campfire, on the range, or at the ranch, music played an important role in the life of all western people. Fortunately, the abundance of western music produced during the heyday of the cowboys has preserved an oral history of the early West. One omission noted in western music is the mention of a wife. Cowboys often fell in love, but their ballads told of heartbreak rather then marital bliss because the typical roaming western cowboy was not the marrying kind.

Even at dances the absence of women was obvious but that didn't stop the cowboys from having a good time dancing. When there were not enough female dance partners, a cowpoke would tie his bandanna around his arm and pretend he was the lady in the square-dancing duo.

As different ethnic groups settled in the West, each influenced the music. The freed slaves brought the fiddle and the banjo. The old ballads from England and Scotland were the tunes for many songs about the cowboy's lonely life.

You will hear the western influence in many types of American music today: country western, pop, show tunes, and classical.

Activities

- Research song titles with a country western flair. Compile a list of titles. Read or listen to the lyrics and stories of the pieces of music.
- Display instruments that were popular on the western ranches.
- Play a word game with the letters of the musical scale. Give the students the note names (C,D,E,F,G,A, and B) and challenge them to rearrange the letters into a list of words.
- Form the class into two teams. Have each team take turns writing the notes to melodies of familiar tunes on a musical staff on the chalkboard. At the same time, the other team should try to guess the song titles.

Some suggested song titles for classroom enjoyment during morning work or creative writing experiences follow:

"John Henry"	"Home on the Range"
"She'll Be Comin' 'Round the Mountain"	"I've Been Workin' on the Railroad"
"Polly Wolly Doodle"	"Don't Fence Me In"
"Clementine"	"The Red Pony"
"Billy the Kid"	"Oklahoma"
"Giant"	"Git Along, Little Dogies"

Music and Poetry

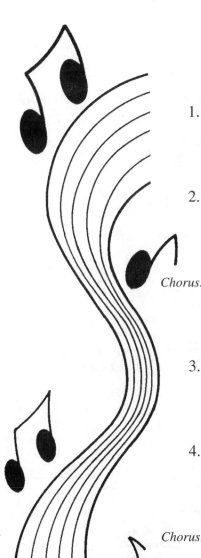

Old Brass Wagon

1. Circle to the left, the Old Brass Wagon,
   Circle to the left, the Old Brass Wagon,
   Circle to the left, the Old Brass Wagon,
   You're the one, my darling.

2. Swing, oh swing around, the Old Brass Wagon,
   Swing, oh swing around, the Old Brass Wagon,
   Swing, oh swing around, the Old Brass Wagon,
   You're the one, my darling.

   Chorus: Promenade to right, the Old Brass Wagon,
   Promenade to right, the Old Brass Wagon,
   Promenade to right, the Old Brass Wagon,
   You're the one, my darling.

3. Walk it up and down, the Old Brass Wagon,
   Walk it up and down, the Old Brass Wagon,
   Walk it up and down, the Old Brass Wagon,
   You're the one, my darling.

4. Break and swing around, the Old Brass Wagon,
   Break and swing around, the Old Brass Wagon,
   Break and swing around, the Old Brass Wagon,
   You're the one, my darling.

   Chorus: Promenade to right, the Old Brass Wagon,
   Promenade to right, the Old Brass Wagon,
   Promenade to right, the Old Brass Wagon,
   You're the one, my darling.

The music for this song can be found in *America Sings,* a musical collection edited by Carl Carmer and published by Alfred A. Knopf in 1942.

Two Little Apples

Way, way up in an apple tree
Two little apples smiled at me.
I shook that tree as hard as I could,
Down came those apples—
Ummmm, they were good!

- Anonymous

Teacher Note: To perform movements with the poem, do the following. At line one, stretch both arms high overhead. At line two, clench both fists to represent apples. At line three, shake your body all around. At line four, stoop to the floor, touching the floor with your fists. Finally, at line five, rub your stomach to show how delicious those apples were.

Music: Preferences

Complete this activity after reading *The Outsiders* by S. E. Hinton (Bantam Doubleday Dell, 1968). The Greasers like Elvis Presley, the Socs like the Beatles, and Buck Merrill likes Hank Williams. Who do you like?

For this activity, your teacher will play three recordings: one by Elvis Presley, one by The Beatles, and one by Hank Williams Sr.

Rate each selection on a 1 to 10 scale, with a 10 being what you enjoy most. After you have finished your individual ratings, graph the class scores. Include your teacher's score, too.

Who emerges as the favorite recording artist in your class?

ELVIS PRESLEY

song: _____

_____

ranking: _____

THE BEATLES

song: _____

_____

ranking: _____

HANK WILLIAMS, SR.

song: _____

_____

ranking: _____

Shakespeare and Music

More of Shakespeare's plays and poems have been the inspiration for the music of major composers, both classical and modern, than have the writings of any other author. *A Shakespeare Music Catalogue* lists more than 21,000 musical compositions inspired by his works, 1,405 of them inspired by *Hamlet* alone.

Many of the compositions are operas which were based on the plays. Shakespeare was 33 when the first opera was written. Although he probably never heard one, the plots of many of his plays, particularly the tragedies, are very suitable for adaptation to that musical genre. Twenty-three of his 37 plays have been made into operas, many of them more than once. One of the best is probably Verdi's *Otello,* with its growling trumpets, screaming flutes, and pounding tympani. Verdi also wrote his *Falstaff* based on Shakespeare's *The Merry Wives of Windsor.*

Prokofiev's ballet of *Romeo and Juliet* is one of the most beautiful pieces of musical theater ever composed, and the meeting of the two lovers at a masked ball is awesome. Mendelssohn's *A Midsummer Night's Dream* is quite magical; after all, is there anyone who has never heard its "Wedding March" to which millions of newly-married couples have walked down the aisle?

Several modern musical comedies have been based on Shakespeare plays. *The Boys from Syracuse* is a musical takeoff on *The Comedy of Errors.* *Kiss Me Kate* is based on *The Taming of the Shrew,* and *West Side Story,* the heartbreaking story of star-crossed lovers in New York's Spanish Harlem, was based on *Romeo and Juliet.*

Shakespeare himself wrote many song lyrics within his plays. Some of these songs were sung by the prepubescent boys who played girls and women on the English stage when females were not allowed to perform. Many of the songs are rather like interludes which distill the atmosphere of a play. "Under the Greenwood Tree," from *As You Like It,* "When Daffodils Begin to Peer," from *The Winter's Tale,* and "For the Rain It Raineth Everyday," from *Twelfth Night,* are three such songs. Can you find the song in *Much Ado About Nothing*?

Activity

Do some research to find a recording of a piece of music which was inspired by Shakespeare or which has come down from Elizabethan times. Your school librarian or the public librarian should be able to help you. Once you have the music, play it for your class. As a group compare it to some contemporary music. Does it sound alike or different? Do you think it might be popular today? Give your reasons.

A Poem About Me

In *The Mixed Up Chameleon* by Eric Carl, the chameleon wanted to be many things it was not. Yet being what it was not did not make it happy. It found out that being itself was best. Find out about yourself by completing the poem below.

I am _____

and _____

But I am not _____

I like _____

and _____

But I do not like _____

I am happy when _____

and _____

But I am not happy when _____

I feel good about myself when _____

and _____

But I do not feel good about myself when _____

If I could be anything, I would be _____

and _____

But, even though I could be anything,_____

I would not be _____

"I'm As..."

Read *The Talking Eggs* by Robert D. San Souci (Scholastic, 1991). Then brainstorm a list of nouns and adjectives on the board. Have the children use the patterns below to create their own simile poems.

Adjectives (*describing words*)	**Nouns** (*naming words*)

Use the pattern frame below to write your simile poem to show all the different ways you are you.

I'm As...

I'm as quick as a_____ .   I'm as slow as a _____ .

I'm as large as a _____ .   I'm as small as a_____ .

I'm as loud as a _____ .   I'm as quiet as a_____ .

I'm as lazy as a_____ .   I'm as busy as a _____ .

Put them all together and you've got me!

I'm As...

I'm as _____ as a_____ .

I'm as _____ as a_____ .

I'm as _____ as a_____ .

I'm as _____ as a_____ .

I'm as _____ as a_____ .

I'm as _____ as a_____ .

I'm as _____ as a_____ .

I'm as _____ as a_____ .

I'm as _____ as a_____ .

Put them all together and you've got me!

Extension for older students: In a revision of one of their creative writing projects, ask the children to incorporate one or two similes in their descriptions.

Journal Topics

1. Write a sequel to *Frog and Toad Together* and describe their next adventure together.

2. Pretend you are a frog hibernating in the pond. What are you dreaming about?

3. Describe the scariest/funniest/nicest dream you have ever had as a toad.

4. Make a list of the froggy things you do everyday.

5. If you were in charge of the world, how would you keep our ponds clean for all the animals?

6. Write about two different pond animals and how they became friends.

7. Become a pond animal and write a paragraph about your life, telling both the good and the bad.

8. You are an amphibian. Describe your life from egg to childhood.

9. One day while standing beside the pond/river, you shrink to the size of a small fish. You dive in the water. Write about what you find there.

10. You and a friend make a raft from old trees and launch it on the river. Tell about your trip and your adventures with some of the river animals you find there.

11. Complete a research report on an animal of the river or pond. Describe its appearance, eating habits, enemies, and unusual characteristics. Diagram the parts of the body.

12. You are a raindrop. Tell about your life starting with life in the clouds to where you land, where you go, and how you end up back in the clouds.

13. Make up your own fairy tale with a river dragon and a pond giant as main characters.

14. You are a fish and have just been caught by a fisherman. Persuade the fisherman to let you go.

15. You take a magical submarine to the pond/river. Narrate your adventure.

16. You are the river. Tell about the things you see from the time you begin in a small mountain pond and move along all the way to the ocean.

17. Write a dialogue between two animals of the river/pond. They can be either friends or enemies.

A Quilt Story of My Very Own

Read *The Patchwork Quilt* by Valerie Flournoy (Dial Books, 1952).

Imagine that you have been asked to design your very own quilt. The quilt should tell something about yourself, your family, your pets, or things that are special to you. What types of things would you put on your quilt?

In the space below, list some things you would like to add to your quilt. These things should "tell a story" about you. Use the Idea Bank to help you think.

Idea Bank

1. Describe your family. Do you have brothers and sisters? a mom and a dad?
2. Do you want a pet or have any pets?
3. What does your house look like? Is it one story or two?
4. Does your family have any hobbies that it does together?
5. Do you have any hobbies that you do alone?
6. Have you gone on any special trips? What do you remember the most about them?
7. Have you read any books that were special to you?
8. What is your favorite subject in school?
9. Do you have any favorite foods? Would you eat them all the time if you could?
10. Do you have a dream about your future? What do you hope to do? Tell about it.

My Ideas

_____

_____

_____

_____

_____

_____

Now, on separate paper draw a quilt picture that shows some important things from your list, things that will tell a quilt story about you.

Picture Journals

Picture Journals provide an opportunity for young children to respond to stories, concepts, and personal experiences, or to answer a general question posed by the teacher. Children should be encouraged to present stories in the proper sequence, and older or more advanced students may add words and/or simple sentences, referring to the posted word banks for spelling.

Make a book for each child, using construction paper for the covers and several sheets of unlined paper. You may wish to create a shape book. Older or more advanced children can assemble their own books. Demonstrate how to assemble the journal and ask students to decorate the cover.

Some questions and topics for journals are the following:

1. Ask the children to draw pictures of activities they like to do with their families.
2. Ask the children to think about the happy and sad times with their families and then illustrate these times.
3. Draw a picture that shows a family tradition.
4. Draw a favorite relative. Include something in the picture that shows what you do with this person.
5. Illustrate a scene from your family's favorite holiday.
6. Draw a picture of a place you like to visit with your family (zoo, amusement park, playground).
7. Draw a picture of the family pet.
8. What is your favorite place in your house? What do you do there?
9. Think about a place you have visited with your family. Draw a picture of it.
10. Draw a picture of someone in your family working.

Family Acrostics

Write the letters that make up the word *family* vertically on the chalkboard. Then ask the children to think of words that begin with each of these letters that would describe something about families. For example:

F—friendly, father
A—attentive, always there, aunt
M—mother
I—interested
L—loving
Y—you

Extend this activity by creating descriptions of family members: father, mother, sister, brother, etc.

What You Do Best

Try the following activity after reading *The Adventures of Huckleberry Finn.*

Huckleberry Finn is able to do many things well. He can fish, navigate a raft, and take care of himself. He also has the ability to understand other people's problems and is able to change his attitude as he learns more about Jim. He seems like a person that most kids would like to call a friend.

Everyone has the ability to do many things well.

- What do you do well?
- What can you do that almost no one else in your class can do?
- What do you know about which only a few people or perhaps no one else in your class knows about?

You might be thinking, "I really don't know what to write. I can't do much." Think of Huck—he feels the same about himself. Yet he has many special abilities. So do you!

Make an I AM booklet.

1. Cut four or five sheets of notebook paper down the center, lengthwise.

2. For the front and back, make a cover of construction paper that is just a bit wider than the notebook paper.

3. Staple the notebook paper inside the construction paper.

4. Write I AM (which stands for "INTERESTING, AWESOME ME!") on the cover.

5. Open to the first sheet and start listing all the things you can do and your special qualities.

6. As you think of more during the next week, continue your list. Don't be satisfied until you reach at least 100.

Don't think you can do it? Yes, you can. You just don't realize how many great qualities you have. Are you a good friend? Write it down. Do you understand what you read? Write it down. Can you figure out word problems? Do you help with chores at home? Can you cook? Play a musical instrument? Dance? Saw a board?

What Do You Think?

After reading *Matilda* by Roald Dahl (Penguin, 1990), comment on the following quotes from the book:

It's a funny thing about mothers and fathers. Even when their own child is the most disgusting little blister you could ever imagine, they still think that he or she is wonderful. (page 7)

...The way he tells it I feel I am right there on the spot watching it all happen.
"A fine writer will always make you feel that," Mrs. Phelps said. "And don't worry about the bits you can't understand. Sit back and allow the words to wash around you, like music." (page 19)

The books transported her into new worlds and introduced her to amazing people who lived exciting lives. (page 21)

"No one ever got rich being honest," the father said. (page 23)

"Do you think that all children's books ought to have funny bits in them?" Miss Honey asked. "I do." Matilda said. "Children are not so serious as grown-ups and they love to laugh." (page 81)

I'm not in favor of blue-stocking girls. A girl should think about making herself look attractive so she can get a good husband later on. Looks are more important than books, Miss Hunky...
"Now look at me," Mrs. Wormwood said. "Then look at you. You chose books. I chose looks."
(page 97)

They gazed in wonder at this goddess, and suddenly even the boil on her nose was no longer a blemish but a badge of courage. (page 108)

"That's the way to make them learn, Miss Honey," she said. "You take it from me, it's no good just telling them. You've got to hammer it into them. There's nothing like a little twisting and twiddling to encourage them to remember things. It concentrates their minds wonderfully." (page 155)

...The whole object of life, Headmistress, is to go forwards... (page 217)

...Your brain is for the first time having to struggle and strive and keep really busy, which is great... (page 230)

Reading Response Journals

One reason avid readers are drawn to literature is what it does for them on a personal level. They are intrigued with how it triggers their imaginations, what it makes them ponder, and how it makes them see and shape themselves. To assist your students in experiencing this for themselves, incorporate Reading Response Journals in your plans. In these journals, students can be encouraged to respond to the story in a number of ways. Here are a few ideas.

Provide the following response statements on a chart for the students. Tell them the purpose of the journal is to record their thoughts, ideas, observations, and questions as they read the book.

Response Statements

1. Write your feelings about what you read.

2. Write how you feel about a character.

3. Write what you think a character is like, compare characters, compare a character with yourself.

4. Make a prediction.

5. Compare to another story or event.

6. Illustrate a favorite scene.

7. Write about what you liked or disliked; always explain why.

8. Write about what you wish would happen.

9. Tell about something you feel the author should have included in the story.

10. Give your opinion of the illustrations.

11. How did you feel as you read the book? What do you notice about how you read?

12. Write any questions you have after reading.

- Provide students with, or ask them to suggest, topics from the story that may stimulate writing. One example is for students to rewrite *Alexander and the Terrible, Horrible, No Good, Very Bad Day* by Judith Viorst with events from the book about a terrible day experienced by one of the main characters in another book.

- Ask students to draw their responses to certain events or characters in the story.

- Suggest to your students that they write "diary-type" responses to their reading by selecting a character other than the main character and describing events from that character's point of view.

- Give students quotes from the novel and ask them to respond to each quote.

The Road Not Taken

Use the following poem with the activity on page 77.

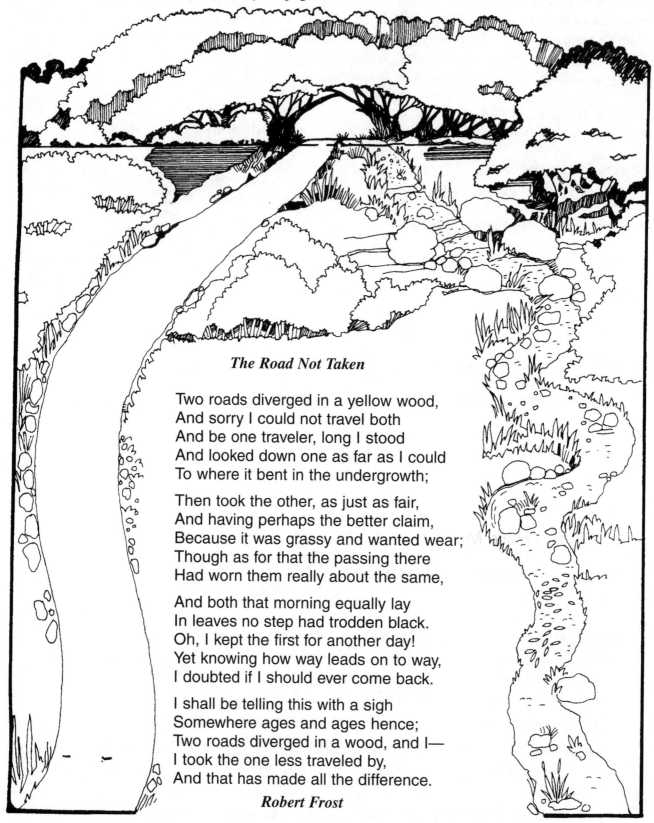

The Road Not Taken

Two roads diverged in a yellow wood,
And sorry I could not travel both
And be one traveler, long I stood
And looked down one as far as I could
To where it bent in the undergrowth;

Then took the other, as just as fair,
And having perhaps the better claim,
Because it was grassy and wanted wear;
Though as for that the passing there
Had worn them really about the same,

And both that morning equally lay
In leaves no step had trodden black.
Oh, I kept the first for another day!
Yet knowing how way leads on to way,
I doubted if I should ever come back.

I shall be telling this with a sigh
Somewhere ages and ages hence;
Two roads diverged in a wood, and I—
I took the one less traveled by,
And that has made all the difference.

Robert Frost

Where the Road Splits

After reading "The Road Not Taken" on the previous page, brainstorm a number of events in your life where you were faced with important decisions. Review your list and select what you feel was a major decision. Next, on a separate piece of paper, write about how things might have been different if you had made a different choice.

Decisions I Have Made Today:

_____

_____

_____

_____

Decisions I Have Made in the Past Year:

_____

_____

_____

_____

Decisions I Have Made in My Life:

_____

_____

_____

_____

Put a star next to the decisions you feel were major life decisions.

Share a Bedtime Story With a Grandparent

To encourage your students to share some special quality time with a grandparent, use a Grandparent Tote. Choose a favorite children's book, such as *Goodnight Moon* by Margaret Wise Brown. Put a copy of the book into a medium-sized tote bag or child's backpack. For added fun, also include a small stuffed animal that correlates with the book, such as the bunny from *Goodnight Moon*. (A book and bunny set is commercially available.) Also include a copy of the note below and the response form from page 79 into the tote. This will explain the activity to the grandparent and provide the child with a project to work on with the grandparent after reading the book together. Send the tote home on a rotating basis with each child in your class, or make several totes to have more than one circulating at a time. (You might make several totes, with each one having a different book.)

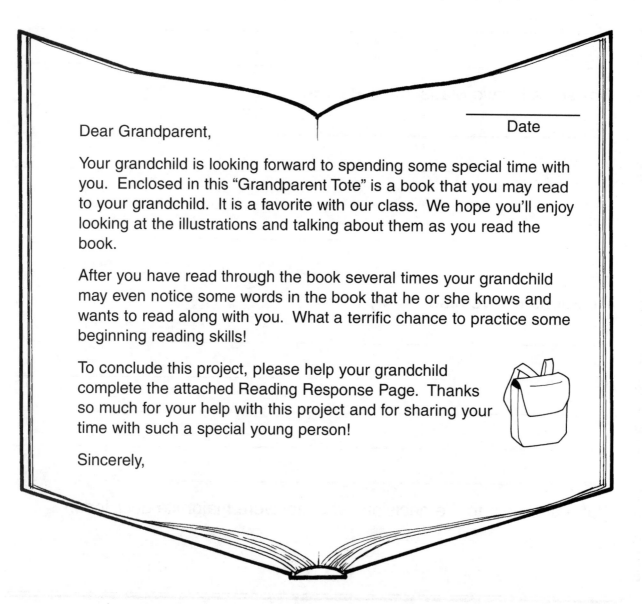

Date

Dear Grandparent,

Your grandchild is looking forward to spending some special time with you. Enclosed in this "Grandparent Tote" is a book that you may read to your grandchild. It is a favorite with our class. We hope you'll enjoy looking at the illustrations and talking about them as you read the book.

After you have read through the book several times your grandchild may even notice some words in the book that he or she knows and wants to read along with you. What a terrific chance to practice some beginning reading skills!

To conclude this project, please help your grandchild complete the attached Reading Response Page. Thanks so much for your help with this project and for sharing your time with such a special young person!

Sincerely,

Share a Bedtime Story with a Grandparent *(cont.)*

Reading Response Page

My grandparent and I read the book _____

_____.

It was written by _____.

It was illustrated by _____.

We liked this book because _____

_____.

Our favorite part of the book was _____

_____.

Here is a picture of our favorite part of the book.

This page was completed by _____ and
  (child's name)

_____ on _____.
  (grandparent's name)   (date)

Recipe for a Perfect Friendship

Read *Frog & Toad Together* by Arnold Lobel (HarperCollins Child Books, 1979). Toad baked some cookies for his friend Frog. Think about what it takes to make a friendship. Make up a recipe for a perfect friendship. Write it on the lines below.

─ A Perfect Friendship ─

Ingredients

_____

_____

_____

_____

Directions

_____

_____

_____

_____

_____

_____

_____

_____

Bake at_____degrees for_____. Share it with a friend.

Fun and Games

Fairy Tale Tag

In this simple game of tag, children are paired in twos. On a deck of cards, write the names of the fairy tale characters listed below. Before play begins, each child must find his or her partner by matching his or her character with a character from the same fairy tale.

Cinderella/Fairy Godmother
Goldilocks/Baby Bear
Red Riding Hood/Grandma
Jack/the Giant
Hansel/Gretel
Elves/Shoemaker
Beauty/the Beast

Snow White/the Dwarves
Mirror/Snow White's Stepmother
The Gingerbread Boy/the Old Woman
First Little Pig/Second Little Pig
Hansel's and Gretel's Stepmother/Hansel's and Gretel's Father
Big Billy Goat Gruff/Little Billy Goat Gruff

Directions: This tag game can be played in a large group or with as few as two children. One child in each pair is designated "It," while the other partner has to keep from being tagged. All children are moving constantly.

Play begins with a signal from the teacher (a whistle or special word). If the child who is "It" tags his or her partner, the partner becomes "It." Play continues for any teacher specified time.

Fairy Tale Switch

Have everyone find a partner in the manner listed above. On your signal, each pair walks about a designated area, the back person following the front person. When you say the name of a fairy tale and the word "Switch" (e.g., Jack and the Beanstalk switch!), everyone does an about-face (turns around) and the game continues with the other partner leading. When you say the word "Rotate," the back person moves ahead to be the front person. Repeat several times and mix up your commands. The game can be changed to include groups of three or even four.

Giants, Wizards, and Elves

This is similar to "Rock, Paper, and Scissors." Giants raise their arms above their heads and make a giant "AAAAAAAAH" sound. Wizards bend their knees and shake their hands out straight in front of them, as if casting a spell and Wizards say, "OOOOOOH!" Elves bend their knees, open their arms out to the side and yell, "EEEEEEEH!"

Giants can crush Wizards, Wizards can cast a spell on Elves, and Elves can trip Giants. Divide students into two equal groups. Each group decides which character they will all be and forms a line side by side, facing the opposing team. On your signal, the groups display their character, and, depending on their combination, will either chase or flee until the signal to end the round is given. A tagged player sits out one round.

Sharing the Responsibility

Complete this activity after reading *Where the Red Fern Grows* by Wilson Rawls (Dell, 1996). The characters in the book knew that responsibility to get the job done must be shared. Old Dan and Little Ann knew that working together as a coon hunting team made them more effective than hunting individually. Billy realized his place in the coon hunting team and held up his end of that responsibility. He also knew he had a responsibility to his family, and unquestioningly gave his father every cent he earned from his coonskin sales and his coon hunt jackpot.

Are there many jobs that are better done if the responsibilities are shared?

Work in groups of two to four to think of ten jobs that are better and more easily done if there is a group effort to complete them. In your list include at least one classroom job and one job at home. When you have finished completing the chart below, choose one of the jobs, and, working in your groups, do it!

Sharing the Responsibility Job Chart

Type of Job	Number of people needed	Completion time if work is done alone	Completion time if work is shared
1.			
2.			
3.			
4.			
5.			
6.			
7.			
8.			
9.			
10.			

Fun and Games

The Whipping Boy by Sid Fleishman (Greenwillow, 1986) is full of adventure and excitement from the point when Jemmy and Prince Brat are kidnapped by two highwaymen in the forest to the final chase through rat-infested sewers. Have students brainstorm a list of highlights from the book and then divide students into cooperative groups in which they work to create a board game.

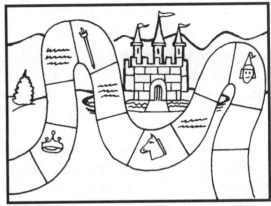

Instruct students to fill in the Brainstorm Worksheet below and then draw their game on poster board. Each group should write a complete set of instructions to accompany their game.

Brainstorm Worksheet

Game name _____

For _____ to _____ players

Ages _____ to _____

Objective _____

_____

Game pieces _____

Procedure _____

_____

_____

_____

Rules _____

_____

_____

Variation _____

_____

This activity may require two sessions to complete. Upon completion, have the groups trade their game boards with one another for a fun-filled afternoon. As an added treat, you might wish to provide a few snacks for the players such as Captain Nips' Potato Chips, Petunia's Popcorn, and Prince's Punch.

Tell a Story

Complete this activity after reading *I Heard the Owl Call My Name* by Margaret Craven (Dell, 1980).

People have told stories for a very long time. Before written language was invented, storytelling was the principal way people passed down their history, traditions, laws, and religious beliefs. In the village of Quee the Indian language is an oral one. No one even knows how words should be written. The young people are gradually losing their oral tradition as they leave the village and go into a world which emphasizes the written word.

People in our country once told stories more than they do today. Before the invention of radio and television, people told stories while sitting around the fireside. Stories were passed down from one generation to the next about family adventures and histories. One could know a lot about one's ancestors by the stories that were told about them. Storytelling became an art as people learned to dramatize and embellish the tales they told.

Today, many people devote a great deal of time to keeping the art of storytelling alive. For example, in Jonesborough, Tennessee, thousands of people get together each year to tell and hear stories at the National Storytelling Festival. The stories that are told at this festival, and others like it, include the following: anecdotes, fish stories, tall tales, ghost stories, tales of true events that are stranger than fiction, animal stories, tales of the supernatural, sad stories, stories of romance and adventure, and tales of famous historical figures. Any kind of story is apt to be told at a storytelling festival because the appeal of a good story remains strong.

Activity

Work with two or three other students to select a story you would like to tell the class. Choose a story you know well. It can be a children's story or any other kind of story you wish. You may want to go to the library to look at a variety of stories. After you choose your story, decide who will tell each part. Then rehearse it together. Be sure to learn your story well, so you won't have to stop in the middle and try to think of what to say next. Find ways to make your story more exciting and interesting. For example, you may wish to use props as part of your storytelling. Props, short for properties, is a stage term used to indicate objects other than costumes or sets which are used in a play. Props can be used to make your story more realistic or more dramatic. Even an object as simple as a hat can add to your performance.

After your group feels comfortable telling the story, perform it for the class. Be sure to look around at your audience so you keep their attention. Relax and have fun telling your story.

Create a Commercial!

At the advertising agency where Peter's dad works, he helps create TV and radio commercials for different products. A commercial is designed to get people to buy a certain item instead of buying another company's item. Commercials use persuasion to get their point across. *Persuasion* means to influence people in a way so they will believe what you are telling them. Some of the methods that commercials use are:

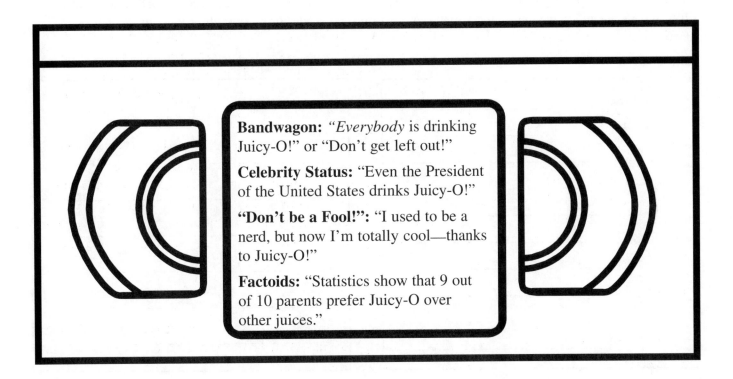

Bandwagon: *"Everybody* is drinking Juicy-O!" or "Don't get left out!"

Celebrity Status: "Even the President of the United States drinks Juicy-O!"

"Don't be a Fool!": "I used to be a nerd, but now I'm totally cool—thanks to Juicy-O!"

Factoids: "Statistics show that 9 out of 10 parents prefer Juicy-O over other juices."

Team Assignment: Your team needs to create a commercial for your drink concoction. Work together in creating a persuasive advertisement that will make the audience want to buy your drink more than any other beverage! You can utilize one of the strategies listed above or a combination of these and your own ideas. Compose a "jingle" for your drink. Take the tune to a well-known or popular song and change words to tell about your drink! Make a poster or do a dance. Be serious, be silly, be outrageous, be sophisticated—but above all, be PERSUASIVE.

Options and Extensions:

- Ask your teacher to videotape the commercials so you may view them at a later time.

- Invite another class to come and watch the commercials.

- Make arrangements with other classes and present the commercials there. Start with, "We interrupt this lesson to bring you a word from our sponsor!"

- Sing the jingles over the school intercom system.

Mock Trial: Who Is Shiloh's Rightful Owner?

Complete this activity after reading *Shiloh* by Phyllis R. Naylor (Bantam Doubleday Dell, 1992).

Imagine Marty were to take Judd Travers to court for the right to own Shiloh. Who do you think would win the case? What would Marty's argument be? What would Judd's argument be? What witnesses would be called upon? What would the judge and jury decide?

Now it is your opportunity to find out. Your class will have a mock trial between Marty and Judd. First, with your teacher's help, choose students to play the following characters in your courtroom drama:

Marty Preston _____

Marty's lawyer _____

Judd Travers _____

Judd's lawyer _____

Judge _____

Witnesses _____

_____

_____

_____

_____

Jury
(12 people)

_____   _____

_____   _____

_____   _____

_____   _____

_____   _____

_____   _____

The next step is for both sides to gather evidence. Using accounts from the book and real documents, try to gather as many facts as possible. Both sides should try to use the laws about animal ownership to strengthen their argument. Remember, speculation and emotion do not go far in a courtroom! Although most readers probably feel Shiloh belongs to Marty, an objective jury may not. Finally, both sides should study the opposition's argument and be ready to counter it.

There should be an equal number of witnesses for both sides. If someone claims to have seen Judd beating his dogs, for example, then someone else should vouch for the dogs' well-being. Lawyers for both sides should prompt witnesses on what questions to expect. When the day of the trial arrives, participants wear appropriate costumes and play out the trial in character. Do you think Judd would dress up nicely for a day in court? What about Marty? David Howard?

The jury has a very important responsibility. They must listen to the facts and go by the letter of the law as they understand it, even if they think it is unfair.

Finally, consider videotaping the proceedings and showing the tape to parents during an open house.

Find It

Questions

Define the word diversity. How much animal diversity is present in everyday life?

Setting the Stage

- Have students compare their ideas of what an animal is with the ideas of others in the class.
- Discuss with students various kinds of animals such as amphibians, arthropods, birds, corals, fish, jellyfish, mammals, mollusks, reptiles, sea urchins, starfish, sponges, and worms.

Materials Needed for Each Individual

- pencil and paper
- animal data chart (page 88)

Procedure (Student Instructions)

1. Walk around the school yard looking for different kinds of animals.
2. On your data-capture sheet, write down the name of each animal and draw a picture of each animal that you find, including the type of animal it is. For example, a cat is a mammal and a lizard is a reptile.
3. Write two descriptive words for each animal. Each descriptive word may be used only once during the investigation.
4. Consolidate all student lists into one list on the board.
5. List animals by their types.
6. Determine which type of animal was seen most.
7. Work together as a class to come up with a list of traits all animals have in common.

Extension

Have students use a camera to take pictures of the animals to compare and classify in class.

Closure

Have students make animal journals in which to write their ideas about animals. Have each student draw a picture of his or her favorite animal seen.

Find It *(cont.)*

Complete the chart below.

Name of Animal	Type of Animal	Picture of Animal	Descriptive Words

Language Arts

Reading, writing, listening, and speaking experiences blend easily with the teaching and reinforcement of science concepts. Science can be a focal point as you guide your students through poems and stories, stimulating writing assignments, and dramatic oral presentations. If carefully chosen, language arts material can serve as a springboard to a plant lesson, the lesson itself, or an entertaining review.

There is a wealth of good literature to help you connect your curriculum. Two of these choices are briefly reviewed for you on this page.

Science Concept: *Plants need certain things to live and grow.*

Flowers, Fruits, and Seeds by Jerome Wexler (Simon & Schuster, 1987)

A simple explanation of how flowers produce fruits and fruits produce seeds.

- Discuss with students what a plant needs to live and grow. Have them conduct plant growing experiments.
- Have students draw a picture of what happens to a seed when it gets the things it needs to grow.
- Have students draw a picture of what might happen to a seed if it does not get what it needs.

Science Concept: *Plants have a cycle of life.*

The Big Tree by Bruce Hiscock (Atheneum, 1981) and *The Fall of Freddie the Leaf* by Leo Busgalia, Ph. D (Slack, 1982).

Both stories tell how a tree changes. *The Big Tree* focuses on the life of a tree historically. *The Fall of Freddie the Leaf* focuses on a tree's yearly cycle.

- Have students draw the life cycle of any plant.
- Have students stage seed races. Include a variety of seeds as their contestants. Determine how different seeds travel most effectively.
- Have students as individuals, in small groups, or as a class write their own story about a plant in each stage of its growth.
- Discuss with students seasons and plant growth.
- Have students stage a plant growth cycle drama based on ideas from *The Big Tree* and *The Fall of Freddie the Leaf.* Assign people to play the parts of the flying seeds, sun mountains, ocean, desert, bird, mouse, big weed, child who steps on the flower, boy, girl, giant flower, birds, bees, butterflies, seedpods, and seeds. Have students present their drama for others.

Language Arts *(cont.)*

SCIENCE CONCEPTS: *Many plants grow from tiny seeds.*
Read the following guided imagery to the class. Discuss with students how they felt as they "grew." Use the guided imagery and discussion as a writing prompt.

Script

Imagine yourself to be a tiny, tiny seed inside a seed packet with hundreds of other seeds. It is very dark inside the packet—you can't see anything. You feel very, very crowded with all the other seeds in there pushing up against you, squ-e-e-zing you between them. Suddenly, you hear a loud tearing noise—RRRRIP— and light flashes in your eyes. It is the sun.

But—LOOK OUT!—Two big fingers are reaching into your seed packet, and they are coming straight at YOU! PINCH! They got you! The fingers pull you up, up, up and out of the seed packet, into the sunlight. Then, all of a sudden, they let you go. Down, down, down you drop—into a hole in the earth. A giant hand pushes soil on top of you. Now it is dark again.

It is cool in the earth, and your body can feel and smell the dampness of the ground.

Pause

Time passes. You fell a need to stretch. First your seed coat cracks open and you send out a tiny, tiny root down, down, down, down even deeper into the wet, cool soil, to find the minerals and water you somehow know you need to live and grow.

Pause

Time passes. Now you start to feel warmer, warmer, warmer. You feel a need to stretch again. This time, you grow up, up, up, up with your stem, up toward the surface of the earth. You break through!

Pause

Aaaaahhhh! You feel the sun's warmth on your face. It feels so good. You breathe deeply now, and stretch out even more. Your leaves slowly grow out, uncurling to catch even more of the sun's light. You feel yourself growing stronger with the sun's touch. The sun is giving you the power you need to mix together the things you need to make food—your chlorophyll, the water and minerals from the soil, and the carbon dioxide from the air. These will be things that will help you grow stronger and stronger.

Pause

It is quiet now. You have made a beautiful flower. Feel yourself rock gently back and forth, back and forth, as the wind pushes softly against your stem and leaves. Feel your roots stretching deeper into the soft, moist soil, keeping you from falling over in the wind. You feel warm, comfortable, and very, very, very peaceful.

Visit a Nursery

In this activity you will need to visit a nursery in order to receive some general information to be used in a later assignment. Follow the instructions below and then answer the questions.

Preparing for your visit

- Locate the yellow pages or telephone directory.

- Find several local nurseries that you and a friend could visit.

- Phone these nurseries and ask what their business hours are.

- Based on the information gathered, choose the nursery that you will visit.

- Arrange for you and a friend to get to the nursery.

- Prepare questions that you may have about plants and gardens so that you can ask the attendant at the nursery.

    1. _____

    2. _____

    3. _____

While at the nursery:

- Read *The Science Garden* by Frances Hodgson Burnett (Dell, 1990). Ask to see some of the flowers mentioned in the book or some that you have researched. Make a sketch of what you saw.

- Ask how you would go about choosing flowers for a garden. Take notes on this information for use in a later assignment.

- Choose several flowers that you would like to plant if you have your own garden. List them below along with their price. This information will be useful to you when you begin to plant flowers in your own garden.

_____

_____

_____

_____

Arctic Animals

Complete this activity after reading *Kävik the Wolf Dog* by Walt Morey (Viking Penguin, 1997). To survive in the harsh tundra environment, Arctic animals must develop special physical traits called adaptations. Through the years of evolution, each type of animal has developed its own ways of coping with its environment. Here are some interesting facts and information about some of the many animals that live in the Arctic.

Lemming

The lemming is a very small herbivore, which means it eats only plants. It is grayish-brown in the summer and changes to white in the winter. This camouflage helps it to hide from predators. This mammal's thick, waterproof fur helps to keep it warm. Strangely, every three or four years the lemming population greatly increases. This trend toward population growth can cause drastic events to occur, such as a large number of lemmings suddenly running off cliffs. As a result of these drastic events, the lemming population rapidly decreases over the next three or four years.

Caribou

The caribou is a large, light brown herbivore. It migrates throughout the Arctic searching for food. Its short tail and small ears help it to conserve heat. It has the widest feet of all the deer, to help it run across the snow. The caribou is also called the reindeer. Sometimes thousands of caribou travel together in a herd.

Polar Bear

The polar bear is a very large animal and can weigh up to 1,700 lbs (771 kg). It is an omnivore that eats mostly meat along with some plants. Its fur is yellowish-white in the summer, and turns to pure white in the winter. This coloring helps the polar bear blend in with its surroundings. The thick, furry hair on its feet provides warmth and works like snowshoes. It has webbed feet so it can swim easily. This mammal eats large amounts of food in the autumn in order to produce the fat it needs for warmth and stored energy to survive the winter. Since the polar bear does not hibernate, it builds a den in the snow or rocks to protect itself from the cold while it rests.

Walrus

The walrus is a carnivore, which means it eats only meat. It is very large and can be gray or cinnamon colored. Its skin has a thin fur coat and a thick layer of fat, or blubber, underneath it to help provide warmth. The walrus with the largest ivory tusks has the greatest status in the community. The tusks are used for weapons and as ice choppers. The walrus has sensitive whiskers that help it search for food in the darkness at the bottom of the ocean.

Narwhal

The narwhal is a large bluish-gray sea mammal. It is a carnivore and migrates to search for food and avoid frozen waters in the Arctic. This animal is virtually waterproof because of the oil glands in its skin.

Arctic Animals *(cont.)*

Ptarmigan

The ptarmigan is a medium-sized bird that usually eats plants but sometimes eats meat, making it an omnivore. Its feathers provide camouflage since they are mostly brown in the summer and white in the winter. The feathers on its feet provide extra warmth and help it shuffle through the snow. This bird spends most of its time on the ground. During the winter it will burrow into snowbanks for warmth.

Snow Goose

The snow goose is a large bird that is a herbivore. It comes in two colors—all white or dark gray with a white head. The snow goose has large number of feathers to trap air for better insulation. In the autumn, this bird consumes large amounts of food to produce a heavy layer of fat so it will have enough energy to migrate south in the winter. Sometimes you will see a snow goose with a white body and an orange head. This occurs when a bird eats large quantities of plants from Arctic waters. These plants are high in iron content, causing the bird's head feathers to turn orange.

Activity

Use the chart as an example to show how adaptations help the animals described in this activity.

ANIMAL	ADAPTATION	PURPOSE OF ADAPTATION
Lemming		
Caribou		
Polar Bear		
Walrus		
Narwhal		
Ptarmigan		
Snow Goose		

Teaching the Social Sciences Through the Multiple Intelligences

Teaching an Alien

Think of an everyday thing you do, like washing dishes, brushing your teeth, making a sandwich, etc. Explain how to do this regular and ordinary thing to an alien who might never have even heard about the process. Be as complete and specific as you can.

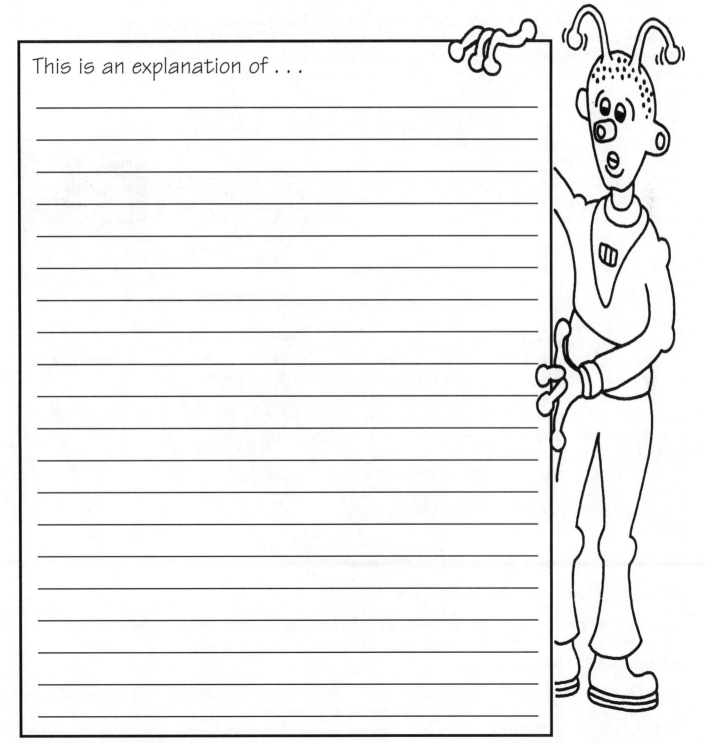

This is an explanation of . . .

Logs and Journals

Rationale

In order to enhance student understanding of historical events and to provide motivation for learning about events, you should read to students at least one historical picture book for each unit of study. If you feel your students are capable, then have them read an additional historical picture book on their own. With the abundant selection of wonderful historical literature available, students can be allowed to self-select the book they will read. However, if we allow students to select their own books to read, how do we keep track of their progress? Student logs and journals can be an excellent way of charting student work, progress, and attitudes for both self-selected books, and for whole class studies of particular historical literature.

Reading logs are designed to track progress and the specific amount of time spent reading. The time limit is set at your discretion. It may include the time spent during a particular unit of study. Or you may simply choose to track on a monthly basis.

A journal is one step beyond a log. In the journal, students respond to the books they are reading rather than just keeping a list of the titles. By reading your students' journals you can get a good idea of not only their reading comprehension ability but also their ability to communicate in writing. The motivation for keeping the journal is the personal response you write back to the students. When teachers and students write back and forth to each other, a more personal relationship can develop. With class sizes constantly increasing, the journal may be the only opportunity for teacher and student to have a one-to-one correspondence on a regular basis. Students will undoubtedly enjoy this special attention.

How To Use Logs and Journals

The log is simple to use. It merely requires that students record what they read during a period of time. The reading log included in this guide is for a one-month period, but you can adjust that if you wish.

Journals have a more complex purpose. After reading a story on their own, or as a class, you may ask your students to respond to the story in their journals.

Readers' Theater

Readers' Theater is a performance of a book or a story, using only the voices of the actors to create the setting, action, and characters of the play.

An entire book can be adapted for Reader's Theater if it is relatively short. Usually it is best to adapt only one chapter of a book, hoping that the Reader's Theater will stimulate the students to read the story from cover to cover.

Now . . . let's turn your students into script writers! Use these guidelines to convert your story into a script.

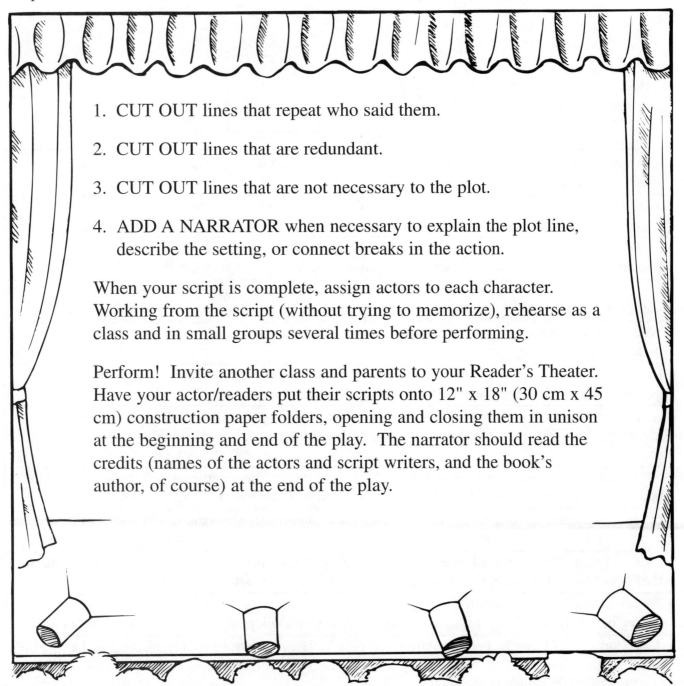

1. CUT OUT lines that repeat who said them.

2. CUT OUT lines that are redundant.

3. CUT OUT lines that are not necessary to the plot.

4. ADD A NARRATOR when necessary to explain the plot line, describe the setting, or connect breaks in the action.

When your script is complete, assign actors to each character. Working from the script (without trying to memorize), rehearse as a class and in small groups several times before performing.

Perform! Invite another class and parents to your Reader's Theater. Have your actor/readers put their scripts onto 12" x 18" (30 cm x 45 cm) construction paper folders, opening and closing them in unison at the beginning and end of the play. The narrator should read the credits (names of the actors and script writers, and the book's author, of course) at the end of the play.

Write About It

Complete this activity after reading *The Great Little Madison* by Jean Fritz (G. P. Putnam's Sons, 1987). Reproduce this page as many times as you need to and cut out the creative writing topics along the lines. Place the cut-apart topics into a shoebox or other container and let students draw one. Have pairs of students brainstorm ideas for their stories. Set a timer for twenty minutes and direct the students to write on their chosen topic for that time period.

It is the year 1824. General Lafayette is coming to your hometown to visit. Tell what preparations your family and town will make for his tour.
You think your best friend would make the perfect wife for the unmarried James Madison. In an introductory letter to your friend, describe Madison and tell her about his accomplishments.
As Daniel Shay, write a speech convincing your fellow farmers why they must march to the federal arsenal in Springfield, Massachusetts, and what they must do when they get there.
As the wife of an important delegate, you have been invited to the mansion for one of Dolley Madison's famous parties. Describe the food and events.
Your newspaper has been given the scoop about the Hamilton-Burr duel. As a witness to the event, write a news feature describing the duel.
Madison hated the idea of slavery yet he knew it would be too costly to run a plantation without the help of slaves. What are some alternatives Madison might have explored?
Alexander Hamilton spoke for six hours on why he thought the president of the U.S. should serve a life term. What are some of the things you think Hamilton might have said during that six-hour speech?
At the time of Madison's presidential term, there were two political parties, the Republicans and the Federalists. Which one would you have chosen if you were alive then? Explain why.
In order to protect the U.S. from possible commercial interference by France, Thomas Jefferson bought the Louisiana Territory. How might the U.S. be different if this purchase had not been made?
Captain Oliver Perry captured an entire British squadron on Lake Erie. As Captain Perry, explain to President Madison some of the tactics you used to help win the battle.
President Madison and his wife Dolley knew that the British were going to attack Washington, D.C. Dolley began to pack things for safekeeping. If you were Dolley, what would you have saved?
American lawyer Francis Scott Key witnessed Fort McHenry's victory over the British and even wrote a song about it called "The Star-Spangled Banner." Write a poem describing the events. (Keep in mind the words of the song.)

Creative Writing Topics

Complete this activity after reading *The Usborne Book of Explorers* by Felicity Everett and Straun Reid (Usborne Publishing, Ltd., 1991). Here are some suggested ways for using the creative writing topics below.

1. Write one topic per day on the chalkboard; have students write for a specified amount of time.
2. Present students with three or four topics from which to choose.
3. Provide students with a copy of all the topics for homework; determine a due date for each one.
4. Cut apart the rectangles, place into a bag, and have each student draw one.

* In Columbus' day people thought there were monsters, giants, and mermaids in the ocean. Draw a picture and write a paragraph about a sea creature that you think people then might have imagined.
* You are a fifteenth century explorer. Write a letter to the King and Queen of your country; outline your reasons for wanting to explore unknown regions. Tell what you expect to find.
* When Columbus was in Iceland, he heard tales about the Vikings who had voyages into the western seas. Write your own tale of a Viking journey.
* The thick seaweed of the Sargasso Sea was frightening to the sailors in Columbus' fleet. Pretend you are a sailor. Write a letter home describing this experience.
* When the *Santa Maria* hit a reef and was wrecked, Columbus had to leave 43 men behind because there was no room on the other ships. Tell how you would choose 43 men if you were Columbus.
* Spanish conquistadors believed that they were entitled to the resources of America regardless of who lived there. Write a paragraph telling why you agree or disagree with this philosophy.
* You are an astronaut. Explain how the early explorers of Christopher Columbus' era influenced your decision to become an astronaut.
* The year is 1498 and you are the first female explorer. Write a story about your all-female crew and their important discovery.
* Tell what would be more exciting to you: to be an explorer in the late fifteenth to early sixteenth century or to be an astronaut on a mission to the moon. Explain the reasons for your choice.
* Compare the dangers faced by early explorers and those faced by current space explorers. Which would you rather have to deal with and why?
* You are the gromet on the late night shift. Half way through you fall asleep. When you awaken you sense that the sand has stopped flowing. The captain walks in. Finish this scene.
* What if Columbus and Leonardo da Vinci had met? Write a conversation they might have had. (Think about some things they might have had in common.)
* Pretend you are Magellan. Instead of sailing around the world, your voyage takes you to the future (1900s). How would you and your crew react to all the new technology? Write a story.
* What one modern technological advance in navigation would the explorers of the late 1400s to the late 1500s find the most beneficial? Which advance would surprise them the most?
* Write a story telling about a voyage that Cortés and Pizarro might have planned together. Do you think they would have gotten along well or would there have been arguments?
* Choose any two explorers. Compare their characteristics and personality traits.

Freedom of Speech

Develop speaking skills and synthesize knowledge of Constitutional facts with this activity. Cut apart the topics in the boxes below and place them into a specially decorated shoebox or other container. Call on a student to draw a topic and direct him or her to give an answer. Students may stand by their desks or go to the front of the room when speaking. Encourage students to use complete sentences throughout their explanations. You may want to add your own questions to the topic list.

1. In your opinion, was the Grand Convention a success? Defend your answer.

2. The Constitution is sometimes called a miracle. Explain why you think this a fitting term.

3. If you had been a delegate to the Convention, would you have been for or against a strong central government? Defend your answer.

4. The Constitution was written in secret. Tell why you do or do not think it should have been done this way.

5. Choose a delegate and describe his outstanding characteristics and contributions to the proceedings.

6. Women and slaves were not allowed to vote during this era. Tell when and how each group finally got the vote.

7. If you could have been a delegate, who would you have chosen to be and why?

8. Explain how the meetings of the Constitutional Convention might have been different if women and slaves had been allowed to participate.

9. The delegates worked under some adverse conditions. Which condition do you think was the hardest for them to endure?

10. What if a Bill of Rights had not been added to the Constitution? How do you think it would have affected your rights today?

11. The delegates argued and debated about many issues. Which issue caused the most disagreements; why?

12. Tell why you think the delegates invented the idea of a Supreme Court; explain its purpose.

13. What is the difference between the requirements for candidates to the Senate and candidates to the House of Representatives?

14. James Madison is often called the "Father of the Constitution." Tell why you think he deserves this title?

15. Ben Franklin told a friend he hoped the Constitution would last but that "...nothing is certain but death and taxes." Explain this quote.

"Buffalo Bill Bucks" Program

Make a copy of this list for each student to have for reference. Be generous with letting students earn money. It might also be wise to alert parents of this new system.

Give students an opportunity to spend their money as a culminating activity. Let them know the cost of an activity. For example, a special movie or story time will cost each student $500.00. Have them decide on a goal and then determine if they have enough money.

Students can earn money in these ways:

1. Each Monday, you will receive $100.00 for being in school or $20.00 a day for being in school and completing your work.
2. Any time you do outstanding class work or show good citizenship you can earn $5.00 to $20.00.
3. If the whole class has worked hard all day long, you may earn a bonus of $5.00 to $20.00.
4. Receiving 100% on classroom tests can earn from $1.00 to $20.00.
5. If you hold any type of classroom responsibility such as messenger or monitor and complete it daily, you will receive $10.00 a day.
6. If you are elected to be banker for this program and fulfill the job, you can earn $20.00.
7. Dividend payments for a Bull Market day will earn $20.00.

Students can lose money in these ways:

Breaking any class rule $10.00

Incomplete assignments (missing name, messy work) $10.00

Not following instructions $10.00

Misbehaving $15.00

Out-of-control noise $10.00

Asking if you will receive money $10.00

Tattling $5.00

Out of seat without permission (drinks, at pencil sharpener) $10.00

Bathroom privileges $5.00

Tardiness $5.00

Lost pencils replaced $10.00

Unexpected school-time problem . . . . From $1.00 to unlimited

Fun With Math

Here are some fun math activities to incorporate into your thematic unit. Each of the assignments below is related to the text of *A Picture Book of George Washington* by David A. Adler (Holiday House, 1989).

* One-to-One Correspondence

After the war between the colonies and England ended, the 13 colonies became 13 states. Direct the students to draw 13 squares—one for each colony. Then tell them to draw 13 stars—one for each state. Draw a line from each colony to each state.

* Sets

The war between England and the colonies lasted *eight* years. George was *eleven* years old when his father died. At *sixteen* George was very tall. Present one of these facts (or any other of your choosing) to the students. Give each child a paper plate and some markers (dried beans, cereal, buttons, etc.). Tell them to make a set on the plate to represent the number in the sentence. Read another sentence and follow the same procedure.

* Measuring and Estimating

George used his father's surveying tools to measure a turnip field and a pine forest. Let students measure their heights, waists, wrists, or ankles using this method. Give students rolls of string or yarn and scissors. Direct them to cut off the amount of string they think will just fit around the wrist or to cut a piece they estimate to be the same length as their height. (You may want to have partners work together for this project.) Have them then compare their estimates with strings cut to actual lengths. Afterwards, discuss how well they were able to estimate.

* Number Names

Pair students for this activity. Direct them to find examples of number names in the text (e.g., "In 1753, when George Washington was twenty-one…"). Have them write the number name and its corresponding numeral.

* Calendars

In April 1775, fighting broke out between England and three colonies. One month later, leaders of the thirteen colonies met in Philadelphia. Have students identify the next month. Ask what month it is now and which month is next. Give each student a blank calendar. Have them fill in the dates for the coming month.

Lincoln's Homes

Abraham Lincoln was born in Kentucky. When he was seven years old, his family moved to Indiana. Fourteen years later they moved to Illinois.

1. Write the answer for each problem in the circle provided.
2. Connect the numbers in the circles in 1-2-3 order to trace Lincoln's route from home to home.

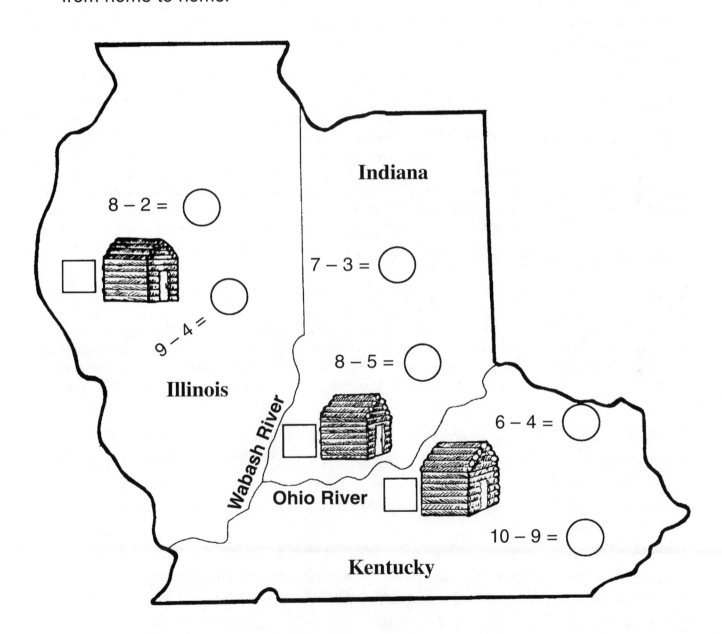

* Write a 1 in the square next to Lincoln's first home.

* Write a 2 in the square next to Lincoln's second home.

* Write a 3 in the square next to Lincoln's third home.

Doing Without

"Use it up, wear it out, make it do, or do without."

During World War II the needs of the soldier came before the needs of the consumer on the home front. To prevent prices from skyrocketing due to shortages of consumer goods, a governmental agency called the Office of Price Administration (OPA) did two things.

1.   The OPA sets price limits on many items.

2.   The agency began rationing products such as sugar, coffee, gas, shoes, meat, fish, flour, and canned goods.

Under the OPA's system of rationing, each American was given ration coupons every month. These coupons were worth 48 Blue Points which could be used to buy processed foods, and 64 Red Points, which could be used to buy meat, butter, and fats. In addition to paying the price of an item, consumers also had to give up the required number of ration points.

The rationing schedules of the OPA were always changing as a result of supply and demand. To help consumers keep track of these changes, the OPA provided tables that gave an updated listing of food point values. Pages 105 and 106 contain information from the actual OPA rationing schedules for September, 1944. Have students use these schedules for the following activities. Remind students that they are only allowed 64 Red Points (meats, butter, fat) and 48 Blue Points (processed foods) per month!

Rationing Activities

1.   Ask students how many total ration points were used to purchase the following items: 1 lb. (0.4536 kg) porterhouse steak, ½ lb. (226.8 g) of cheddar cheese, 10 oz. (300 g) canned apricots, 8 oz. (226.8 g) tomato juice, and 1 can of whole kernel corn. Ask how many of these points were red and how many were blue and then ask how many ration points were left for the rest of the month.

2.   Explain to students that consumers tried to purchase foods that did not require any ration points in order to make their points last an entire month. Have students list three items from each schedule that did not require points.

3.   Have students plan a meal for their family. Ask them to figure out how many red points and blue points the meal would cost.

4.   Plan how you would use your 64 Red Points and 48 Blue Points for an entire month. What foods would you buy that did not cost any points? **Note**: Each person could automatically purchase 2 pounds (1000 g) of sugar per month without using ration points.

5.   Have students write word problems that can be solved using the Rationing Schedules.

6.   Have students set up algebraic rationing equations such as the following for classmates to solve:

   1 T-bone steak + 1 lb. (0.4536 kg) of shrimp = 8 oz. (226.8 g) container of applesauce + x.

Doing Without *(cont.)*

Rationing Schedule

Red Stamp Consumer Point Values, September, 1944

Meats, Fish, Fats, and Dairy Products

BEEF	Grades AA, A,B	LAMB	Grades AA, A,B	PORK	Points per lb. (453.6 g)	VEAL	Points per lb. (453.6 g)
Porterhouse Steak	14	Loin Chops	10	Tenderloin	8	Loin Chops	0
T-Bone Steak	13	Leg Chops and Steaks	8	Roast Loin	8	Shoulder Chops	0
Sirloin Steak	13	Sirloin Roast	7	Ham-Boneless	6	Rump Roast	0
Boneless Rump Roast	12	Shoulder Chops	5	Shoulder	0	Shoulder Roast	0
Short Ribs	0	Chuck Crosscut	3	Knuckles	0	Flank Meat	0
Hamburger-ground beef	0	Lamb Patties	0	Spareribs	0	Ground Veal and Patties	0

BACON	Points per lb. (453.6 g)	FISH	Points per lb. (453.6 g)	SAUSAGE	Points per lb. (453.6 g)	OTHER MEATS	Points per lb. (453.6 g)
Canadian	8	Shrimp	6	Dry	0	Luncheon Meats	0
Sides, aged dry-cured	2	Tuna	6	Semidry	0	Tamales	0
Sliced	0	Oysters	2	Fresh, Smoked	0	Meat Loaf	0

FATS, OILS, DAIRY	Points per lb. (453.6 g)	FATS, OILS, DAIRY	Points per lb. (453.6 g)	FATS, OILS, DAIRY	Points per lb. (453.6 g)	FATS, OILS, DAIRY	Points per lb. (453.6 g)
Creamery Butter	20	Margarine	2	Cheddar Cheese	12	Cottage Cheese	6
Country/Farm Butter	12	Shortening	0	Colby Cheese	12	Cream Spread	6
Process Butter	12	Salad/Cooking Oil	0	Creamed Cheese	6	Canned Milk	1

Doing Without *(cont.)*

Rationing Schedule
Blue Stamp Consumer Point Values, September, 1944
Processed Foods

	Over	0 oz (0 g)	7 oz (210 g)	10 oz (300 g)	14 oz (420 g)	1 lb. 2 oz (.5136 kg)	1 lb. 6 oz (.6336 kg)
CANNED or **BOTTLED** including		7 oz (210 g)	10 oz (300 g)	14 oz (420 g)	1 lb. 2 oz (.5136 kg)	1 lb. 6 oz (.6336 kg)	2 lb. (.9072 kg)
FRUITS Apples		10	20	20	30	40	60
Apricots		10	20	20	30	40	60
Fruit Cocktail		10	20	30	40	50	80
Peaches		10	20	30	40	50	80
JUICES Grape Juice		10	10	10	20	20	30
Orange Juice		0	0	0	0	0	0
Tomato Juice		10	10	10	20	20	30
VEGETABLES Corn (whole kernel)		0	0	0	0	0	0
Spinach		0	0	0	0	0	0
Tomatoes		10	10	10	20	20	30
SPREADS Jams, Preserves, Marmalades		0	0	0	0	0	0
Jellies		0	0	0	0	0	0
Fruit Butters		0	0	0	0	0	0
SPECIAL PRODUCTS Tomato Catsup		20	30	50	70	90	130
Tomato Sauce/Paste		0	0	0	0	0	0

Grandmother's Quilt

Display a patchwork quilt (brought into the classroom by you or a student) in an area where it can be easily seen and measured. Write the following questions on the board or use them to discuss the quilt.

1. What are the outermost measurements of the quilt?
2. What is the area of the quilt?
3. What are the predominant colors of the quilt? Are the colors primary, secondary, or tertiary? Are any of the colors in the quilt complementary?
4. What is the predominant shape used in the quilt?
5. How many quilt squares are in the quilt?
6. What are the measurements of each quilt square?
7. What is the perimeter of each quilt square?
8. Is a border used around the quilt? What is the perimeter of the border?
9. Name all the shapes that are used to make this quilt.

Bonus: Quilt patterns were often given names to describe what they represented. Examples include Ohio Star, Card Trick, Flying Geese, and Morning Star. Bring in books about quilts and ask the students to identify the block names in the example quilt.

Patchwork Quilt Math

Patchwork quilts were among the few belongings that traveled west with the early settlers of the United States. Since fabric was scarce and expensive, the creative women of the West sewed scraps of fabric into quilts that were used as blankets. These practical items were also intricate works of art.

Have each student make a 6" (15 cm) square that will serve as his or her quilt block. Allow students to fill their blocks with geometric patterns of their choice. For example, they may cut out:

2" (5 cm) squares	1" x 6" (2.5 cm x 15 cm) rectangles	6" (15 cm), 3" (7.5 cm),
3" (7.5 cm) squares	2" x 6" (5 cm x 15 cm) rectangles	and 2" (5 cm) squares cut on diagonals to make
	3" x 6" (7.5 cm x 15 cm) rectangles	triangles

Students may use any combination of shapes to fit their blocks.

Additional Ideas:

1. Have the class assemble all of the paper blocks together to make a class quilt as a display on the bulletin board. Have students assemble four or six squares of their own as samplers.
3. Using a copier, reduce the students' patterns to use them as note cards. Each can be colored or painted.

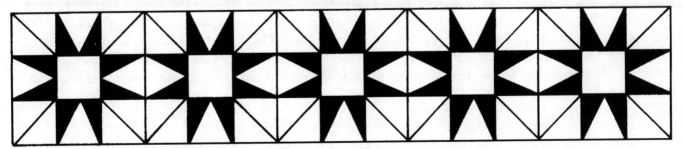

Native American Games

All games can be played indoors or outdoors, except for Danger Signal which should be played outdoors.

Tossing and Catching Games

◆ *Bowl Catch:* Variations found in all areas of the Americas

The Native Americans played this game with a bowl and pottery disks, beaver or muskrat teeth, fruit pits, or bone depending on the area. One side of the object was plain and the other had designs which established its value.

Materials: shallow basket (8" to 10" or 20 cm to 25 cm across); 6 large lima beans

With a marker draw a Native American symbol on one side of each bean. Put the beans in the bowl. Sitting cross-legged, hold the bowl in both hands. Toss the beans into the air. Catch them in the bowl. Count those that land design side up, this is your score. Depending on the age and ability of the students, the symbols can be assigned a value and it can become a math game.

◆ *Toss and Catch:* Played by Plains, Woodlands, and Northwest Coast Tribes

This game, played with sticks or reeds about 3 to 4 inches (7.5 to 10 cm) long and ⅛ to ¼ inch (.3 to .6 cm) in diameter, was popular with boys and girls. Using craft sticks, balance two on the back of your hand at waist level. Toss the sticks straight up into the air to about the height of your head and catch them in the palm of your hand. To increase difficulty add more sticks, turn around before catching the sticks, or catch the sticks with your palm open.

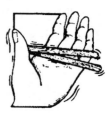

Hunting and Stalking Games

◆ *Danger Signal:* Played by Plains, Woodland, and Northwest Coast tribes

To develop hunting skills, young braves were taken into a fairly dense forest and told to spread out in various directions. They were told to listen for danger signals such as those given by alarmed birds or animals. At the sound of the alarm, they were to freeze or head quickly for the cover of a tree or rock. Divide the class into thirds: braves, rocks, trees. Position yourself (as chief) at the finish line. Rocks and trees are stationary. The braves begin at the starting line. The chief turns his back and the braves move from rock to tree quickly and quietly. The chief blows a whistle, turns around, and tries to spot a brave. Braves should be frozen behind a tree or rock or they are out. The winner is the first brave to cross the finish line.

⊗ Chief (teacher)
○ Braves
○ Student "rocks"
△ Student "trees"

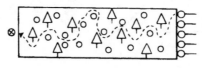

Native American Games *(cont.)*

◆ ***Rattler:*** Played by Plains, Woodland, Northwest Coastal, and Southwest tribes

Since rattlesnakes are found throughout the Americas, this game was developed in many forms by numerous tribes.

Have the class form a large circle, about 20 feet (6 meters) in diameter. Select two volunteers: rattlesnake and hunter. Blindfold the snake and the hunter. Place them about 10 feet (3 meters) apart within the circle. Give the rattlesnake a baby rattle or a maraca. Both students start moving. At a given interval, approximately 15 seconds, the group hisses. The rattlesnake needs to rattle at each hiss. The hunter tries to touch the snake to win the game. After this happens, select a new rattler and hunter.

Important Safety Precaution: Since the players are blindfolded, they need to move slowly and carefully, listening for each other. If the chief (you) shouts "STOP!", all action must freeze.

◆ ***Guardian of the Fire:*** Played by Plains, Woodland, and Northwest Coastal tribes.

Student sits cross-legged and blindfolded in the center of the circle. In front of him or her, within easy reach is a dowel or a ruler. This is the fire stick! The Guardian listens carefully with his or her hands on his or her knees. If he or she touches the person in the act of taking the stick, he or she wins the game. If not, the Guardian tries to guess who stole the fire stick. If he or she doesn't, the thief becomes the next Guardian.

◆ ***There!:*** Played by Plains and Woodlands tribes

Counting coup was a way in which a warrior could prove his or her bravery. Often this was accomplished by touching an enemy.

The "enemy" sits like the Guardian above. All others form a circle. The chief signals someone from the circle to be a stalker who tries to touch the enemy on the tips of the fingers without being heard. The "enemy" listens. When he or she thinks he or she hears a stalker, he or she points in the direction of the sound and shouts, "There." If he or she is right, the chief selects a new stalker. If the "enemy" points in the wrong direction, the stalker can keep approaching and the "enemy" needs to keep listening. Be sure that the students know they cannot rush the "enemy" and count coup before the person has time to say, "There!" Not only is this not fair, but it does not demonstrate bravery!

Hand Signals

The following activity can be used as part of a unit on bicycle safety.

Materials

- hand signal picture (below) for each student

Activity

Pass out the hand signal pictures and have everyone lay them down on the desks.

Ask students to stand and practice the hand signals. Call out "left turn," "right turn," and "stop." Repeat the commands and mix them up. (Stand in the back of the room so you can observe the signals.)

Repeat this practice at intervals throughout the safety unit and review the signals all year.

Left Turn   Stop   Right Turn

Extension

Watch *I'm No Fool on a Bicycle* (Disney safety film starring Jiminy Cricket). Discuss the film to culminate the unit on bicycle safety.

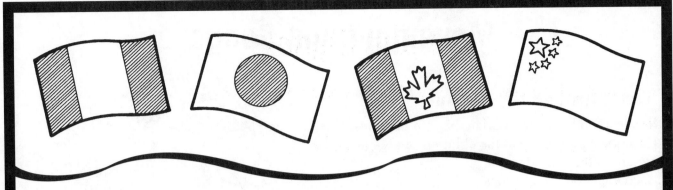

Hoops—Greece

Equipment:
- a hoop of plastic, rubber, or an inflated tire tube for each player
- a stick for bowling (rolling) for each player

Where to Play:

outdoors

Number of Players:

one or more

Directions:

Hoop rolling has been a form of exercise for many years. Historically, there are references to it dating back to Ancient Greece (300 B.C.). To begin this modern version of the game, a player holds the hoop with one hand, fingers pointed downward. The player then bends slightly and flings the hoop forward. He or she runs after the hoop and tries to keep it rolling with one hand or a stick. Once two or more individuals have mastered hoop rolling, then a variety of games may be played. Try Hoop Races, Hoop Relays, Hoop Targets, Follow the Hoop Leader, etc. If the hoop is big enough, the player may even try to jump through it while it is rolling.

Movement and Songs

A Tree Through the Seasons

* Set the mood with appropriate background music.
* Describe a scene so that the children can see a picture in their minds.
* Encourage the use of props.
* Suggested movements for each season:

Summer

* A bird is building a nest in your uppermost branches. (Pair the children. One partner is the tree swaying slowly, happily. The other partner is the bird building a nest in the other's hair. Use cotton, small twigs, and fabric scraps. Trade roles.)

Fall

* The wind is beginning to sway your branches. Your leaves are falling off. (Give each child a number of paper leaves or let them make their own. Have them sway and drop their leaves.)

Winter

* It is very cold outside now. Snow is falling on your branches. (Pair the children. One partner is the tree; arms are extended and the body is shivering. The other partner drapes snow, use white yarn or fabric on the outstretched arms. Have the children exchange roles.)

Spring

* Days are getting warmer now. Buds are beginning to open on your branches. (Children keep their arms at their sides as they dance joyfully. Slowly they open their hands to show the buds opening.)

A Palm Tree During a Tropical Rain Storm

* The rain is coming down slowly and splashing on all your branches. Now the rain is hitting you harder and harder. (Give each child a section of newspaper. Tell them to hold the paper with both hands as they wave it through the air faster and faster to make rain sounds.)

Here We Go Round the Mulberry Bush

* Sing and play a game of "Here We Go Round the Mulberry Bush." Music for this song can be found in *Tom Glazer's Treasury of Songs for Children* (compiled by Tom Glazer, Doubleday, 1964).
* Substitute other tree names for mulberry bush—Joshua tree, cypress tree, cottonwood tree, etc.
* Make up your own verses or use some of the following ideas.

> This is how the leaves fall off, the leaves fall off, the leaves fall off.
> This is how the leaves fall off, all autumn long.
> (One child is the tree. The others can hold handfuls of real or paper leaves and drop them as they sing and dance around the tree.)
> This is how the branches sway, branches sway, branches sway.
> This is how the branches sway, all during spring.
> (The children can move their arms gracefully as they sing this verse.)

Origami Fun

Origami is the ancient Asian art of paper folding. At one time it was believed that paper contained spirits and could not be cut. Follow these directions to make an origami boat. Enjoy!

How to Make a Floating Boat

This paper boat will not last long. You can float this boat in the sink, in the bath, or even in a bucket of water.

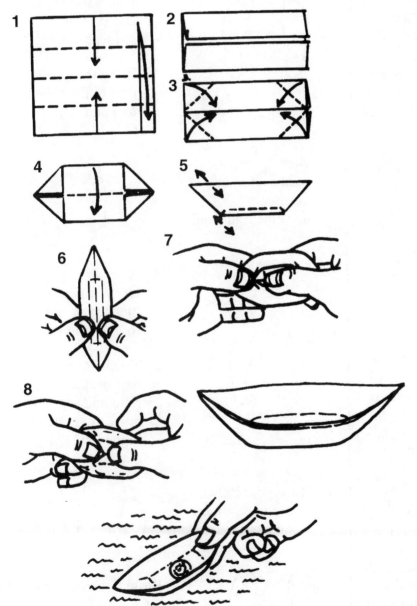

1. Hold the paper vertically. Fold the paper in half.

2. Open the paper and fold both ends of the paper inward to the middle fold. Make sure the ends touch but do not overlap.

3. Turn the paper over and fold the four corners.

4. Fold in half.

5. Pull the layers apart at the top, by opening two layers to one side and one layer to the other.

6. Press on the bottom to form the shape of the boat.

7. Turn over and make a crease across the seam at one end with one thumb and flatten the point with the other thumb. Do the same thing at the other end.

8. Round out the boat and raise the sides to complete.

Floating Your Boat

One side of the boat will be heavier than the other and the boat will tip to the heavier side. To steady your boat, place a coin or two on the lighter side of the boat. You may or may not need to tape the pennies onto the boat.

Do a Little Dance

Discotheques, nightclubs that featured recorded music for dancing, became popular in the seventies. Teach students a basic disco dance. Make a transparency of the patterns and directions on this page for use on the overhead projector. Read them together and then demonstrate the steps to the class. Let students practice the steps without music and then play a disco tune and do a little dance!

Boys

4. Now move your left foot in a diagonal movement in front of you.

1. Move your left foot to the left on a diagonal.

6. Step forward to your basic position and start the sequence over.

5. Bring the right foot next to the left foot and step together.

3. As soon as your right foot is planted, touch your left foot next to it.

2. Touch your right foot next to your left and begin to move your right foot to the right on a diagonal.

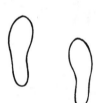

Basic Position: Both feet side by side, shoulder width apart

(Start Here)

Girls

4. Now move your right foot in a diagonal movement in front of you.

1. Move your right foot to the right on a diagonal.

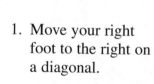

6. Step forward to your basic position and start the sequence over.

5. Bring the left foot next to the right foot and step together.

3. As soon as your left foot is planted, touch your right foot next to it.

2. Touch your left foot next to your right and begin to move your left foot to the left on a diagonal.

Basic Position: Both feet side by side, shoulder width apart

(Start Here)

Resource

Disco Dancing by Joetta Cherry and Gwynne Tomlan (Grosset and Dunlap, 1979)

Ball Games

Pelota

There were many versions of this ball game which looked like a cross between basketball and soccer. Although the rules varied from tribe to tribe, it was a highly significant and difficult game. Winning teams were richly rewarded. The losers may have been sacrificed to the gods. Almost every archaeological site uncovered contains a ball court. Two good books to read are *Rain Player* by David Wisniewski and *A Quetzalcoatl: Tale of the Ball Game* by Marilyn Parke. Here is a simplifed version:

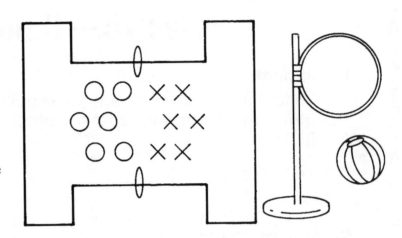

Materials: 2 volleyball poles, 2 hula hoops, 1 beach ball

Purpose: to hit the beach ball through the hoops without using your hands or forearms

Play: two teams of six players on a large "H" shaped court (drawn with chalk, or marked with tape)

Indian Ball

The game of kickball demonstrated the endurance and skill of the players. Different types of kickball were played in local villages and on days of celebrations. Here is a simplified version of one type of kickball.

Materials: 3-inch (7.5 cm) diameter rubber ball, books, cardboard boxes and tubes to make the obstacle course, stopwatch

Purpose: to complete the obstacle course in the fastest time, using only your feet to maneuver the ball Work in relay teams of two persons each. Team members must alternate kicking the ball, working together to complete the course.

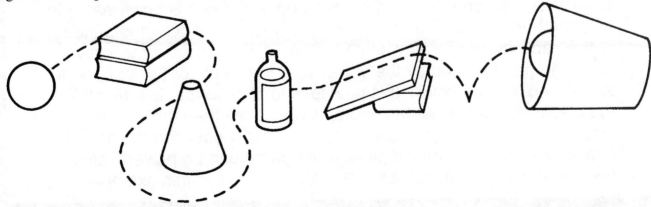

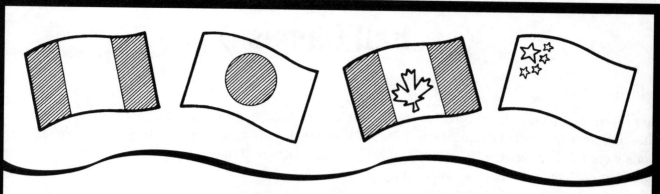

Tac Tix—Denmark

Equipment:

- 16 toothpicks (Matches are traditionally used to play Tac Tix, however, for safety purposes, toothpicks are substituted in this game.)

Where to Play:

indoors

Number of Players:

two

Directions:

Tac Tix is a Danish game invented by Piet Hein, a mathematician, inventor, and poet. He also invented the board game of Hex. To begin the game, 16 toothpicks need to be arranged in a square formation (four four columns).

The players alternate taking turns. The first player takes one or more toothpicks from any one row or column, but the toothpicks taken have to be adjacent, with no spaces in between. For example, suppose that the first player takes all four toothpicks from the second row. The second player may then take any number of adjacent toothpicks from one of the other rows, but he or she is now unable to take the three remaining toothpicks from any of the columns because of the gap—he or she may only take any one toothpick or the lower two. The game is won by the player who forces his or her opponent to take the last toothpick. It is pointless to play so that the winner is the player who takes the last toothpick because then the second player can always win by playing symmetrically opposite the first player. For more advanced players the game can be played using a 5 x 5 or 6 x 6 square instead of the 4 x 4 square in this example.

Lesson Planning Activities

The following is a list of activities that you can use when creating a visual/spatial lesson or when you plan to strengthen this intelligence. Use these activities in combination with those listed under other intelligences to develop a well-rounded curriculum.

- Brochures
- Collages
- Color Cues
- Color/Texture Schemes
- Designs
- Drawing
- Fantasy
- Flow Charts
- Graphic Symbols
- Guided Imagery
- Idea Sketching
- Imagination
- Labeling
- Mapping

- Mind Mapping
- Molding Clay
- Montage
- Painting
- Patterns
- Photography
- Pictures
- Picture Metaphors
- Posters
- Pretending
- Sculpting
- Texture
- Visualization

Star-Spangled Banner Class Book

Cut out the lines below and distribute to the class. Each student can illustrate one line using watercolors. Assemble the pictures together to make your own "Star-Spangled Banner Class Book."

Oh! say, can you see by the dawn's early light,
What so proudly we hail'd at the twilight's last gleaming?
Whose broad stripes and bright stars,
through the perilous fight,
O'er the ramparts we watch'd were so gallantly streaming?
And the rocket's red glare, the bombs bursting in air,
Gave proof through the night that our flag was still there.
Oh! say, does that Star-Spangled Banner yet wave
O'er the land of the free and the home of the brave?
On the shore, dimly seen through the mists of the deep,
Where the foe's haughty host in dread silence reposes,
What is that which the breeze, o'er the towering steep,
As it fitfully blows, half conceals, half discloses?
Now it catches the gleam of the morning's first beam,
In full glory reflected, now shines in the stream.
'Tis the Star-Spangled banner. Oh! long may it wave
O'er the land of the free and the home of the brave!
Oh, thus be it ever when freedom shall stand
Between their lov'd home and the war's desolation,
Blest with vict'ry and peace,
May the heav'n-rescued land
Praise the power that hath made
And preserved us a nation.
Then conquer we must,
When our cause it is just,
And this be our motto, "In God is our Trust,"
And the Star-Spangled banner in triumph shall wave
O'er the land of the free and the home of the brave.

I Have a Dream

Martin Luther King Jr. had a dream that some day all people of all colors would be able to live together in peace. Tell about your dream for peace. Draw a picture to go with your story.

Match the Home

Directions: Cut out each home and paste it in the correct habitat.

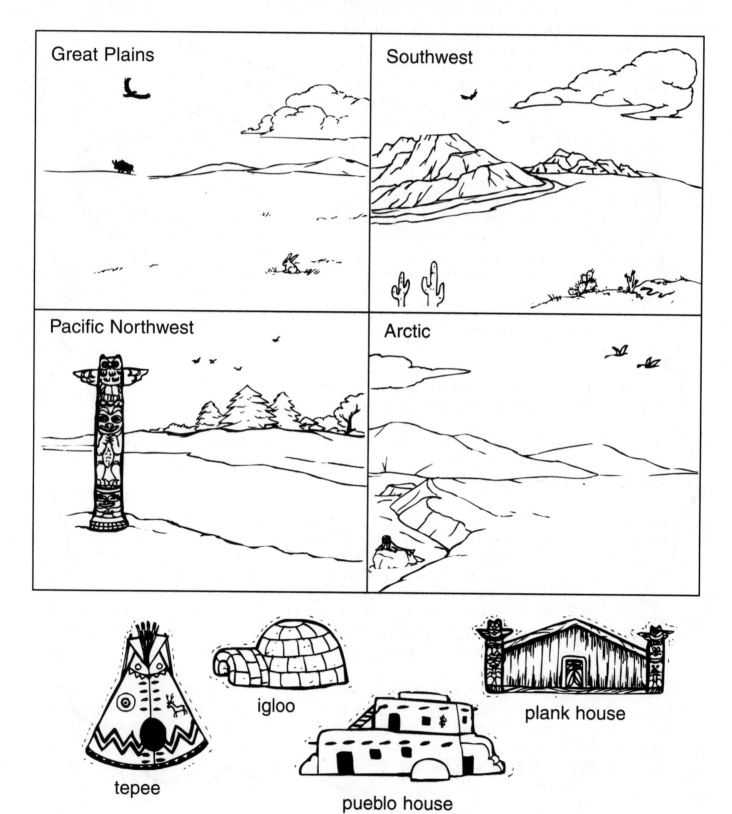

Bulletin Boards

Create a Constitution bulletin board with any of these easy ideas.

1. **The Preamble.** Line a bulletin board background with stripes of red, white, and blue butcher paper or construction paper. Make a copy of the Preamble and glue it to the inside lid of an appropriate-sized box for an instant frame. Attach the Preamble to the center of the bulletin board. Surround it with student-made copies of the paragraph.

2. **Graffiti.** Cover the classroom door with butcher paper. Assign students to make a patriotic border of stars and stripes or other appropriate symbols. The door can then be used as a graffiti board. Tell students that this a covered window in the Philadelphia State House. Have them write statements about the Constitutional proceedings as if they were one of the city's residents. For example, "No kings for us!" or "We demand to know what is transpiring."

3. **Hornbook Lessons.** Cover a bulletin board background with red and blue paper. Create a border with intertwined red, white, and blue crepe paper. Draw a hornbook pattern on a piece of paper. Direct the students to complete a handwriting assignment or a Constitutional studies-related lesson onto the paper. Attach the cutout hornbook shapes to the bulletin board. Make a title for the board out of a strip of white tagboard or construction paper. It could say "Constitutional Lessons," for example.

4. **On the Ropes.** A rope can be used to make an interesting three-dimensional bulletin board. In a corner or other safe area of the classroom, suspend a rope (or twine or craft yarn) form the floor to the ceiling. Decide on a theme such as a "Time Line of Events that Led to the Constitution." After deciding on the events which you wish to focus on, write them on separate sheets of construction paper. Along with the title, include a paragraph explaining the significance of the event. Arrange the events in chronological order on the rope from top to bottom. Attach the events to the rope with clothespins. (You may want to assign different events to each student pair or group. Have them include pictures, diagrams, or drawings.)

5. **Appliance Boxes.** Cut open a large appliance box to use as a bulletin board. Paint one section red, the next white, the next blue, etc., until all sections have been covered. When the sections are dry, stand the box up. Assign a different topic to each section and make appropriate headings for each one. For example, one section might be used for Current Events, another for Terms to Know, another for displaying student work. Add to the sections throughout the unit.

PICTURE PUZZLE

Cut out the individual pieces to make a picture of an important event in American history.

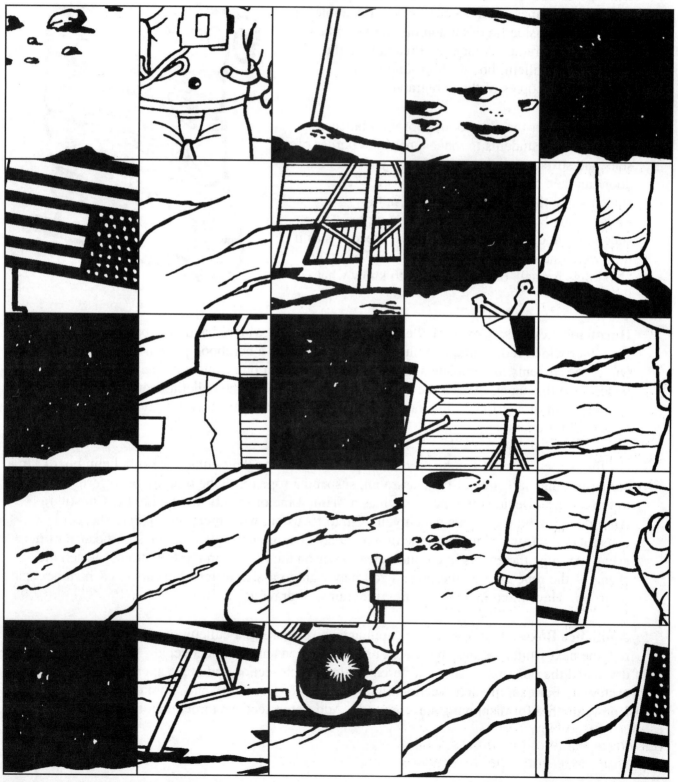

Art Experiences

Students can experience the different styles of artists Jackson Pollock and Willem de Kooning with these two art projects.

Action Painting

Introduction: Display a copy of Pollock's *No.1, 1950 (Lavender Mist)*. Call attention to the black, white, and silver lines. Note the lack of perspective, focal point, or recognizable images.

Materials: black, white, and silver paint; an old sheet or length of white butcher paper taped together; old newspapers; small cans or margarine cups; funnels; craft sticks; etc.

Directions:

- Spread newspaper on the floor to cover the working area completely.
- Place the sheet or paper in the center of the newspaper.
- Dip the can, funnel, or other instrument into one of the paints. Drizzle paint onto the canvas.
- Dip another can into a different color paint and again drizzle the paint onto the canvas.
- Continue until all colors have been used and the artist is satisfied with the design.

Note: Students can create individual murals or small groups can work on one together.

Slash Strokes

Introduction: Display a copy of de Kooning's *Woman, I*. Ask students to share their observations of the artist's style.

Materials: yellow, pink, and buff paints; wide paintbrushes; butcher paper

Directions:

- Dip the paintbrush in a color.
- Apply paint to the canvas with wide brush strokes.
- Dip the paintbrush in another color and apply to the canvas with wide strokes.
- Continue in this manner until all three colors have been used to create a figure.

═══ Suggested Activity ═══

Museums Jackson Pollock's *No. 1, 1950 (Lavender Mist)* can be seen at the National Gallery in Washington, D.C., while Willem de Kooning's *Woman, I* can be viewed at the Museum of Modern Art in New York City. If possible, visit these museums and view these art works. Find out where some of these artists' other paintings are located or find library books that contain copies of these and other abstract expressionist artists' work.

Music and Movement

"One Little, Two Little, Three Little Candles"
(Sing this song to the tune of "One Little, Two Little, Three Little Indians.")
One little, two little, three little candles,
Four little, five little, six little candles,
Seven little, eight little, nine little candles,
In my Hanukkah lamp.
The first night, one little candle,
The second night, two little candles,
The third night, three little candles in my Hanukkah lamp.
The fourth night, four little candles,
The fifth night, five little candles,
The sixth night, six little candles in my Hanukkah lamp.
The seventh night, seven little candles,
The eighth night, eight little candles,
The shammash makes nine little candles in my Hanukkah lamp.

Sing "One Little, Two Little, Three Little Candles" again. This time line up eight children and have them all curl over or squat down. Choose another child to be the shammash. As the song is sung, the shammash lightly taps each "candle," who then rises.

Repeat, letting all children have a turn to be candle.

"The Dreidel Song" (Traditional)
I have a little dreidel.
I made it out of clay.
And when it's dry and ready,
Oh dreidel I shall play.
Dreidel, dreidel,
I made it out of clay.
When it's dry and ready,
Oh dreidel I shall play.

Let children spin around as if they were dreidels. One child can start out in a crouching position, and another can pretend to be turning him or her. As the top spins faster, the child gets to spin more.

Musical Ideas

The following ideas and projects can easily be incorporated into a thematic unit on the environment.

Easy Listening

As a class listen to Camille Saint-Saens' "*The Carnival of the Animals*" or Igor Stravinsky's "The Rite of Spring." Have the children make up their own body movements to match the mood of the songs. Let the children paint an abstract picture after they have listened to the music. Brainstorm a list of words inspired by the music; use the list of words to write poems.

Sing a Song

Teach students the words and melody to "The Animal Fair" (A copy can be found in Tom Glazer's *Treasury Songs for Children,* Doubleday, 1964. rev. ed. of *Treasury of Folk Songs*). Illustrate it with a class mural. Substitute forest animal or ocean animal names for the jungle animals listed in the song.

Music Makers

Make your own musical instruments (see suggestions below). Divide students into small groups. Assign each group a different topic, e.g. jungle noises, forest noises, ocean animals noises, etc. In turn, have each group perform an original composition for the class; see if the others can determine the names of the animals and/or environment.

Soft Drink Bottle Horn

Gently blow into the top of an empty soft drink bottle to produce a hollow sound.

Sandy Blocks

Wrap and tape sandpaper around two wood blocks. Gently rub them together.

Milk Carton Rattle

Clean a half-pint milk carton. Put a handful of dried peas or beans in the carton; staple shut. Shake to make rattling sound.

Coffee Can Drum

Use any size coffee can (empty) with a plastic lid. Drumsticks can be pencils, straws, fingers, brushes, etc.

Encourage the students to invent their own musical instruments and to experiment with the different sounds the instruments can make.

Native American Musical Instruments

Drums

Music plays an important part in the lives of Native Americans. From the time they are born until they die, their lives are marked by dances and ceremonies. The drum provides the rhythm and is often joined by rattles and rasps to furnish the background for the chants and dances accompanying tribal ceremonies.

There are four major types of drums:

1. the small hand drum which could be carried into battle

2. the larger drum usually made from a hollowed log

3. the water drum used by the Apache

4. the basket drum used by Southwestern tribes

Native Americans make drum heads from animal hides. The drums are decorated with printed symbols and designs having significant meanings. The Native American never plays the hide drums by tapping them with his or her hands, as is done in Africa. A drumstick is always used.

Quick and Easy Drums

1. Coffee cans with plastic lids are instant drum material. First remove the metal bottom for a better sound. Cover with construction paper. Add Native American symbols and designs.

2. Oatmeal boxes, salt boxes, or paper ice cream containers make drums with a different sound.

3. Pottery jars, flower pots, and metal buckets also make excellent drums. Attach a head of light 100% cotton canvas by using a rubber band or tightly tied string. Dampen the fabric to shrink it. When struck, it will make a drum-like sound.

   These drums should be struck with drumsticks. Wooden kitchen spoons with painted Native American designs work well.

4. For a basket drum, use any size woven basket. Turn it over. This can be struck by hand or with pine needles to make a whisk-like sound.

International Women's Day Theme Song

1. Make up a song that women can feel good about singing on International Women's Day.

   - Some song writers like to have the melody first. You can make it up or use one that is well-known.

   - Other song writers like to write the words first and then fit the melody to the words.

2. Write the words on the lines below. Make a note of the tune if it is familiar. If you make up the tune, record it on tape.

3. Teach the words to volunteers and perform it for your class (or for the school).

Song for International Women's Day

_____ Sung to the tune of_____

or

_____ Tape of original melody attached. _____

_____

_____

_____

_____

_____

_____

_____

_____

Songs of the Gold Rush

"Oh, Californy!" *(to the tune of 'Oh, Susanna!')*

I come from dear old Boston with a washbowl* on my knee,
I'm going to California, the gold dust for to see.
It rained all night the day I left, the weather it was dry,
The sun so hot I froze to death, dear brother, don't you cry.

> *(CHORUS)*
> *Oh, Cal-i-for-ny!*
> *Oh, that's the land for me!*
> *I'm going to Sacramento*
> *With a washbowl on my knee.*

I jumped aboard the largest ship and traveled on the sea,
And every time I thought of home, I wished it wasn't me!
The vessel reared like any horse that had of oats a wealth,
I found it wouldn't throw me, so I thought I'd throw myself!
(CHORUS)

I thought of all the pleasant times we've had together here,
And I thought I ought to cry a bit, but I couldn't find a tear,
The pilot's bread was in my mouth, the gold dust in my eye,
and I thought I'm going far away, dear brother don't you cry.
(CHORUS)

I soon shall be in Frisco, and there I'll look around,
And when I see the gold lumps there, I'll pick them off the ground.
I'll scrape the mountains clean, my boys, I'll drain the rivers dry,
A pocketful of rocks bring home, so brother, don't you cry.

*A washbowl—the pan miners used to separate gold from sand.

"Around Cape Horn" *(to the tune of 'Camptown Races')*

A bully ship and a bully crew
Dooda, dooda,
A bully mate and a captain too,
O, Dooda, dooda, day.

> *(CHORUS)*
> *Then blow ye winds hi-oh*
> *For Cal-i-for-ny-o,*
> *There's plenty of gold so I've been told*
> *On the banks of the Sacramento.*

Oh, around Cape Horn we're bound to go,
Dooda, dooda,
Around Cape Horn through the sleet and snow,
O, Dooda, dooda, day.
(CHORUS)

Oh, around Cape Horn in the month of May
Dooda, dooda,
Oh, around Cape Horn is a very long way,
O, Dooda, dooda, day.
(CHORUS)

Ninety days to Frisco Bay,
Dooda, dooda,
Ninety days is darn good pay,
O, Dooda, dooda, day.
(CHORUS)

I wish to God I'd never been born,
Dooda, dooda,
To go a-sailin' round Cape Horn
O, Dooda, dooda, day.
(CHORUS)

To the Sacramento we're bound away
Dooda, dooda,
To the Sacramento's a heck of a way,
O, Dooda, dooda, day.
(CHORUS)

Music Migrated Too!

As immigrants traveled to new lands, they brought with them the musical traditions of their homelands. Some of these traditions remained intact in the new country, but others were combined, modified, and then exported around the world only to return, modified again. Below are some examples to share with your class.

Italian Opera

Modern opera began in Italy in the late 1500s. By the end of the 1600s, it had spread throughout Europe and from there to America by way of European immigrants. Introduce your students to opera through *Aida*, one of the most popular operas of all time. In *Aida* Italian composer Giuseppe Verdi (1813-1901) tells the story of an Ethiopian princess who was captured and forced into slavery by the Egyptians.

Leontyne Price, renowned African-American opera singer, is known throughout the world for her exemplary portrayal of Aida. She has retold the story of the opera in a beautifully illustrated book for children, *Aida* (HBJ, 1990). Read the book to students beginning with Ms. Price's "Storyteller's Notes" found at the end. Then play selected portions of a tape of the opera. A recording of Giuseppe Verdi's *Aida* (1971), conducted by Leinsdorf, with Leontyne Price, Placido Domingo, Grace Bumbry, and Sherrill Milnes, is available through Classical Recordings Department, RCA Victor Red Seal.

Russian Symphonies

Russian immigrants in the 1900s brought with them a strong, classical musical tradition. One of the major Russian composers of this period was Sergei Sergeyevich Prokofiev, who lived in New York City from 1918 to 1923. His classic symphonic fairy tale, *Peter and the Wolf* (1936) is beloved by children and adults alike the world over. Introduce the symphonic form to your students by using one of the many book/tape combinations, for example, *Peter and the Wolf* by Sergei Prokofiev, illustrated by Jorg Muller (Knopf, 1986).

Caribbean Calypso

The musical style of calypso originated on the island of Trinidad in the Caribbean Sea before 1830 during singing competitions held by African slaves during carnivals. It is a combination of several heritages—African, Spanish, and American rhythm and blues. After 1920 this style became widely know around the world. Later it was popularized in the United States with such songs as "Day-O," "Banana Boat Song," and "Mary Ann." Appeal to record-collecting parents and grandparents for recordings of these songs or call a local oldies radio station with your request. When you play them in class, let students keep beat with the rhythm using homemade or commercial rhythm instruments.

God Bless America

One of the most popular patriotic songs in the history of the United States, "God Bless America," was composed by a Russian immigrant, Irving Berlin. Mr. Berlin wrote this song in 1918. It was not until 1938 when singer Kate Smith performed it on the radio on Armistice Day (now Veterans Day) that it became popular. As a way to say thank you to his adopted country, Irving Berlin donated the money he made from the song to the Boy Scouts and Girl Scouts of America.

Sing Me a Song

Can you sing in Latin? Here are some songs for your class to perform at a special Roman dinner party.

Mica, Mica, Parva Stella

Mica, Mica, parva stella:
Miror quaenam sis tam bella!
Super terra in caelo
Alba gemma splendido.
Mica, Mica, parva stella,
Miror quaenam sis tam bella!

Barcam Remiga

Barcam remiga
lente in aqua
Hilare, hilare, hilare, hilare
Somnium est vita.

Tres Caecae Mures

Mures tres, mures tres
caecae currunt, caecae currant
Sequuntu sponsom agriculae,
Ab ea abscissae aunt caudulae
est plenius nihil stulitiae
quam mures tres.

Twinkle, Twinkle Little Star

Twinkle, twinkle little star
How I wonder what you are!
Up above the world so high
Like a diamond in the sky.
Twinkle, twinkle, little star,
How I wonder what you are!

Row, Row, Row Your Boat

Row, row, row your boat
gently down the stream.
Merrily, merrily, merrily, merrily
Life is but a dream.

Three Blind Mice

Three blind mice, three blind mice,
See how they run, see how they run!
They all ran after the farmer's wife,
She cut off their tails with a carving knife;
Did you ever see such a sight in your life,
As three blind mice?

Latin Pronunciation

Classical (Roman) Latin uses the same letters as English except for w. The letters y and z are not used often. Every letter is pronounced, and there is only one pronunciation for each consonant. Vowels may be long or short, but the difference is how long it takes to say each one.

Vowels	**Diphthongs**
a as in father: trans	**ae** as in aisle: aes-tas
e as in they: me	**au** as in ouch: au-tem
i as in ski: si	**oe** as in oil: coe-pi
o as in note: non	
u as in rule: tu	

Consonants: Most consonants have the same sound as in English, but c, g, and t are always hard.

c as in cat: ca-sa	**v** is pronounced as w, as in wine: vi-num
g as in get: gens	**qu** is a single sound, pronounced kw as in queen: e-quus
t as in tin: tamen	**b** before s or t has the sound of p

Writing a Song

Complete this activity after reading *Caddie Woodlawn* by Carol Ryrie Brink (Macmillan, 1990). When it was too cold for the Woodlawn children to walk to school, Robert Ireton hitched the horse to the sledge and drove them. Robert often enjoyed singing as they rode along, and the children joined in by echoing the last line. The songs they sang often had silly lyrics, or lines, and usually related to things in their everyday lives.

Work together with three or four other students to write a song that Robert Ireton and the Woodlawn children might enjoy singing. When writing your song, try to make the lyrics humorous and have the last word in every set of two lines rhyme.

Example: I once saw a pig,
            Who tried to do a jig.
            But he was so fat,
            That he just fell flat!

Songs of the Period

Much of the essence of the culture of the United States can be found in its popular songs. Students will enjoy knowing the kinds of songs heard on the riverboats and in the theaters of the pre-Civil War period.

I. Stephen Foster, America's most famous song writer of the nineteenth century, wrote many of his compositions around the time of Huck's journey down the Mississippi River. Certainly passengers on the paddlewheelers would have been hearing his famous melodies. The music is easily obtainable at your local library.

"Oh, Susanna"

Chorus
Oh! Susanna, don't you cry for me;
I come from Alabama, with my banjo on my knee.
Verses
I come from Alabama with a banjo on my knee;
I'm goin' to Lou-siana my true love for to see.
It rained all night the day I left, the weather it was dry;
The sun so hot I froze to death, Susanna don't you cry.
I had a dream the other night, when everything was still
I thought I saw Susanna dear, a-comin' down the hill.
The buckwheat cake was in her mouth, the tear was in her eye,
Said I, I'm comin' from the south
Susanna don't you cry.
I soon will be in New Orleans, and then I'll look all 'round
And when I find Susanna, I'll fall upon the ground.
But if I do not find her, this man'll surely die,
And when I'm dead and buried,
Susanna don't you cry.

Other Stephen Foster favorites include "Jeanie With the Light Brown Hair" and "Camptown Races."

II. Some older songs still popular during Huck's day were these:

"Froggie Went A-Courtin"
(a sample of its many verses)
Oh, Froggie went a-courtin' and he did ride, uh-huh, uh-huh.
Froggie went a courtin' and he did ride,
A sword and pistol by his side, uh-huh, uh-huh.
He rode up to Miss Mousie's door uh-huh, uh-huh.
He rode up to Miss Mousie's door.
Where he had often been before, uh-huh, uh-huh.
He took Miss Mousie on his knee, uh-huh, uh-huh.
He took Miss Mousie on his knee,
And said, "Miss Mouse, will you marry me?" uh-huh, uh-huh.

"Shenandoah"
Oh, Shen-an-doah, I long to hear you.
Away, you rolling river!
Oh, Shenandoah, I long to hear you,
Away, I'm bound away,
Cross the wide Missouri.

III. There is a modern musical version of the novel called *Big River* with music and lyrics by Roger Miller. The CD or tape is available. Your students would enjoy hearing the numbers. Preview first.

Social Studies Survey

Name _____

Circle your answers.

1. How do you feel about studying history?

I like it.   It is O.K.   I don't like it.

2. Is it important to know about the past?

Yes   I'm not sure.   No

3. Is it important to know about other people and cultures?

Yes   I'm not sure.   No

Roses for Valentine's Day

Directions: Many people give roses or other flowers to show they care. Using information available in reference books or on the Internet, find out the modern meanings of the different colors of roses. Color these roses to show what you mean.

Friendship

Purity of the Mind

Love

Friendship or Sweetheart

Topics for Discussion

Discuss methods of transportation to which you are accustomed. Also discuss reasons for travel today. Review the contrasts between modern day shopping and traditional trade and barter in North America. (Make sure that the students understand that Native Americans today use the same methods of transportation and "trade" as does everyone else.)

Use some or all of the following questions for discussion topics.

1. Do you travel?

2. Where do you travel?

3. When you travel, what mode of transportation do you use?

4. Why do you travel?

5. What is your favorite kind of transportation?

6. Who carries your clothes and other possessions when you travel?

7. How much could you take along with you if you had to carry all of your possessions yourself when you traveled? How far could you carry them?

8. How did the early Native Americans travel?

   (by canoe, raft, horse, sled, on foot, etc.)

9. Why did the early Native Americans travel?

   (to trade, to hunt, to gather wild crops, etc.)

10. Which types of traditional travel are still practiced today?

    (walking, running, skiing, sledding, tobogganing, horseback riding, boating)

11. What did the early Native Americans use for money when they shopped?

    (shells, beads, furs, etc.)

12. What kind of goods did the early Native Americans trade?

    (furs, feathers, shells, food, beads, jewelry, etc.)

13. Could you invent a new way to travel and shop in the future?

14. If you were a trader, what would you trade?

15. Who would make your goods?

16. With whom would you trade?

Japan

Launch this Web site: http://www.jinjapan.org/kidsweb/

Directions: Click on one of the links around "Kids Web Japan." (There are twelve from which to choose.) Read the information at the link you chose and then write a sentence or two telling what you learned about Japan.

What's Important

Think about something that is really important to you. It might not be important to many other people, but it is to you. Write about this important thing. What makes it important? Is it something that should be important to other people? Why or why not? (It might be a thing, or an idea, or an event—or anything else that is important to you).

_____

_____

_____

_____

_____

_____

_____

_____

_____

_____

_____

_____

_____

_____

_____

_____

_____

_____

If You Were There

Ask the students to imagine themselves as some of the famous people of the sixties. For example, what might it have been like to be the first woman in space, or how might it have felt to perform the first heart transplant surgery? Discuss these and other hypothetical situations with the class. Have each student choose one of the situations listed below and complete the assignment.

1. Even though you have little higher education, you want to become a cosmonaut. Write a letter to Russian space authorities volunteering your services. Tell them about your parachuting abilities and explain how you feel about the cosmonaut program.

2. You are an art critic for the *New York Times* and have been sent to Britain to review Henry Moore's latest work, *Reclining Mother and Child.* Write a news article detailing the flowing lines and hidden beauty of this sculpture.

3. Pretend that you are the young Dr. Albert Schweitzer. For a year you have been planning your clinic in Africa. Although you are not sure what to expect, you are taken aback by what you do find. Write a diary entry about your first day at the clinic site.

4. Sickly as a child, you were never expected to walk. Now you, Wilma Rudolph, are at the 1960 Olympic Games. In 1956 you were part of the bronze medal winning relay team, but today you hope to take home the gold. Write a letter to your mother expressing your hopes for this competition.

5. You are Auguste Piccard, inventor of the bathyscaphe *Trieste,* and you have been invited to speak to a group of sixth graders. Write a speech you will give to the class, explaining how the craft is able to descend to the ocean floor.

6. The city in which you live has just been divided into two sections with a heavily guarded wall. You want to visit your grandparents who live on the other side. Write a plan for a daring balloon escape to visit your grandparents.

7. Because of a life-threatening heart disease, you must undergo a heart transplant. Dr. Christiaan Barnard has been assigned to your case. You know he is a respected surgeon, but you still have some questions. Write a conversation you might have with him before surgery.

8. Recent tests indicate that there might be oil in Antarctica, and your country is sending you there on a fact-finding mission. You are an avid environmentalist and believe that searching for oil may upset the ecological balance. Make a list of your concerns.

9. Advisors are telling you to bomb or invade Cuba, but as president of the United States you are not convinced that either choice is correct. Instead, you set up a blockade to prevent more weapons from entering Cuba. Explain the reasons for your choice to your advisors.

10. When you first see the Aborigines, you can barely believe your eyes. They are living in primitive conditions and have not even invented the wheel yet. In a paper for the geographic society, describe the culture of these ancient people.

Socrates' Hot Seat

Socrates was one of Greece's most famous scholars and philosophers. He asked probing questions of his students to try to help them observe, analyze, and think. By doing this he felt the absolute truth could be found. Choose three of the following quotes by well-known philosophers and describe them in your own words on another sheet of paper. Write a thorough description and be ready to support your reasoning.

1. *Much learning does not teach understanding.* (Herodotus)

2. *Words have a longer life than deeds.* (Pindar)

3. *Time eases all things.* (Sophocles)

4. *A bad beginning makes a bad ending.* (Euripedes)

5. *Know thyself.* (Socrates)

6. *Strive not to become a god; mortal aims befit mortal men.* (Pindar)

7. *The life which is unexamined is not worth living.* (Plato)

8. *Education is the best provision for old age.* (Aristotle)

9. *Nothing in excess.* (Socrates)

10. *All is flux, nothing stays still.* (Herodotus)

Pretend you are at the Agora and that your teacher is Socrates. Take turns taking the "hot seat" in front of the class, just like a pupil of Socrates would be singled out and questioned in front of the gathering. Present one of your quotes and explanations to the group and then answer the questions posed by "Socrates." "Socrates" will attempt to find contradictions and flaws in your reasoning, so do not get discouraged. Be prepared to defend your position with logical and well-elaborated details that answer "Why?" and "What do you mean?"

What's Your Philosophy?

After Socrates died many other philosophies evolved that may describe a person's outlook on life. Read the descriptions of the philosophies below. Which one best fits your attitude towards life? Why? Write a paragraph on another sheet of paper explaining your reasoning.

SKEPTIC—You reject the idea that truth can ever be found, so you doubt everything.

CYNIC—You believe that we are powerless to control the world, therefore you reject all civilization and want to return to a state of nature.

STOIC—You believe in complete self-control and accept everything that life brings to you since you believe that you cannot control fate.

HEDONIST—You believe that one should seek pleasure and avoid anything that is unpleasant, no matter what the consequences are.

EPICUREAN—You believe that pleasure is good, but one must balance it with work and learning to lead a successful life.

What's in a Name?

Octavian had many names in his lifetime. Make a chart on the board like the one below. Have students refer to reference books to help them a list his different names and describe each stage in his life and the reason for his name change.

Have students make a chart for themselves and list the different names that they might go by at home or at school (nicknames, family names, etc.) Why might different people refer to them by a different name? (relatives might use one name, pet names used by parents, nicknames by friends, etc.) What names or titles might they use in the future? (Mr./Mrs., Dr., Sam, Sir, different married name, hyphenated name, etc.) What is the purpose of using different names or titles? (to show affection, respect, etc.)

Name	During what part of his life?	Why?
Gaius Octavius	Birth and early childhood	Legal name
Gaius Julius Caesar Octavianus	When adopted by Julius Caesar	To show he was the son of Julius Caesar
Caesar Octavian	When he inherited power after Caesar died	Shortened name
Princeps	When he was secretly plotting to gain total control	To fool the Senate
Augustus Caesar	When he became Emperor	To show the power and respect he enjoyed

Name	Who calls you this?	Why are you called this?
Colton James	School records	Legal name
Cole	Family and friends	Shortened name
C.J.	Friends on soccer team	Another Cole on team
Pumpkin Head	Parents	Baby nickname

Autobiographical Incident Organizer

Crossing the Rubicon

When Julius Caesar made the decision to lead his army across the Rubicon River, he knew his life would forever be changed. Today when someone says they have "crossed the Rubicon," it means they have made an important decision that they won't be able to change and which will affect the rest of their life.

Recall a time in your past in which you made an important decision that has affected your life ever since. It might be choosing a friend, deciding how to spend your money, turning down cigarettes, alcohol, or drugs, or helping to make a family decision. Write about the event and tell why you feel it was a "Rubicon" for you.

Introduction/Opening Statement—The opening statement tells what you are going to write about. You can restate the prompt and add your event, or start with an action from your story.

_____

_____

_____

_____

_____

Specific Supporting Details/Sequence Statements—The body of your composition must include a clear sequence of what happened, the setting of the event, and the reactions and feelings of the characters involved. Jot down a brief sequence of events you can expand in your composition.

1. _____

2. _____

3. _____

4. _____

5. _____

Conclusion/Summary Statement—Summarize the decision you made, say whether or not you're glad you made it, and tell why it was your "Rubicon." Write a strong closing sentence.

_____

_____

_____

_____

Jigsaw Task Season: Identification

Group Members   Season

_____   _____

_____   _____

_____   _____

_____   _____

You will be assigned to an "expert" group. In your expert group you will be given the name of a season. Your group needs to find out what the weather is like in that season and which months of the year are included in that season.

After you have learned that information in your "expert" group, you will return to your "home" group. Tell the members of your "home" group what you learned about your season.

After everyone has described his or her season, have your group make a calendar. Use the calendar below as an example. Make a label and picture for each month, naming and describing the season.

_____
MONTH

SUNDAY	MONDAY	TUESDAY	WEDNESDAY	THURSDAY	FRIDAY	SATURDAY

General Group Task: Classroom Rules

Group Members

_____   _____

_____   _____

_____   _____

We have rules and laws that allow us to have a civilized society. In order to be a good citizen, you must obey these rules and laws. You have rules in your classroom that must be followed. These rules must be followed so that everyone can learn and be safe. Being a good citizen is very important. Being a good citizen in your classroom is also very important.

Suppose that your teacher decided that the students should make the classroom rules. In your group, make a list of rules that you feel are very important for your classroom. They should be rules that help everyone learn and be safe. Write your rules at the bottom of this page.

Our Rules

_____

_____

_____

_____

_____

_____

Declaration of Classroom Rules

Using the form below, draft a list of classroom rules within your small group. You must agree on all the rules within your group before they can be placed on the list. When your list is complete, all members of the group should sign it just like the Declaration of Independence.

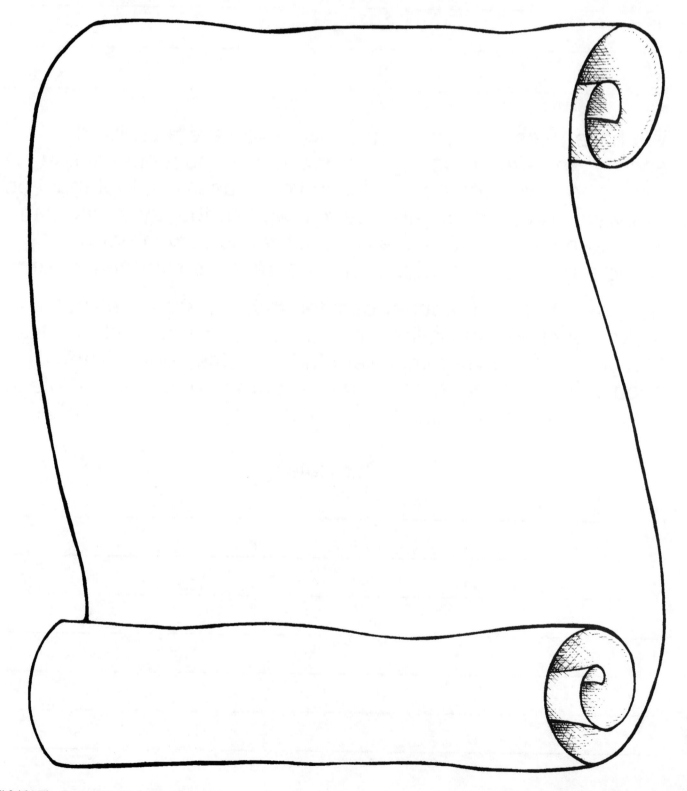

Multicultural Calendar—An Internet Research Activity

Many of the holidays that we celebrate originated in different cultures. Research the traditions of different cultures through the creation of a multicultural calendar.

Grades: 2–3

Duration: three 30-minute sessions

Instructional Objective: The students will research the traditions of different cultures and create a multicultural calendar.

Materials: Internet access; CD-ROM encyclopedias

Computer Software: *ClarisWorks, Microsoft Works,* CD-ROM encyclopedias

Procedure:

Before the Computer:

Discuss the holiday traditions that students celebrate and the country in which they originated. Brainstorm a list of cultures students would like to know more about. Divide the class into groups of two or three and assign a culture to each group.

On the Computer:

During session one, have groups use the Internet and CD-ROM encyclopedias to find important calendar dates in the traditions of their assigned cultures.

During session two, assign each group a month. Have the students create a calendar and fill in the dates for holidays and other important dates for their assigned culture for that month. Students can decorate the calendar month with patterns and symbols from their assigned cultures.

After the Computer:

Have the students choose one holiday or important date from their month to illustrate. Students mount their calendars and illustrations on pieces of 11" x 17" colored poster board. The poster boards can be bound together to make a classroom multicultural calendar.

Extended Activity:

Have students create a "How We Celebrate Special Days" book.

Make a Senet Game

Senet was a popular board game in ancient Egypt. It is played on a square board with 25 squares called "oyoon," or eyes. The two players each have 12 playing pieces called "kelbs." The object is to capture your opponent's kelbs. The player with the highest number of kelbs at the end of the game is the winner.

Making the Playing Board and Kelbs:

1. Using a square sheet of heavy tagboard and a ruler, measure and draw 25 squares, five across and five down. Draw an X in the center square.

2. Gather 12 identical playing pieces for each player. These can be shells, checkers, stones, coins, or other objects that will fit in a square.

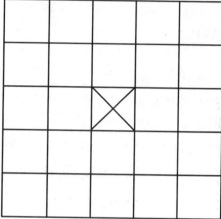

Playing Board

Placing the Kelbs:

1. Roll dice, flip a coin, or draw cards to see who places pieces first.

2. The first player sets 2 kelbs on the board in any square except the center one. (There is an advantage to placing kelbs on the outside edge.)

3. The second player then sets 2 kelbs on the board. Repeat this process until all squares except the center are covered.

Playing the Game:

1. Roll dice, flip a coin, or draw cards to see who moves first.

2. Kelbs can move forward, backward, or sideways, but not diagonally. Kelbs cannot jump over other kelbs. In one turn, a player can move only one kelb one space. The player who moves first must move a kelb into the center square.

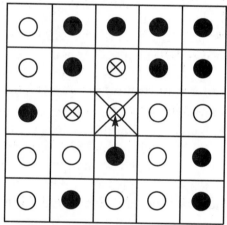

Ⓧ =captured on first move

3. To capture an opponent's kelb, a player must trap it between two of his own kelbs. If a player voluntarily moves his own kelb between two of his opponent's kelbs, his kelb cannot be taken.

4. As the board clears, the game grows more complex. If a player is blocked on all sides and cannot move, he must forfeit his turn. However, his opponent must open a space for the player on his next move.

5. If a player captures a kelb, he may take another turn—if and ONLY IF in that next turn he can capture another kelb.

6. Play continues in this manner until one player cannot move his kelbs, refuses to move his kelbs, or when all of his kelbs have been captured.

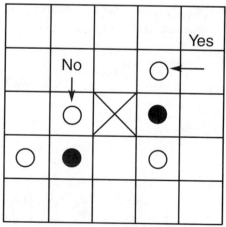

How to capture kelbs

Who Has the Vote?

Athens is known as a democracy, but the Athenian notion of democracy was quite different from ours. This exercise will give students direct knowledge of what it meant to be a citizen, or what it meant to be deprived of the rights of a citizen.

Materials: photocopies of page 148 for the class. (Assuming that your class has 30 students, the following distribution would approximate the percentages of each class in Athens during the classical period.)

Adult male citizens:	5 students
Adult females married to citizens:	4 students
Female children of citizens:	4 students
Male children of citizens:	5 students
Metics:	3 students
Slaves (*all ages and sexes*) :	11 students

Directions

1. Explain that many histories of Athens concentrate on just one section of the population, the people who were allowed to be citizens. Explain that you will show them some of the limitations of the Greek democracy.

2. Cut apart the photocopies so you have enough for the class. Randomly pass them out. Have the class read them aloud and discuss the differences in their rights. Explain that you have handed out the slips so that it will be proportionate to the numbers of each class in Athens. List the classes on the board and gather a few predictions about which one will be the most numerous.

3. Ask the students to divide so that each group stands together in a different part of the room. Discuss what the numbers mean.

Extension: Select some real-life decision that the class will be making. You are going to give them a 20-minute free period. What do they want to do? Allow the students who were citizens to make the decision. How do the other sections of the class feel about the process?

Who Has the Vote? *(cont.)*

Citizen

You are a male, and your father was also an Athenian citizen. (After 451 B.C. your mother's father also had to be a citizen.) At 18 you served two years in the armed guard. After that you are always available to join the army when there is a war. You may take part and vote in the Assembly, as every citizen has the right to. You may also serve in juries. You are eligible to serve in the Council of Five Hundred, which reviews ideas before they are presented to the Assembly. You also work as a farmer, craftsmen or merchant.

Citizen's Wife

You have none of the rights of your husband. Legally, you are considered his property and he may punish you as he sees fit. You spend most of your time in the house, weaving cloth and overseeing the household servants. Ordinarily you are never seen outside the house. If your husband brings guests home, they eat in a separate room. You join your husband only for religious festivals and for plays in the city's theater.

Female Children

Some infant girls are left at the city's gates because their fathers decide they do not want to raise a girl. Other people may take these girls home, or they may starve. You do not attend school. You stay in the home and learn from your mother how to run the house and how to raise children.

Male Children

Many male children attend school for some period of time. Boys of a wealthy family may attend for many years. You receive training in athletics, reading, writing, arithmetic, and literature. You know one day you will be a citizen.

Metics

You are a person, usually a male, who was born in another city, who is allowed to live in Athens. You have no voice in the government, but you are free to run your own affairs. You may make money, and you might conceivably become quite rich. You can move back to your home city if you wish, and you can take your money along if you wish. You will never be made a citizen, no matter how successful you become.

Slave

Male or female, adult or child, you have no rights whatsoever. The kind of life you have depends solely on the kind of person who owns you. You need your master's permission to marry or have children. Your master may permit you to work for money, and (for a male) it is possible, though rare, for a slave to purchase his freedom. Other slaves are worked to death in the silver mines near Athens.

Mind Your Manners

Directions: Make a copy of this page. Cut apart the boxes. Give one to each group and have the groups think of two or more solutions to the problem. Let one group at a time present their problem and their solutions to the whole group. Have your students decide which solution they would most likely use and explain why.

1.	You have just completed building a four-foot skyscraper out of blocks. It took you a long time to make the skyscraper. For no reason a classmate comes along and kicks the bottom blocks; the building comes tumbling down.
2.	Your older sister has cooked her first meal for the family. She is very proud of her hard work. You do not like the way that the meatloaf looks or tastes. The potatoes are pretty good, though.
3.	Everyone is supposed to contribute ideas in your science group. One person (who sometimes has some good ideas) insists on interrupting anyone else who is talking.
4.	You had a friend over for a sleepover, and the friend insisted on having his or her own way the whole time. He or she wanted to play only certain games, did not like the dinner your mom prepared, and did not say thank you afterwards.
5.	A classmate has brought her new game to show the rest of the class during sharing time. When it is your turn to look at it, you take one of the playing pieces and put it in your pocket.
6.	The telephone rings at home, and you pick up the receiver. A voice at the other end asks for Mr. Swenson, but there is no Mr. Swenson in your household. You react angrily to the person's mistake.
7.	In the school cafeteria you are sitting next to someone who has awful table manners. He slurps his spaghetti, chews with his mouth open, and leaves his crumpled napkin behind.
8.	A group of your friends is standing around, talking about the newest kid in the class. Some of the things they are saying are unkind, and other things are untrue and you know it.
9.	Your bedroom window faces a neighbor's. One summer night when your window and his are both open, you hear loud music blaring from his room. It is past your bedtime, and the music is still loud and strong.
10.	During free time you and a classmate both try to sit at the same computer. You decide that you were there first, and you try to take the disk away from your classmate.

Group Writing Projects

This page lists eight different creative writing projects related to the 1970s. They can be assigned to large or small groups. Give students a choice of assignments. Let the groups present their completed projects to the rest of the class.

Pet Rocks　Pet rocks were a popular fad in the seventies. They came packaged in their own carryall with a set of tongue-in-cheek directions for their care and were priced at just $5 each. With your group go outside to find a suitable rock. Create a container for the rock, name your pet, and write directions for the care and feeding of the rock.

Inventions　All of the following were invented during the seventies: Sony Walkman personal cassette players, pocket calculators, inexpensive (under $10) digital watches, video games played on the TV screen, prerecorded video cassettes, and miniature TV screens. Pretend it is the year 2025 and you are writing about inventions of the 1990s. Make a catalog of these innovations complete with pictures and descriptions of how each is used.

How To　How-to books were popular in the seventies. As a group, determine a topic that interests you and write a how-to book. Some suggested titles include *How to Write a Term Paper, How to Look Good on a Budget, How to Make Friends, How to Disco Dance.*

T-Shirts　In the mid-seventies plain T-shirts were out and T-shirts decorated with words or slogans were in. Brainstorm a list of words or phrases that might have been popular in the seventies. Think of events then such as Watergate, the oil embargo, the Twenty-sixth Amendment, etc. Draw and cut out large T-shirt shapes from a piece of butcher paper and decorate each one with some seventies lingo and/or pictures.

The Environment　With your partners brainstorm a list of things you can do to clean up and protect the environment at home or at school on a daily basis. Create a group book using 25 of these ideas. Draw pictures to illustrate the ideas.

CB Lingo　Citizen band radios were popular during the seventies, especially among truckers. They invented their own vocabulary or lingo to communicate with one another. Divide the students into groups, and direct them to make a dictionary of CB terms and their meanings. You may be able to find a prepared list of terms from a CB supply store. Check your phone book for possible sources.

Fads　Mood rings were another popular fad of the seventies. Group the students and instruct them to invent a new fad for the seventies. Tell the groups to draw a picture of this new fad and develop an advertising poster that will prompt others to purchase the item.

Special Effects　The 1977 movie *Star Wars* set a new standard for visual effects in motion pictures. With the students brainstorm some of the new visual effects that are currently being used in films. Have pairs of students write about an innovative special effect for the next decade. For example, smellovision would allow movie goers to smell what is on the screen, from the exhaust of cars to the food the characters eat.

Discussing the Fifties

Create student interest with a lively discussion. Suggested topics and some methods for implementing them follow.

A Woman's Place During the fifties, the prevailing philosophy was that a woman's place was in the home caring for her husband and children. Ask students to brainstorm some pros and cons of this position; have them defend their answers.

Forgotten War The Korean War has often been referred to as the "forgotten war." Discuss with students how this title originated and why the Korean War remains in the background of United States history.

DNA One of the most important scientific breakthroughs of the decade occurred when Crick and Watson developed a model for DNA. Discuss with the class why DNA is important. Have them look for current newspaper and magazine articles to see how it is being used in crime detection and genetics.

Civil Rights During the fifties the civil rights movement was just beginning. When Rosa Parks refused to give up her bus seat for a white man, she sparked a whole new battle for equality. Tell students that they are Parks' attorney and have them explain to the judge why their client should be cleared of all charges.

Space Race When Russia launched *Sputnik I*, Americans were caught off guard. The event showed how seriously America lagged in space technology. Not wanting to be outdone, agencies were created to work on future United States spacecraft. The government also allocated millions of dollars to be spent on scientific education in schools at all levels. Discuss how more science instruction would help the future space program.

McCarthyism Senator Joseph McCarthy started a one-man war on communism. He wrongfully accused innocent people and caused thousands to lose their jobs. Pair the students for some role-playing. One partner is McCarthy, while the other is the accused communist. First McCarthy explains the charges, and then the other partner defends himself or herself.

Fifty States Both Alaska and Hawaii became states in 1959. As a class discuss the natural resources of each state. Group the students and assign each group either Alaska or Hawaii. Direct them to write a 1950s TV ad whose message tells why the state should be admitted to the union.

Campaign '52 Dwight David Eisenhower was a former career military man with no political party while Stevenson was a governor, a Democrat, and well-spoken. Ask the students to explain who they think was the better choice for president. Tell them to defend their views.

Spying In 1951 the Rosenbergs were executed for spying against the United States. Historians still argue over their guilt or innocence. After students research the story of the Rosenbergs, conduct a class debate in which they discuss evidence to support guilt or innocence.

Building a "Recyclable" Playground

Goal:

to make children aware of recycling as a way to protect the Earth; to create a model playground using recyclable materials

Materials:

Variety of recyclable materials, large cardboard carton, glue, scissors, tape, large cardboard boxes or poster board, green paint, paintbrush

Directions:

Before starting the project, talk about recyclable materials. Set up a recycling center in your class. Explain that recycling is an important thing to do especially if one considers that every day so many Styrofoam cups are used that they could circle around the globe. This project can be accomplished with boxes that are labeled "Recyclable."

Discuss with children that all over the world children play in playgrounds and what type of play equipment is found there. Then, in small groups, have them brainstorm about equipment they might like to see on a playground. What would the equipment do? Would it move? How would it be made safe?

Challenge each group to use recyclable materials from the recyclable boxes and make one piece of playground equipment. Place all the equipment on a poster board or bottom of a box carton painted green. Display.

Extensions:

This can be a cross-grade activity where older students work with younger students in creating a new playground.

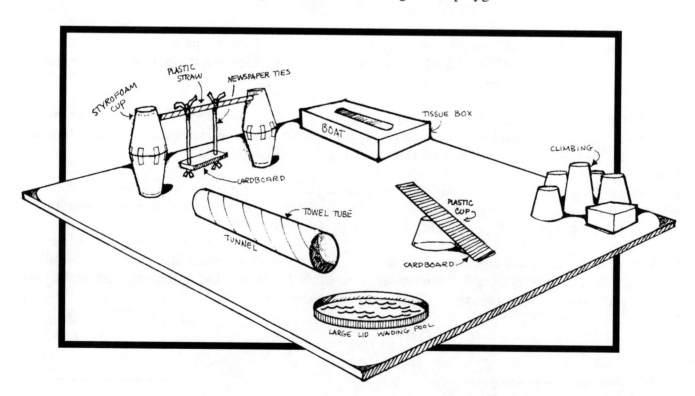

First Day of Spring

Background

The first day of spring usually falls on March 21. It is the day when the sun is directly above the equator and the hours of daylight are exactly equal to the hours of darkness. Another name for the first day of spring is the vernal equinox. Since the seasons are reversed below the equator, the first day of spring in the northern hemisphere is the first day of fall in the southern hemisphere.

Making It Work

Make the season a firsthand experience for your students by going for a nature walk to observe the signs of spring: nesting birds, new plant growth, blossoms, etc.

Nature Walk

Materials

- copies of observation form below

Activity

Go for a nature walk around your school or neighborhood. Even in the most urban environment, you will see budding trees and returning birds.

Name _____   Date _____

Nature Walk Observation Form

What I Saw   Where I Saw It

_____   _____

_____   _____

_____   _____

_____   _____

_____   _____

_____   _____

_____   _____

Animals of the Rain Forest

Goal: To develop awareness of some of the many creatures that live in the rain forest

Materials: magazines such as *National Geographic* and *Ranger Rick*, picture books about the rain forest, encyclopedias

Directions: Talk about animals of the rain forest with your class. Explain that many are in danger of losing their homes unless people all over the world become more aware of taking care of rain forests. As a class, create a background that shows the layers of the rain forest which include a top layer, canopy, understory, and floor. These can be represented by using different colors of construction paper for each and having children draw in trees.

Have each student choose an animal found in the rain forest. A list is provided below. Each child draws his or her animal. Cut around the animal and place it on the rain forest background.

Extensions: Have students make "Save the Rain Forest" posters.

- emerald tree boa
- spider monkey
- morpho butterfly
- tarantula
- arrow-poison frog
- three-toed-sloth
- hawk
- tapir
- orangutan
- jaguar
- toucan
- boa constrictor
- bee
- anteaters
- porcupines

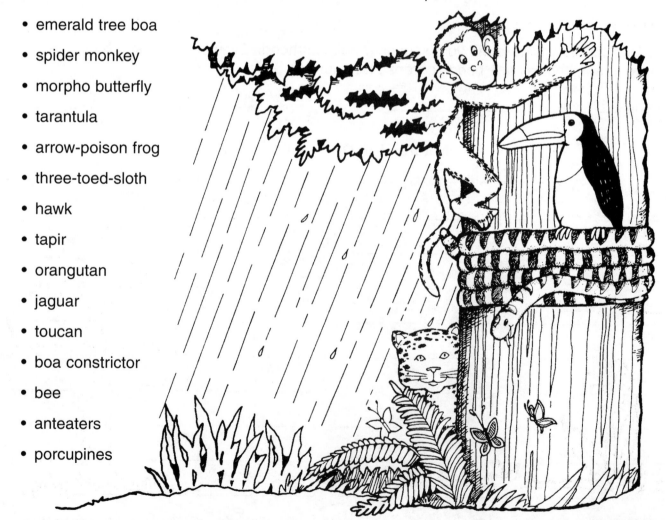

Imagine . . .

Use your imagination. Imagine that trees and flowers could speak to each other.
What would a tree have to say to a flower, and how would a flower reply?
Create a conversation between a tree and flower and write it below.

_____

_____

_____

_____

_____

_____

_____

_____

_____

_____

_____

_____

_____

_____

_____

Interviewing an
Endangered Species

Research the following information pertaining to the endangered species assigned to you or your group. Use more paper if necessary.

Endangered Species _____

General Characteristics _____

Predators _____

Food Requirements _____

Habitat _____

Size/Weight_____

Skilled Senses _____

Mobility _____

Longevity_____

1. Describe the role in the food chain your species has in its ecosystem.

    _____

    _____

    _____

2. What issues contribute most to the endangerment of your assigned species?

    _____

    _____

    _____

3. Describe thoroughly the *biomes* in which your species can live and interact. Also, what adaptations are apparent over the course of time that would suggest that your species' endangerment is not due to natural selection or other natural occurrences but rather to human-induced circumstances?

    _____

    _____

    _____

Earth Day

Earth Day was first held in the United States on April 22, 1970, and was founded by United States Senator Gaylord Nelson. The second Earth Day, held on April 22, 1990, was celebrated in over 140 countries. Earth Day is a day to remind us of the need to care for our environment. It is a time to become actively involved in many Save-the-Earth projects.

Another related holiday held nationally in the United States on the last Friday of April is Arbor Day, a day to plant new trees and emphasize conservation. It was first held in Nebraska on April 10, 1872, and its founder was conservation advocate Julius Sterling Morton. The date for Arbor Day may vary depending on the state in which you live.

Activities

Start a school-wide recycling program. Collect aluminum cans, plastic bottles, paper, and glass. Put collection points around the school. If possible, have a curbside drop-off point one day a week so the public can support your efforts. Recruit some adults to help with transportation to a recycling center. This may be coordinated by your class or by your school's student government. Decide on a worthwhile organization that helps the earth and contribute the money you earn to it.

Create a bulletin board. Use the classified section of the newspaper as the background for this bulletin board. Title the board "The Daily Planet." Throughout the unit, have students bring in and post articles from newspapers or magazines that tell about environmental problems that the world is facing.

Learn how to read the air quality reports in the newspaper.

Discuss how the air can be cleaned up.

Have students design a mode of transportation that would not pollute the air.

Make a class weather station, including a wind sock, wind vane, anemometer, and rain gauge. Students can make instruments individually or in teams. Then hold an Air, Wind, and Weather Open House to share the products of the unit. Invite the school principal, parents, another class, and/or others.

Experiment to find out what makes a candle flame go out if you put a glass jar over it. Discuss how fire needs air to burn.

Cut long ribbons from tissue or crepe paper. Put music on and let students make up their own ribbon dances. Point out how the wind moves the ribbons. This is now an Olympic event in the gymnastics category.

Earth Day *(cont.)*

Have your students design posters for Earth Day. They can be displayed in the classroom, in the library, throughout the school, and in the community.

Hold an Earth Day bookmark contest. Have your class make up the contest rules and forms. Select a winner from each grade level. Duplicate the bookmarks of the winners and distribute them to the students at your school. See if your public library will duplicate and distribute them, too.

Set up an art center where students create art work from recyclable material including anything that they can use in a way different from the way it was originally used. This might include old buttons, fabric scraps, or lace trim as well as more typical "trash."

Make seed pictures. Draw simple shapes onto small pieces of colored tagboard. Glue a variety of seeds onto the shapes.

Create fruit and vegetable mobiles. Have students identify a grouping (e.g., vegetables that are seeds or fruits with pits) and draw, color, and cut out representative examples. Attach these to the bottoms of coat hangers with string or yarn. Mount the title from the top of the hanger.

Use the following quick-write topics or brainstorm some with your class: "If I were a seed. . ." "If I were a flower. . ." "I'd like to be a tree because . . ."

Learn about careers related to plants. Be sure to include nursery workers, landscape architects, gardeners, farmers, horticulturists, arborists, and botanists. Have students interview nursery workers or research the occupations and present their findings to the class. Invite some of these workers to school as guest speakers or take field trips to visit places of work.

Bibliography

Javana, John. *50 Simple Things Kids Can Do to Save the Earth.* Andrews and McMeel, 1990.

Lowery, Linda. *Earth Day.* Carolrhoda, 1992

The Tropical Rain Forest

You can create a rain forest environment in a classroom terrarium.

Materials: five or ten gallon aquarium with a glass or clear plastic cover, gravel, ground charcoal, peat-based compost, variety of specimen plants (Refer to the list below or ask students to collect plants and seedlings from their yards.)

- **Sunplants:** marantas, dracenas, ficus, palms, rubber tree, dieffenbachia

- **Shade plants:** fittonia, peperomia, spathyphyllum

- **Epiphytes:** tillandsia, vriesia

- **Vines:** philodendron, spiderwort

Directions: Decide what to plant in the terrarium and the best planting plan. Light-tolerant plants should be taller than the shade plants and placed to represent the canopy layer of the rain forest.

1. Clean the bottom and sides of the aquarium.

2. Place a layer of gravel in the bottom of the container. Next spread charcoal over the gravel. The charcoal will act as a filter. Last, spread the planting medium over the charcoal.

3. Plant the lower, understory plants first; then, add the taller plants. If you are using epiphytes like bromeliads and climbing vines, provide some branches to support them. To plant one air plant, pack the roots of the plant in sphagnum moss. Press the root bundle into a fork or hole in the branch or tie it to a branch.

4. Mist the plants lightly with distilled water or rainwater and cover the aquarium.

Place the aquarium in a warm, sunny area of the classroom. Within a few days you will notice drops of water collecting inside the top. This means that the ecosystem is functioning and that the water and air are cycling just the way they would in a rain forest.

Individual Terrariums

To make individual terrariums, use clear two-liter soda bottles. Carefully remove the opaque base of each bottle and follow the directions above for planting. Cut the bottle below the neck, making sure that it is taller than the tallest plant. Place the cut end in the base, forming a dome over the terrarium.

Teaching Mathematics Through the Multiple Intelligences

Accessing Logical/Mathematical Intelligence Through Verbal/Linguistic Intelligence

Cause and Effect:

Grades K–1: Cause and effect is not a difficult concept for young students to understand. It is a little more difficult for them to verbalize it, however. For these students, short, simple verbal lessons are appropriate. Find examples of cause and effect in daily life, such as in books that you read and in classroom management situations. Point these out during the end-of-the-day ritual or during a discussion/sharing period. After a few examples, students will be able to identify cause and effect without prompting. Examples of cause and effect:

When the sun shines (cause), I get hot (effect).

When I bump the blocks (cause), they fall down (effect).

When I disobey (cause), I get a time out (effect).

Grades 2–4: Cause and effect can be approached a little more formally with older students. Let the students know that sometimes when something happens, it causes something else to happen. For example, when you turn on the faucet, that will cause water to come out.

Cause   Effect

turning on the faucet   water coming out

Adding One

I'm so smart;

I learned a trick,

An easy way

To add things quick.

One plus a number,

Any number plus one,

Is just like counting.

It's easily done.

One plus one is two;

Count on up, is what you do.

Two plus one is three;

It's easy as can be.

Three plus one is four;

Just count on up one more.

Four plus one is five;

I'm the smartest kid alive!

1+1=2

2+1=3

3+1=4

4+1=5

by Sandra Merrick

Whose Is It?

Can you use the clues in the pictures to figure out what item belongs to each child? **Hint:** Think of the *number* of things. Write what each child owns on the line under his or her picture.

Kami owns_____ **Pablo** owns _____ **Maria** owns _____

wagon   **scooter**   **skates**

A Present for Everyone

Can you match each present to each child? **Hint:** The ones that go together have something in common. Write the present on the line under each child.

Ancient Math

The following math problems are based on facts and figures from the text of *Dig This! How Archaeologists Uncover Our Past.* Give a copy of this page to each group of students to complete together. Direct them to show their work on separate paper. When all the groups have completed this page, orally check the answers and processes used to determine them.

---

1. The Sumerians occupied southwest Mesopotamia from about 4000 B.C. to 2300 B.C. How many years did they occupy the area?

---

2. The Parthenon is 237 feet long and 110 feet wide. What is the area of the Parthenon? Hint: Area = length x width.

---

3. Teotihuacan was a massive urban hub that stretched over 5 square miles and housed more than 20,000 people. On the average, how many people lived in each square mile?

---

4. Arthur Evans began excavating the palace of the Minoan kings in 1906 and continued his work for 35 years. In what year did he complete his work?

---

5. The Parthenon is 237 feet long, 110 feet wide, and 60 feet high. What is the volume of this structure? Hint: Volume = length x width x height.

---

6. Gudea ruled the Sumerian city-state of Lagah from 2144 to 2124 B.C. How many years was Gudea ruler of Lagah?

---

7. Mt. Vesuvius erupted in 79 A.D., burying Pompeii which was not rediscovered until 1728. How many years passed before it was found?

---

8. The ancient city of Tikal covers more than 9 square miles in the rain forests of Guatemala. What is the length of one side of the city?

---

9. The Pyramid of the Sun stands approximately 200 feet high while the Parthenon is 60 feet high. What is the difference in height between the two?

---

10. The Parthenon is 110 feet wide and 237 feet long. What is the perimeter of the Parthenon? Hint: Perimeter = 2 x length + 2 x width.

Character Traits

Character traits describe the unique qualities of a person. Select a character from a book you are reading. Decide whether each trait listed below is *never, occasionally, sometimes, frequently,* or *always* exhibited by that character. Place a check (✓) in the appropriate box. Provide written evidence from the story that supports some of the ratings you have given.

Title of Book: _____

Author: _____

Character's Name: _____

Character Trait	Never	Occasionally	Sometimes	Frequently	Always
1. daring					
2. respectful					
3. talkative					
4. ambitious					
5. proud					
6. persistent					
7. adventurous					
8. self-centered					
9. optimistic					
10. dishonest					
11. lazy					
12. friendly					
13. conceited					
14. bold					
15. energetic					

Number and Numeration

Different Numerals for Numbers

The numerals we use are called Arabic numerals because they were originally brought to Europe by the Arabs. They look like this: 0, 1, 2, 3, 4, 5, 6, 7, 8, 9.

The numerals used by the ancient Romans, called Roman numerals, look like some of the capital letters in our alphabet. Here are some of them:

I = 1	XI = 11	C = 100
II = 2	XII = 12	CCC = 300
III = 3	XIII = 13	CD = 400
IV = 4	XIV = 14	D = 500
V = 5	XV = 15	DC = 600
VI = 6	XX = 20	CM = 900
VII = 7	XL = 40	M = 1000
VIII = 8	L = 50	MC = 1100
IX = 9	LX = 60	
X = 10	XC = 90	

Study the relationship between these two numeral systems and figure out the answers below.

17 = _____	28 = _____	55 = _____
64 = _____	99 = _____	101 = _____
222 = _____	624 = _____	47 = _____
1025 = _____	492 = _____	1995 = _____
XVII = _____	XXVIII = _____	LXIV = _____
LV = _____	CI = _____	XCIX = _____
MCMXCV = _____	MCDXCII = _____	MXXV = _____
DCXXIV = _____	CCXXII = _____	CMXLVII = _____

What did you discover about these two sets of answers?

_____

_____

_____

_____

Number and Numeration *(cont.)*

Translating the Experience

Think about the experience you just had. It was a logical/mathematical experience. You were thinking about numbers, the numerals that stand for them, and their relationships.

Think about your reaction to the experience. In this part of learning about the multiple intelligences you will be translating logical/mathematical experiences by explaining them in written words. Many people feel that logical/mathematical thinking can be made clear by writing about it.

How did you start to figure out the problems? What did you do next? Did you make any false starts? If so, how did you go about figuring out what to do next?

_____

_____

_____

_____

_____

_____

There are two important differences between the way we write numbers in Arabic numerals and the way the Romans wrote numbers. Our system has two things that they did not have. Did you discover what they are? Write about them below.

_____

_____

_____

_____

_____

_____

Cookie-Chip Graph Recording Sheet

Directions: Mix an assortment of different chips in a plastic container. Each person should then pick 25 pieces from the container. Tally up the different types of chips and make a graph that shows your results. Use the information from your graph to fill in the blanks below.

Recording Information

My cookie-chip graph has . . .

_____ dark chocolate chips

_____ butterscotch chips

_____ white chocolate chips

_____ peanut butter chips

Graph Summary

I made these discoveries:

My graph has more _____

than any other kind of cookie chip.

My graph has fewer _____

than any other kind of cookie chip.

My friend's graph has more _____

than any other kind of cookie chip.

My friend's graph has fewer _____

than any other kind of cookie chip.

I like to eat _____

more than any other kind of cookie chip.

YES or NO

Read each of the bubbles on this page. Decide if the things in these bubbles can or cannot be measured in inches. If something can be measured, use green to color the bubble and one "YES" box on the graph at the bottom of this page. If it cannot be measured, use yellow to color the bubble and one "NO" box on the graph. Answer the questions below the graph.

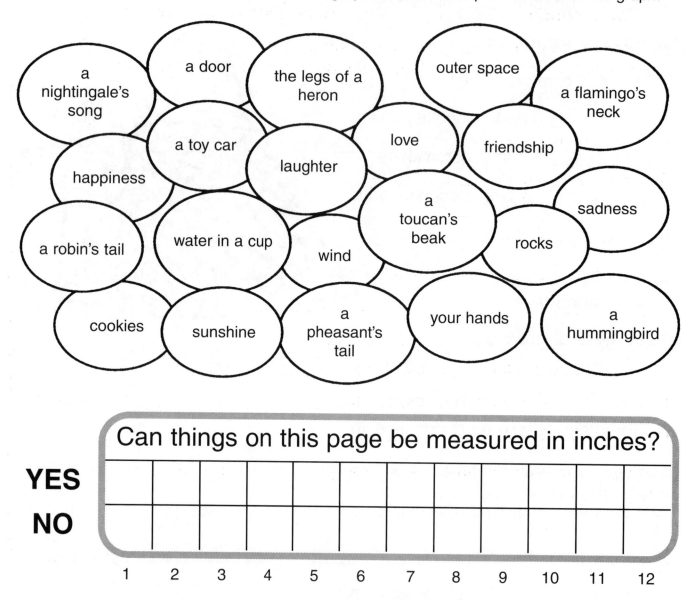

1. How many things on this page can be measured in inches? _____

2. How many things on this page cannot be measured in inches? _____

3. Are there more things on this page that can be measured or that can not be measured in inches?_____ How many more?_____

1 2 3, X Y Z

Some patterns repeat. These are patterns like 1 2 3 1 2 3 and x y z x y z. Some patterns do not repeat, but there is a connection or pattern between one thing and the next thing in a group.

For example: 1 3 5 7 9   **Rule: Skip a number.**

Here are some patterns using numbers and letters. Look for the rule that is used to make the patterns. Add more things to complete each pattern.

1. 2 4 6 8 10 _____ _____ _____ _____

2. AA B CC D EE _____ _____ _____ _____

3. up, cup, at, sat, it, _____, _____, ton

4. Z Y X W V U T S _____ _____ _____ _____

5. a 1 b 2 c 3 d _____ _____ _____ _____

6. December, Saturday, November, Friday, October, Thursday, September,

   _____, _____, _____

7. 30 27 24 21 18 _____ _____ _____ _____

8. Amy, Barbara, Carrie, Debbie, Erin, _____ _____

9. mouse, mice, house, houses, goose, _____, _____, plants

10. 4 2 1 6 3 2 8 4 3 _____ _____ _____

Make your own patterns here. See if your friends can find the rules you used to make your patterns.

1.

2.

3.

How Many Ways?

How many ways can your group think of to divide these objects in half?

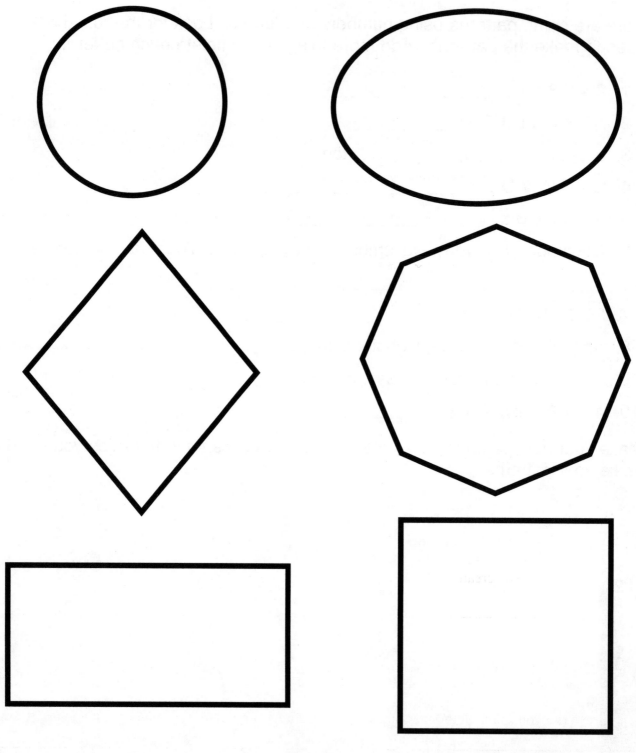

The Cookie Business

Everyone enjoys the cookies that you bake. To earn money, you decide to go into business for yourself by making and selling your cookies. Your mother said that you could use the kitchen and her baking equipment, but you will have to buy your own ingredients. Before you begin, you must make a business plan to see if this really is a good idea. Complete each of the following steps to create a business.

1	Who will buy your cookies? Create a questionnaire asking students, neighbors, and others if they would buy cookies from you. Ask what types of cookies they would buy, how much would they be willing to pay, and how many would they buy from you. Here is your first decision. Are there customers for your enterprise?
2	How much will it cost to make the cookies? After determining the types of cookies that the customers will buy, research the cost of making the cookies by going to the store and getting prices for the ingredients.
3	Add up the cost for all of the ingredients and divide by the number of cookies the recipe will make. How much does it cost to make each cookie? Subtract this amount from what your potential customers said that they would pay for the cookies. This is the amount of profit for each cookie sold. If all the cookies are sold, what would be the profit? What would it be if only $\frac{1}{2}$ of the cookies sold?
4	Now consider different scenarios. Should those who buy more than one cookie receive a discount? Should someone who wants to buy cookies every week receive a discount? Look at some of the ways other business people encourage customers to buy their products and list some creative ideas for marketing the cookies.
5	If the plan looks good, it can be shown to people who might be willing to "invest" in the business or make a loan to get the business started. The plan will show that this is a serious and well thought out enterprise. Write your plan on another piece of paper, and if you are serious, you are on your way.

Chuck Wagon Math

You and your class are going on a cattle drive as one of the activities during your stay at the dude ranch. You'll only be gone overnight, but Cookie, the ranch cook, looks like he's packing for a year!

Your dinner menu for the night consists of:

- pork and beans
- hot dogs
- mustard and pickles
- juice
- hot dog rolls

Cookie is sending you to town to buy his cooking supplies. You must figure out how much money you will need so that Cookie can give you enough cash to buy all the supplies for the cookout.

Using a grocery store flier or prices recorded from a local grocery store, determine the cost for each item. You will need to decide approximately how many servings each item contains and how many "cowpokes" are in your class. (And. . . don't forget your trail boss!)

Item Name	Amount Needed	Cost Per Item	Total Amount
pork and beans			
hot dogs			
hot dog rolls			
mustard			
pickles			
juice			
cups			
plates			
spoons			
napkins			
		Total Cost	

Deductive Reasoning

Can you find a pattern of operations that can be used on any number so that the answer is always the same?

Here is one example:

	4	7	9
• Choose any numbers.			
• Add 5 to each number.	$4 + 5 = 9$	$7 + 5 = 12$	$9 + 5 = 14$
• Double each sum.	$2 \times 9 = 18$	$2 \times 12 = 24$	$2 \times 14 = 28$
• Subtract 4 from each product.	$18 - 4 = 14$	$24 - 4 = 20$	$28 - 4 = 24$
• Divide each result by 2.	$14 \div 2 = 7$	$20 \div 2 = 10$	$24 \div 2 = 12$
• Subtract the original numbers.	$7 - 4 = 3$	$10 - 7 = 3$	$12 - 9 = 3$

Can you write a general rule for the above series of operations? In each step the same operation was done to each number. Use **n** to represent any number, and write the steps as a mathematical sentence or formula.

$$\frac{[(n+ 5)\, 2] - 4}{2} - n = 3$$

Now try this pattern on your own.

- Choose any three numbers.

- Double each number.

- Add nine to each of the products.

- Add the original number to each number.

- Divide each of the sums by three.

- Add four to each quotient.

- Subtract the original numbers.

What is the result in each case? Can you find the pattern and write it as a formula?

Create your own deductive reasoning problem, and write the pattern as a formula. Ask another student to try it to see if you are correct.

The Swinging Pendulum

For this activity you will try to solve the mystery of the pendulum. To make a pendulum, you will need a length of string, a weight for the end of the string, a place from which to suspend the string, and a stopwatch or watch with a second hand. Set up your pendulum as shown in the illustration. Pull the weighted string upward as shown. Hold the string in this position. Measure the angle formed by the new position and the pendulum at rest. Set your pendulum in motion. Now, count the number of swings the pendulum makes in a given time (20 seconds, for example). Record your answer.

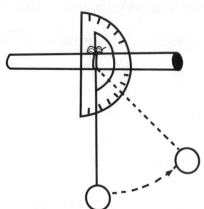

Repeat the experiment two more times. Change the angle each time. Measure the angle and count the number of swings, using the same amount of time as in the first trial.

Complete the chart to show the results for all three pendulums. Use what you discovered to think of a way to make a pendulum that would work as a clock. Write your ideas on the lines provided. Try to solve this problem by testing your ideas.

Trials	1	2	3
Angle			
Number of swings per _____			

_____

_____

_____

_____

_____

_____

_____

_____

Geometry

The Mobius Strip

Most people think of a sheet of paper as having two sides or surfaces. There is, however, a piece of paper with only one side. In 1858, a German mathematician named August Ferdinand Mobius discovered what has come to be called the Mobius strip.

- You can make a Mobius strip with any sheet of paper. A piece that is about two inches (5 cm) wide and two feet (61 cm) long is convenient and easy to handle. Make a ring from the strip but before taping the two ends together, give one end a half-twist.

- Starting anywhere on the strip, draw a continuous line. You will find that you can go all the way around the surface and back to the starting point without ever crossing an edge.

- Draw a line lengthwise through the middle of one surface of the strip. Is there another surface—a back—left to color?

  _____

  _____

- Cut the band lengthwise along the line you drew in the center of the strip. What was the result?

  _____

  _____

- Draw another line down the center and cut the band lengthwise again. What happened this time?

  _____

  _____

- Make another band. This time draw a lengthwise line one third of the way in from one edge. What result did you get?

  _____

  _____

  _____

Geometry *(cont.)*

The Mobius Strip *(cont.)*

Complete the chart below to discover what happens when you change the number of twists and the way you cut the strip. Later, you can compare results with your classmates.

Number of Half Twists	Number of Sides and Edges	Kind of Cut	Results (length and width, number of sides and edges, loops, twists, and knots)
0		center	
1		center	
1		one-third	
2		center	
2		one-third	
3		center	
3		one-third	

Pie Graph

Materials: chalk; paper; crayons; flat paved areas on the playground

Directions: Ask how many children are wearing the color red. Those children will need to form a line and hold hands. The children not wearing red will form a line and hold hands. The children on the ends of each line will hold hands with the children of the other group and form a large circle. One child or the teacher will draw a circle around the inside of the children with chalk. Each group will be standing together on the edge of the chalk circle.

Have the children help locate the center of the circle and place an "X" in the center. Draw lines from the "X" to the beginning and ending of the red group. Which group makes the biggest piece of the pie? This is a pie chart.

Pass out crayons and paper and let each child copy one of the human pie graphs that you made on the playground. This can be done right on the playground so that each child can remember what a pie graph looks like. Label the pie chart.

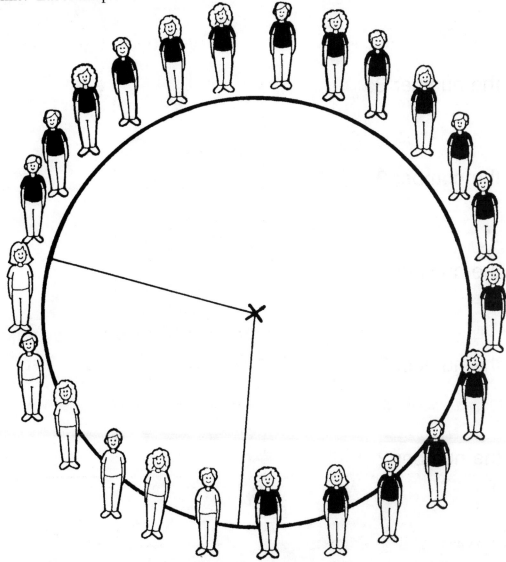

Variation: Divide the class by hair color, eye color, Velcro versus tie shoes, number of siblings, or birth order. Show the children more complicated pie graphs using more than one category.

Counters

Materials: two-sided counters (beans painted on one side work well) and a small paper cup for each student

Example:

Learning the number 6

Put 6 counters in your cup.
Dump your counters on your desk.
Write the sum you see.

2+4=6

1+5=6

Learning the number 4

Learning the number 8

Learning the number 3

Learning the number 5

Learning the number 7

Learning the number 2

Measurement Madness

Materials: paper clips, pennies, beans, ruler

Using the items listed above, measure how long each of the following things are.

	paper clips	beans	pennies	inches
your hand				
top of your desk				
seat of your chair				
cover of a reading book				
around a lunch box				
side of this paper				

Counting, Sorting, and Graphing

Teacher Note: Give each student or group of students a small package of M & M's and red, brown, blue, green, orange, and yellow crayons.

Directions: Sort your candies by colors, count the number of candies in each color group and then complete the bar graph using the matching colored crayons.

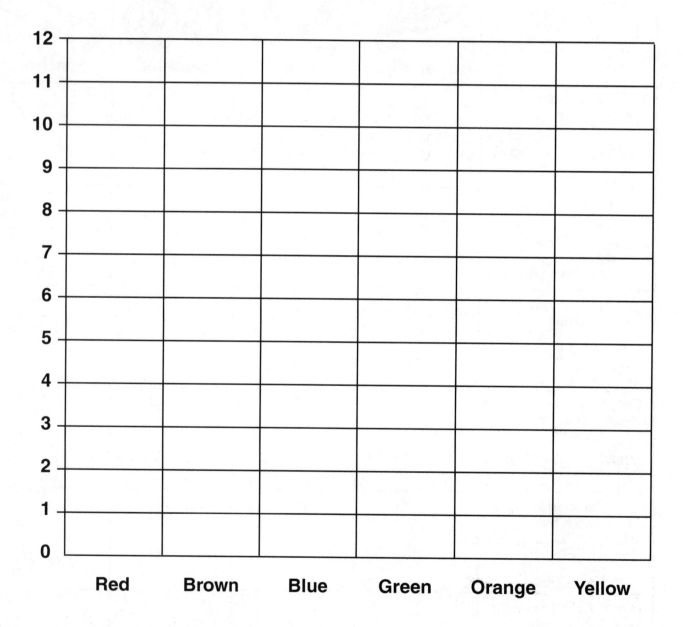

Which color has the most candies? _____

Which color has the fewest candies? _____

Build a Sundae Game

Teacher Directions:

1. Duplicate the game rules and laminate them for durability. Affix them to the front of a large envelope or file folder.

2. Duplicate, color, laminate, and cut out multiple copies of the patterns on the next page. Store them in the envelope or folder.

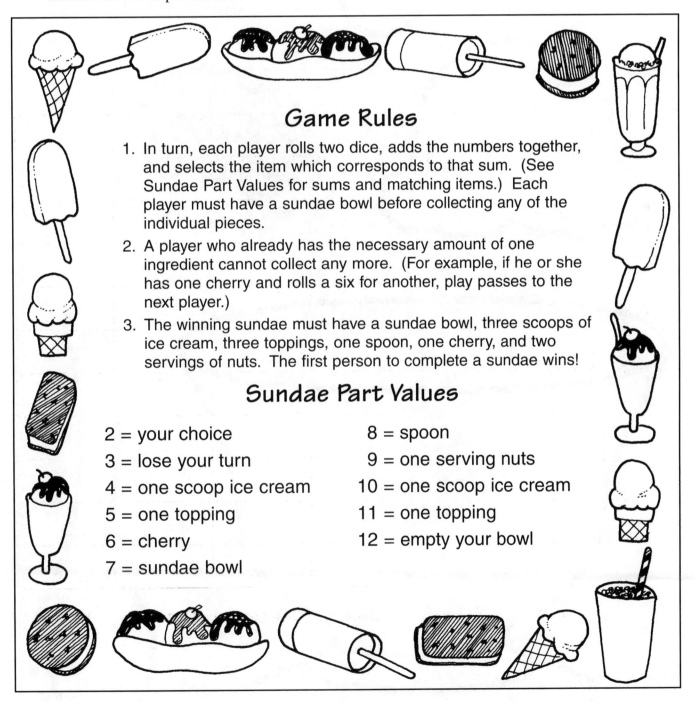

Game Rules

1. In turn, each player rolls two dice, adds the numbers together, and selects the item which corresponds to that sum. (See Sundae Part Values for sums and matching items.) Each player must have a sundae bowl before collecting any of the individual pieces.

2. A player who already has the necessary amount of one ingredient cannot collect any more. (For example, if he or she has one cherry and rolls a six for another, play passes to the next player.)

3. The winning sundae must have a sundae bowl, three scoops of ice cream, three toppings, one spoon, one cherry, and two servings of nuts. The first person to complete a sundae wins!

Sundae Part Values

2 = your choice

3 = lose your turn

4 = one scoop ice cream

5 = one topping

6 = cherry

7 = sundae bowl

8 = spoon

9 = one serving nuts

10 = one scoop ice cream

11 = one topping

12 = empty your bowl

Build a Sundae Game *(cont.)*

patterns

Mayan Math

The ancient Mayans were one of only three civilizations to discover and use the concept of zero. Although their system used only three symbols, the Mayans were able to measure time and record dates with great accuracy. Zero in the Mayan system, and in ours, shows the place value of numbers.

The Mayans based their number system on 20, which probably came from using fingers and toes to count objects. Archaeologists believe that the Mayans moved from counting with fingers and toes to using cocoa beans and bean pods on counting boards, which probably looked like boxes in a column. Five beans would be exchanged for one pod. When the box contained three pods (15) and 4 beans, the box was cleared, and one bean was added to the box on top. It was very easy to see the numbers in this way. This probably also explains why the Mayans wrote their numbers vertically. (In our system, we move from right to left to indicate place value.)

Later, when they wanted to carve numbers on monuments, there was a problem. How would they know whether the single dot (or bean) meant 1 or 20 if it was removed from the box? To solve this dilemma, they invented a symbol that looks like a shell (or a closed fist) to show that a box is empty. This is similar to the way that zero works in our number system. Zero allows us to see the difference between 1 and 10. In Mayan math, the shell tells us whether the dot represents 1 or 20.

Activity

Mayan Counting

Materials: beans, cinnamon sticks, macaroni shells, 3" x 8" (7.5 cm x 20 cm) strips of heavy paper divided into 4 equal boxes

Directions: Divide the class into teams or small groups. Give each team a supply of beans, sticks, and shells, and a counting board.

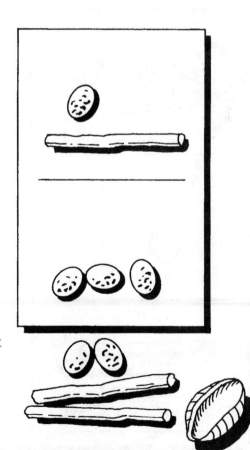

One student will count the beans while the other serves as recorder and banker. As the beans are counted, the recorder draws the missing Mayan numerals on the chart. When the counter has placed five beans in the box, he or she exchanges them for a cinnamon stick. When the box has three sticks and four beans, replace them with a shell and add a bean to the next box up.

Teacher Note: Full lesson plans and additional activities are presented in *Maya Math*, from Sunburst Communications.

More Mayan Math

You have seen that the Mayans used just three symbols and that they never showed more than three bars and four dots in any one place. You have also seen that this system is vertical.

At the lowest level, each dot is one and each bar is five. This box can hold a total of 19. _____

In the next box, each dot represents 20. What does each bar represent? _____

What is the highest number that can be written using the first and second boxes?_____

The third box begins where the second one ends. One dot in the third box means 400.

Follow the example to translate these Mayan numbers into our numbers.

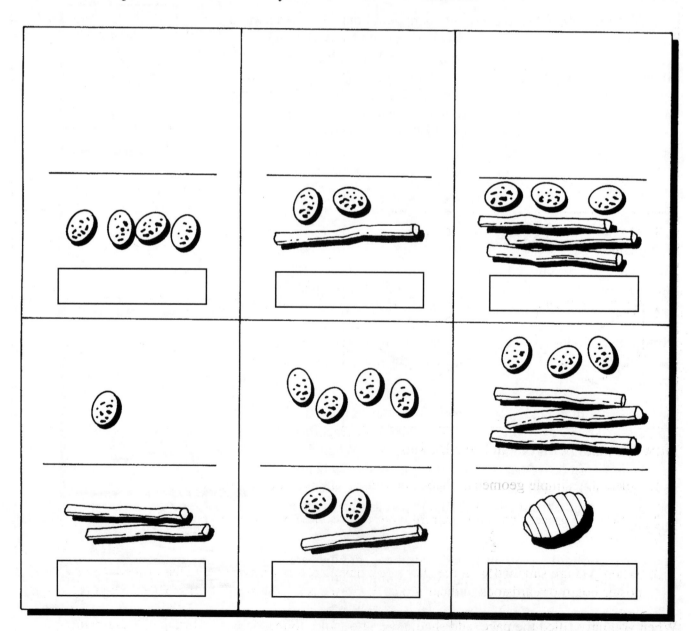

Tessellations

A tessellation is a design that covers a plane. The design does not overlap and there are no gaps in it. Maurice C. Escher, a Dutch artist, was fascinated with tessellations. In many of his sketches he used various forms of tessellations. If you can find prints of his works, look at them carefully. You will see how he rotated and transformed tessellations to create many of his sketches.

The word *tessera* comes from Latin and means the small squares used to make a mosaic. In a tessellation, a pattern is formed from a single shape. The shape is modified in some way and repeated to fill the available space. Many tessellations are very complicated and contain non-geometric figures. The following are directions for one geometric tessellation you can make.

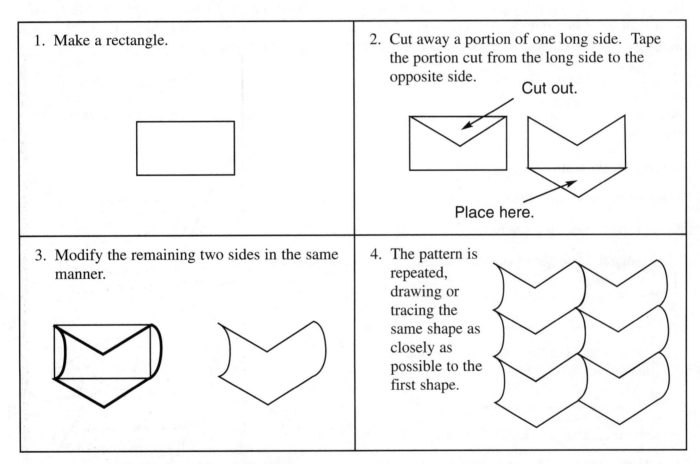

1. Make a rectangle.

2. Cut away a portion of one long side. Tape the portion cut from the long side to the opposite side.

   Cut out.

   Place here.

3. Modify the remaining two sides in the same manner.

4. The pattern is repeated, drawing or tracing the same shape as closely as possible to the first shape.

Now Create Your Own Tessellation

1. Select any simple geometric shape and draw it on a separate piece of paper.

2. Follow the process used above, removing a portion from a side and adding it to an adjacent or opposite side.

3. When you are satisfied with the shape you have created, trace it on a piece of heavy paper like poster board or cardstock and cut it out. Use this as a template and fill a page with your design.

When you have filled the page, add shadings and/or color to make your picture more interesting.

Hearts in Motion

Each individual has a rate at which his or her heart beats. The beating of your heart is called your pulse. When you are resting, your heart rate (pulse) will be different from what it is when you are exercising. You can check your pulse by placing your fingers in certain places on your body. Many people are able to feel the pulse on the insides of their wrists. This is accomplished by placing your first two fingers on top of the veins in your wrist. Your thumb can be used to support the back side of your hand. If you are unable to feel a pulse from this vein, you may want to try the artery in your neck. To find this artery, gently place the same first two fingers in the middle of your neck and then move them to either side of your neck about one inch. You should feel a pulse in this position. It is important that you not press too tightly in this area.

Once you are able to feel your pulse, you should be able to find out what your resting heart rate is and what your heart rate right after exercise is. Have a partner assist you by keeping time for you. You will want to count the number of pulse beats that you feel during a one-minute period of time.

First, you should take your pulse while sitting at your desk. Record your resting heart rate below.

Next, jog in place for a few minutes. Now take your pulse again. Below, record your heart rate after exercising.

Resting Heart Rate: _____

After-Exercise Heart Rate: _____

Answer the following questions:

- When did your heart beat the fastest?

  _____

  _____

- What was the difference between the two heart rates?_____

  _____

  _____

- Does exercise increase or decrease the rate at which your heart beats?

  _____

  _____

- Why do you think it is important to increase the rate of your heart? _____

  _____

Going the Distance

How are time, distance, and rate of speed related? To find the answer you will need books, tape, a toy car, a long board, a protractor, and a stopwatch or watch with a second hand. For this problem, you will work with time, distance, and rate of speed of an object.

Use the books to elevate one end of the board to create an inclined plane. Use tape to mark off a specific distance on the ground from the end of the board. Add this distance to the length of the board to find the total distance the toy car travels as it moves down the plane onto the ground. Keep this distance the same. Start the car at the top of the inclined plane (board). Time how long it takes for the car to reach the finish line. Do this 10 times, varying the angle of the inclined board each time, while keeping the distance the car travels the same for each trial.

Use the chart below to show the results of each trial in terms of feet (stays the same) per second (this varies).

Data Chart

Trial	Angle	Distance	Time	Distance ÷ Time	Results of column 5 (in feet per second)
1					
2					
3					
4					
5					
6					
7					
8					
9					
10					

Make My Quilt Square

Count all the shapes used in the quilt square below.

There are _____ squares.

There are _____ triangles.

There is _____ hexagon.

Trace the pattern blocks from page 191 onto colored paper, making as many of each kind as you need to build the quilt square. Make the square shapes yellow, the triangles blue, and the hexagon red. Cut them out and glue them to a white background. Use the pattern below as a guide.

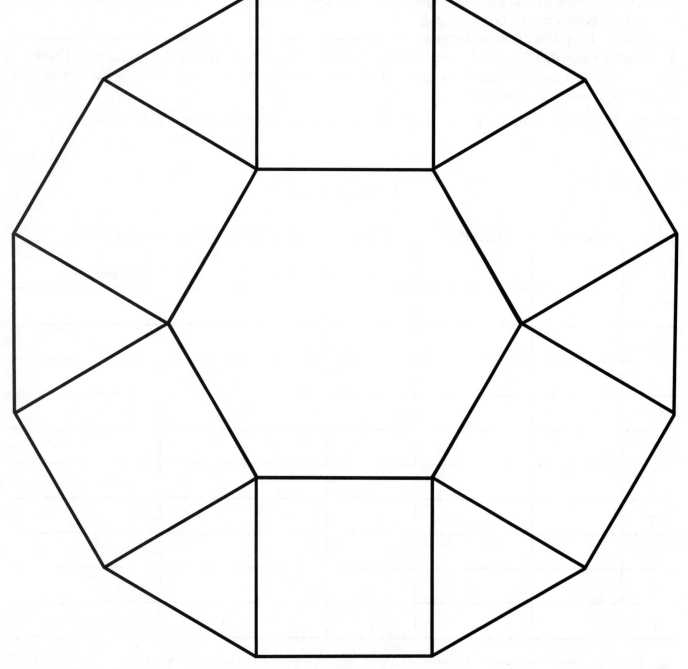

Make My Quilt Square *(cont.)*

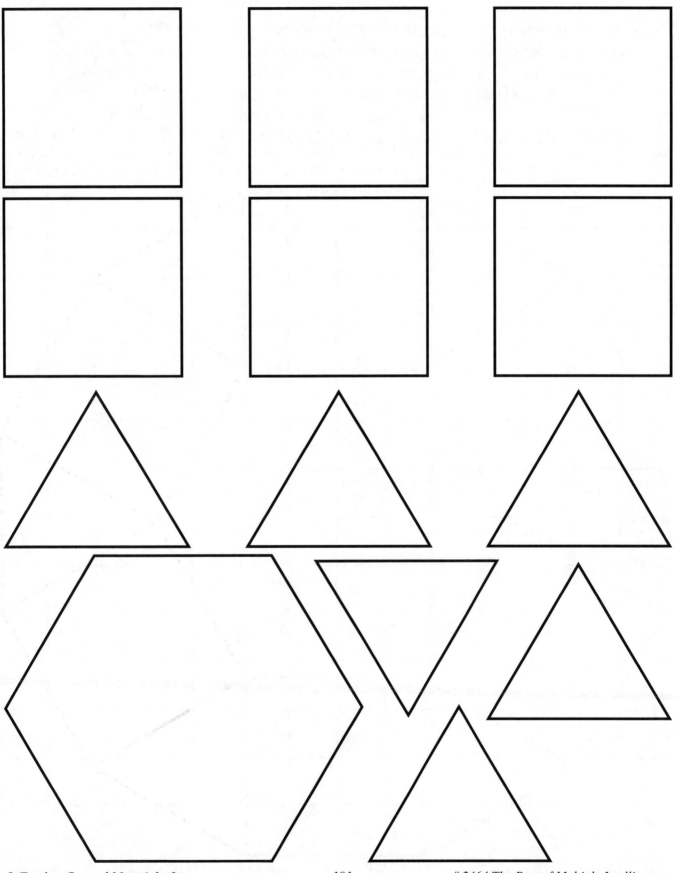

Symmetry

Look at this pattern. This is called a symmetrical pattern. That means that the pattern is balanced on all four sides. The right side is like a mirror reflection of the left. The top half is like a mirror reflection of the bottom half. Color a symmetrical pattern on the grid below. Make sure that the pattern is the same on all four sides.

Marine Math

Draw pictures in the space provided to show these math problems. Color and count them and write your answer.

1. Six clown fish are swimming in the coral reef. Each clown fish has two white stripes. How many white stripes do you see?

_____
white stripes

2. Each starfish has five arms it uses to crawl along the rocky shore. Five starfish are searching for clams. How many arms can you find?

_____
arms

3. Three octopuses are hiding among the rocks. Every one of the "octos" has eight arms. How many octopus arms are there?

_____
octopus arms

4. The inky squids each have ten tentacles. Two squids float past you while you swim. How many tentacles float past?

_____
tentacles

5. The crab has two bulging eyes to see its prey. Four crabs scuttle sideways along the colored reef. How many eyes are looking about?

_____
eyes

Patterns

A pattern is a group of things that repeats. Draw a line through the designs that do not repeat (the ones that are not patterns).

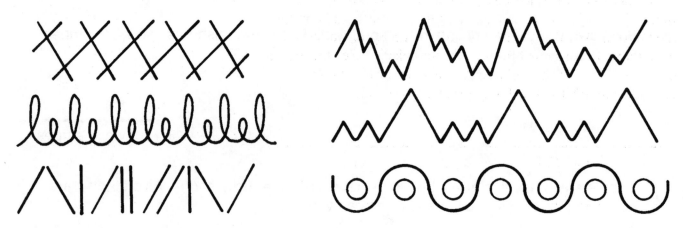

Look for the repeating patterns in each row and add three more things to complete the patterns.

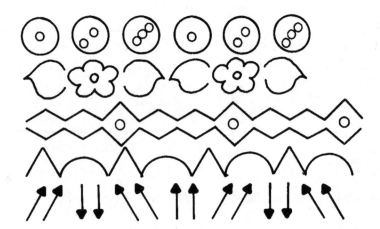

Make your own patterns below.

1.

2.

3.

4.

Three-D Tic-Tac-Toe

Doing three-dimensional problems on a two-dimensional surface requires some imagination. For this problem, you will use the rules for tic-tac-toe. Imagine three 3 x 3 grids stacked on top of each other. Grid A is on the top, grid B is in the middle, and grid C is on the bottom. Any three in a row will win the game, but they do not have to be on the same grid (in the same plane). See the example of one way to win. Use the three-dimensional grids below to play several Three-D Tic-Tac-Toe games with a partner.

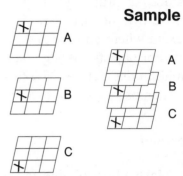

Perspective

How does an artist create a perspective view of telephone poles, trees, or other objects disappearing from view in the distance? The steps below will show you how to create the vertical lines that will represent where you are to draw your objects. You will see how to create your own perspective view of a series of objects. When you are done, the objects will appear equally spaced as they move from large to small in the picture. Use this page to practice making a series of poles, trees, cornstalks in a field, etc. Then use page 197 to design a picture that includes one of these perspective drawings.

Directions

1. Make a horizon line and place a vanishing point (X) on it.

2. Draw a vertical line segment (AB) to represent the first of the series of objects (the one nearest to you as the viewer). Connect AB to the vanishing point.

3. Draw a second vertical line segment (CD) parallel to the first, at the place you would like to draw the second object. Make diagonal lines (BC and AD). Label the point at which they meet (Y).

4. Draw a line from X to line segment AB, passing through point Y. This line will become the center point for each of the objects.

5. To make the vertical line segment for the third object, draw a line from point A through the center point of line segment CD until it touches line BX. This now becomes the base of the next object.

6. Add the rest of the vertical line segments in the same way you made AB and CD. These line segments represent the positions for each of the objects you wish to draw.

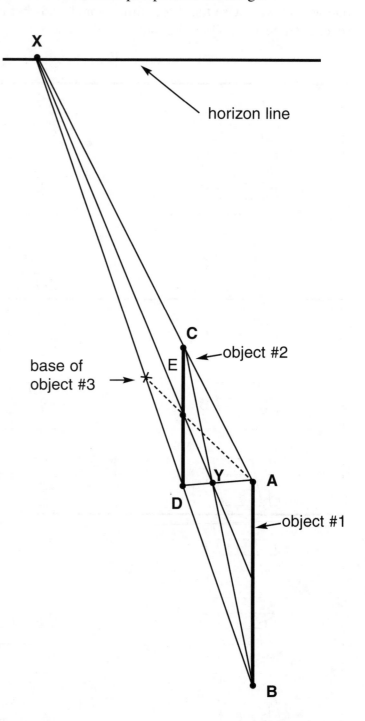

Perspective *(cont.)*

Directions: Use the information on page 196 to help you draw a scene that contains a series of objects moving toward a vanishing point. You could use such objects as rows of trees, telephone poles, or a vanishing road with road signs on each side, or a series of objects of your own choosing.

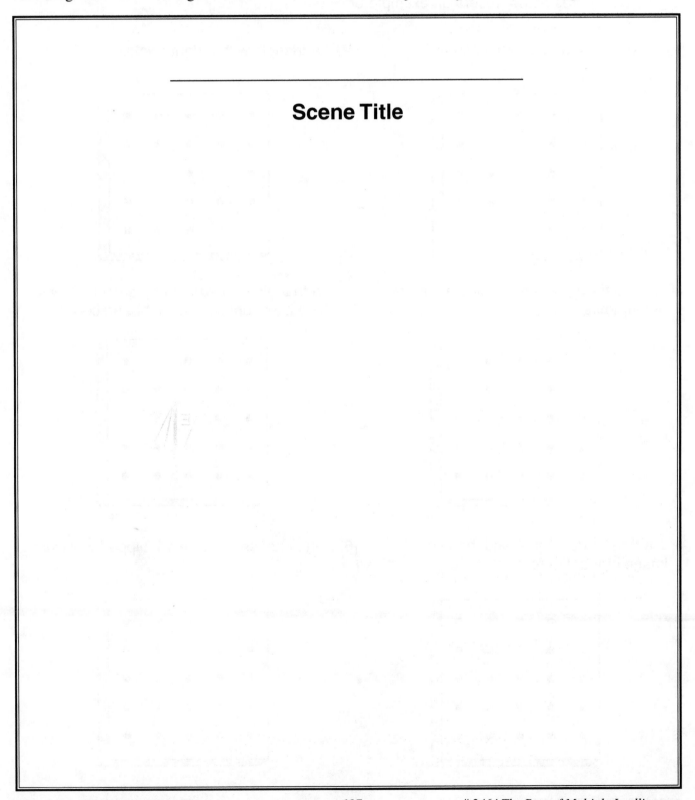

Scene Title

Geoboard Constructions

Name _____ Date _____

On the geoboards below, record an example of...

1. ...two sets of perpendicular lines.

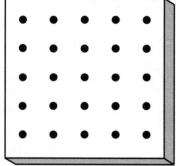

2. ...a triangle with a right angle.

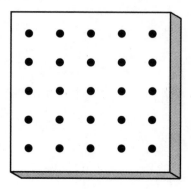

3. ...a square of two units inside a square of four units.

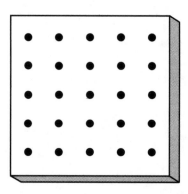

4. ...a triangle with a right angle using 3 pins. Slide it two units left or right and copy.

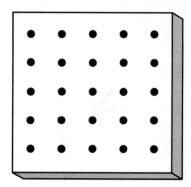

5. ...a three-sided figure and the mirror image of that figure.

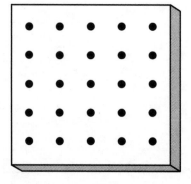

6. ...the images in figure #4, flipped downward.

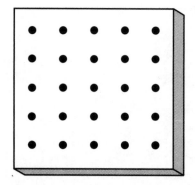

Geometric Figures

Hypatia particularly enjoyed geometry and was fascinated by conic sections. Conic sections are the geometric figures formed when a plane is passed through a cone. After the death of Hypatia, conic sections were neglected until the beginning of the seventeenth century. Only then did scientists begin to realize that many of the natural phenomena, such as orbits, could be described best by the curves formed by conic sections. Below are four cones. A plane passes through each of the cones at a different angle. Look at the dotted conic section formed. Below each figure, write whether the conic section is a circle, an ellipse, a parabola, or a hyperbola.

Circle — a closed, curved line, every point of which is equally distant from the center

Ellipse — a closed curve that is a symmetrical oval

Parabola — the curve formed by the edges of a plane when cutting through a right circular cone at an angle parallel to one of its sides

Hyperbola — the curve produced by the intersection of a plane with the surface of a cone, the plane intersecting both nappes

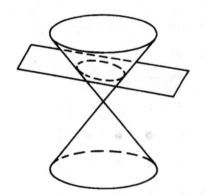

1. _____

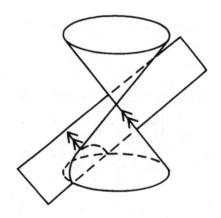

2. _____

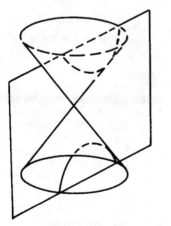

3. _____

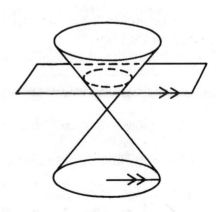

4. _____

Multiplication Songs

Twinkle, Twinkle, Times Tables

Sing each of the times table to the tune of "Twinkle, Twinkle, Little Star."

Three times one is always three.

Three times two is always six.

Three times three is always nine.

And three times four is always twelve.

Three times five is fifteen.

Three times six is eighteen.

Three times seven is twenty-one.

And three times eight is twenty-four.

Three times nine is twenty-seven.

Three times ten is thirty.

Three times eleven is thirty-three.

And three times twelve is thirty-six.

I Can Sing the Times Tables

Sing individual multiplication facts to the tune of "Are You Sleeping, Brother John?"

Six times seven, six times seven,

Is forty-two, is forty-two.

I can sing the times tables,

I can sing the times tables,

Yes, I can. Yes, I can.

Make a Note

Draw a set of notes that has 1 less than the set given.

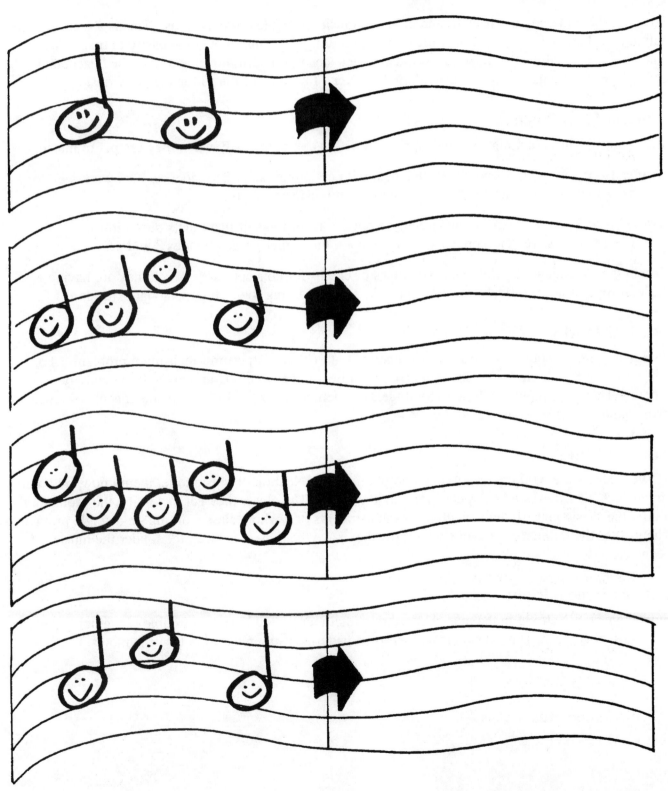

Accessing Logical/Mathematical Intelligence Through Musical/Rhythmic Intelligence

Background Music:

Many teachers already use background classical music during learning periods. This is a great way to help musical students feel at ease while doing something that might not come easily to them. Music that works especially well are selections that have a steady forward movement, like the "Pachelbel Canon." Extend music into the curriculum, however. Try some of the following activities.

Musical Math Facts:

Students can learn counting and other various functions of math easily when they are put to music.

Grades K–1: Fingerplays and chants that deal with counting, patterns, sequence, etc., work well to access the logical/mathematical intelligence through music and rhythm.

Grades 2–4: There are many commercially produced recordings of math facts put to music. Multiplication raps are very popular with students in the higher grades (grades 3 and 4).

Encourage students to develop their own tunes or chants for concepts with which they are having a difficult time or cooperatively develop some classwide learning tools (Interpersonal extension).

Musical Math:

Assign a different sound to various math functions. Let students perform their math problems. For instance, plus (+) might be a clap; equal (=) might be a finger snap. Doing an addition activity repetitively in this manner will help the students remember their facts. Let the students choose their own sounds for the various functions.

Musical Clues:

When students are working on solving a problem, use a selection of music to let them know, by volume signals, whether they are on target or missing the point. The closer they get to solving the problem, the louder the music gets. Use this with individual students or a whole class working on a single problem. The greater the number of students who show they have the correct answer, the louder the music becomes.

Pattern Recognition:

Students who are strong in the musical/rhythmic intelligence will have less trouble recognizing patterns in a musical context. Have them create their own patterns, using musical notes or symbols.

Musical Time

One other very important piece of information included on the staff of any piece of music is called the time signature. This tells the person reading it how long to hold each note and where the stress should be placed. This information looks like a fraction. The top number tells how many beats there are in a measure of music. The measures are indicated by vertical lines drawn through the staff. In most written music there are 3, 4, or 6 beats to a measure.

The shape of each note on the staff indicates its value. A whole note has a value of one. There are also half, quarter, eighth, sixteenth, thirty-second, and sixty-fourth notes.

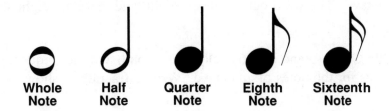

| Whole Note | Half Note | Quarter Note | Eighth Note | Sixteenth Note |

The bottom number in the time signature indicates which kind of note receives one beat. The most common key signature uses four, meaning that a quarter note receives one beat.

On the musical staffs below, see how many different combinations of notes you can make to complete one measure of music. Note that usually this rhythm is consistent throughout a piece of music.

Sound Ideas

Sound is all around us. Vibrating matter produces a wave-like disturbance which is transmitted, usually through air, to a receiver like the human ear. Sounds can be pleasant or unpleasant, depending on a number of factors. Music is sound produced by matter which vibrates in a regular fashion.

In a piano, sound is produced by strings. Pushing the key of a piano causes a hammer to hit a string and produce a sound. Because the strings are of different lengths and diameters, each string vibrates at a different rate, creating a different sound or note. The shorter a string is, the more rapidly it vibrates, and the more rapid the vibration, the higher the sound. If the length of a string is cut in half, the speed at which it vibrates, called the frequency, doubles. In music, the interval between tones that have this half ratio is called an octave. The word octave means eight, and there are eight steps or notes between the two tones.

The frequency of middle C on a piano is 256 cycles per second, and the frequency of high C is 512. Below are the frequencies for the notes of an octave. Write a fraction to show the ratio between middle C and each note.

Note	Frequency	Fraction
middle C	256	
D	288	
E	320	
F	341	
G	384	
A	426	
B	480	
high C	512	

Use eight identical glass bottles, or eight test tubes, to create a scale. Add water to each one. Tune the glasses so that each one is one full tone higher than the previous one. Measure the height of the water for each note. Use ratios to compare the notes. Is there some similarity? Explain your findings.

_____

_____

_____

A Minute Waltz

The time signature is an essential part of written music. The time signature tells us how long to hold each note in relation to the other notes in the same measure or piece of music, but it does not give an exact time. Sometimes phrases are written on the piece of music to indicate how loud or soft and how slowly or quickly a particular piece should be played.

In a concert, the conductor is responsible for setting the tempo (speed). He or she uses a baton or his or her hand to set the tempo. The musicians watch for signals that indicate the downbeat, or first note, of the measure. Serious students of music may use a metronome to establish tempo for their playing.

Listen to several different pieces of music. Include a Strauss waltz like "The Blue Danube," a contemporary waltz like "Moon River," a fast rock and roll song, and a ballad.

Record the name of the music on the chart below.

Listen to several measures and identify the downbeat. Count the beats from one downbeat to the next to find the beats per measure.

Record the time signature.

Use a watch with a minute hand or a stopwatch to time yourself and begin counting the number of measures in a minute. Be as precise as you can.

Record the number of measures per minute and calculate how many beats per minute the song has.

Title	Time Signature	Measures per Minute	Beats per Minute

Music, Maestro!

On every piece of music, there is a time signature: 2/4, 3/4, 4/4, 6/8, with variations. The rhythm of beats is based on a count. Notes are based on fractions. In 4/4 time there are four beats to a measure, and each quarter note gets one beat. A half note gets two beats, and a whole note gets four. In 6/8 time there are six beats to a measure, and each eighth note gets one beat.

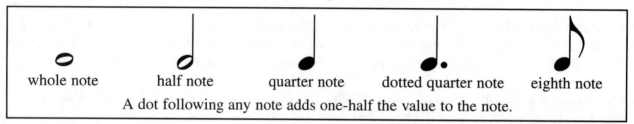

A dot following any note adds one-half the value to the note.

Mozart once wrote a waltz in which he specified 11 different possibilities for 14 of the 16 bars of the waltz and two possibilities for one of the other bars. Thus, there are 2×11^{14} variations on the waltz, only a fraction of which have ever been heard.

Examine the musical measures shown below. Do the notes always conform to the time signature shown at the beginning?

Can you tell what the time signature is in the second set of measures shown below?

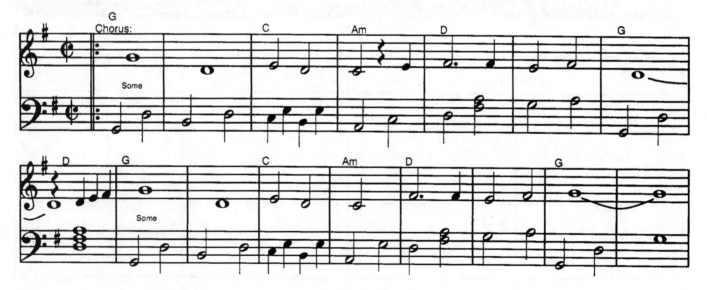

If you play a musical instrument and are learning how to read music, bring your instruments to class and demonstrate to your group how you use math to play and math to listen and math to dance.

How Am I Doing?

Teacher Note: Using the bar graphs provided, encourage your students to chart the number of conflicts they are engaged in throughout the week.

Begin by brainstorming what a conflict is. Develop a working list of ideas that encompasses the class idea of conflict. Help the class by providing certain times immediately following time blocks to do their graphing. Do not let it wait until the end of the day.

Collect at the end of the week.

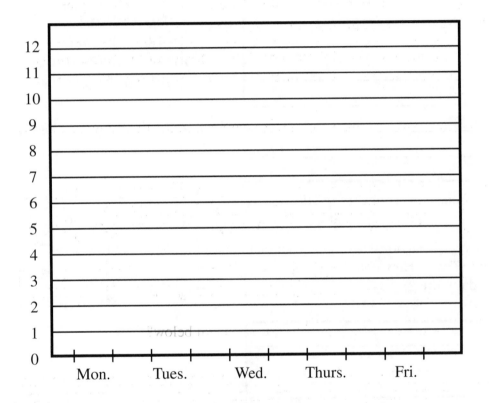

WEEK # 1

My behavior
in the classroom,
on the playground,
and at lunch.

Give students the same graph sheet on the following Monday. Ask them if they see anything they can improve for this week. (*Ideas*: "Maybe I could work on not being so easily teased. I fly off the handle whenever I hear anyone tease me. I make myself a fun target that way." Or "I think that I will not play with Emily for awhile. We are still having some problems after school. I want to work them out first." Or "I want to keep doing what I have been doing because it works just fine for me. I am not involved in outside or classroom conflicts. I work out disagreements as soon as they come up.")

This second week graph is very empowering to the class. It helps them immediately see the importance of their own attitudes in their own behavior. Discuss learnings that have occurred to students.

Note that the second bar graph has an open-ended label. In this way, you could simply fold the top of the page under and copy the bottom graph twice. This way, you will be ready to have an open-ended set of two graphs on the same page. This can be done at other times throughout the year to help students monitor their own behavior. Discuss after each week.

How Am I Doing? *(cont.)*

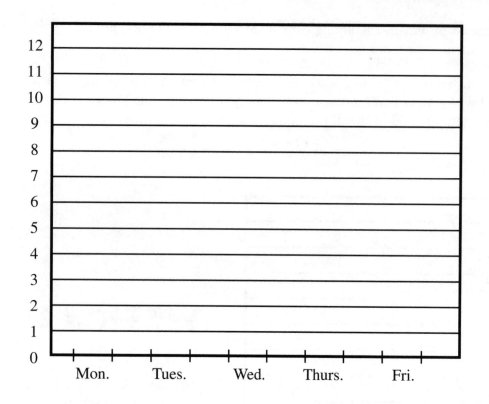

WEEK #1

My behavior
in the classroom,
on the playground,
and at lunch.

Begin with the top graph. Graph your behavior daily. Use your class chart on conflicts to see how many you had throughout the day. *Think:* How could you improve? What could you do to lower the number of conflicts in your own daily life?

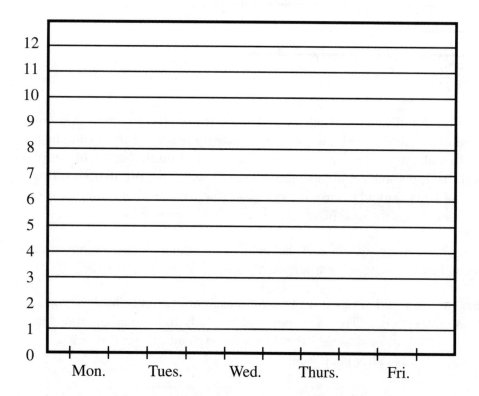

WEEK # ___

My behavior
in the classroom,
on the playground,
and at lunch.

Estimating

Directions:

1. Choose one item and estimate (guess) how many it will take to fill one ice cream scoop.
2. Fill the scoop level with the item.
3. Count and write down the actual number in the scoop.
4. Figure out the difference between your estimate and the actual number. Write down the difference.
5. Do these steps again for another item.

Item	Estimate	Actual	Difference

Pickup Truck from Shapes

1. Tell what each shape is.
2. Cut out the shapes.

3. Put the truck together.
4. Glue the truck to another paper.

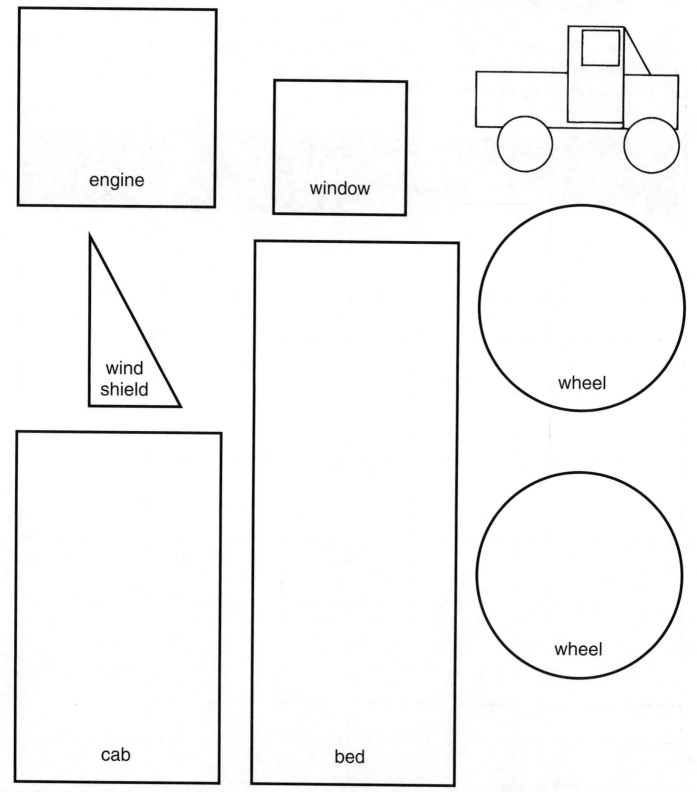

engine

window

wind shield

wheel

cab

bed

wheel

Pattern Quilt

Quilts often use a pattern of colors and shapes to create a beautiful design. Use the grid below to make a new quilt design. A simple pattern may be made by coloring the squares (red, yellow, blue, red, green, etc.). A more complex pattern can be created by dividing the squares diagonally before coloring.

Size is Relative

Student Activity Sheet

Name: _____

Date: _____ Per: _____

Have you ever stood at the bottom of a very tall building and wondered just how tall it was? Think for a moment about the tallest building or the highest mountain you have ever seen. Sometimes it is hard to relate to their massive heights. By comparing a known height, for instance, to how tall you are, you will be better able to understand the relationship between heights of different objects.

How Tall Are You?

A good place to begin your understanding of the height of something is to measure your own height. Work in pairs to measure your heights. Record your height below. Then list your height in inches, feet, centimeters, and meters.

Your height in inches: _____

Your height in feet (use decimals): _____

Your height in centimeters: _____

Your height in meters (use decimals): _____

Washington Monument

Let's see how you compare to the Washington Monument. Use a reference source or the Internet to find out the height of the Washington Monument. List its height in inches, feet, centimeters, and meters.

Washington Monument height in inches: _____

Washington Monument height in feet: _____

Washington Monument height in centimeters: _____

Washington Monument height in meters: _____

Size is Relative *(cont.)*

How Do You Stack Up?

Compare your height to the Washington Monument's height by setting up a ratio in inches, feet, centimeters, and meters. Express your answers as fractions, decimals, and percents. Use the work space at the bottom of the page. Fill in the table with your values.

Inches	Fraction	Decimal	Percent
Your Height ———— Washington Monument			

Feet	Fraction	Decimal	Percent
Your Height ———— Washington Monument			

Centimeters	Fraction	Decimal	Percent
Your Height ———— Washington Monument			

Work Space

Wars Are Hard to Predict

"You'll be home before the leaves have fallen from the trees." This famous quote from Kaiser Wilhelm II proved to be far from correct. Both sides thought World War I would be a short war, but war is filled with unexpected circumstances and problems. Using your best strategies, solve the following story problems.

1. The general called a meeting of lieutenants and sergeants to plan for the following day. Altogether, 178 lieutenants and sergeants attended the meeting, and there were 44 more sergeants than lieutenants. How many sergeants and how many lieutenants attended the meeting?

2. Soldiers Smith, Lutz, and Jones are at the supply tent together. Each of the soldiers has part of the list of things they need for their infantry. As they go to the checkout station, they each decide to get in a different line to save time. As Smith gets in line, he notices that there are three more people in front of him than are in front of Lutz, and there are two times as many people in front of Jones as there are in front of Lutz. The total number of people in front of Smith, Lutz, and Jones is 11. How many people are in front of each of the soldiers?

3. Captains Arthur and Floyd and First Lieutenants Short and Erickson are seated at a square table. Floyd is sitting to Short's left. Short is sitting across from a first lieutenant. Where is each soldier sitting at the table?

4. General Sharp is making his morning rounds around camp on his way to the mess tent. He goes north three tents, stops at Tent A and turns right. He goes east for 2 tents and then turns left and goes one tent north to the supply tent. Then he turns right, goes east one tent, and turns right again. He goes four tents south to the mess tent. When General Sharp leaves the mess tent, what is the quickest way for him to get back to where he began?

How Much Do You Weigh?

How much do you weigh? Your weight depends upon where you are. If you were in orbit around the earth, far away from Earth's gravitational pull, you would be weightless and would float. Mass is the amount of matter that makes up an object. The gravitational pull depends upon mass. Even a pencil has mass. Thus, it has gravitational pull, but since it is far less than the Earth's mass, it falls to the ground when you drop it.

If you were to visit other planets and moons with more or less mass than Earth's, a scale would show that you weigh a different amount than you do on Earth. Complete the chart to find out how much you would weigh on the planets in our solar system and on the moon.

Planet	Surface Gravity	Your Weight on Earth	New Weight
Mercury	.38 x		
Venus	.90 x		
Earth	1.00 x		
Mars	.38 x		
Jupiter	2.64 x		
Saturn	1.13 x		
Uranus	.89 x		
Neptune	1.13 x		
Pluto	.06 x		
Earth's Moon	.17 x		

How Much Do You Weigh? *(cont.)*

Make a bar graph to show the results of your calculations from page 215.

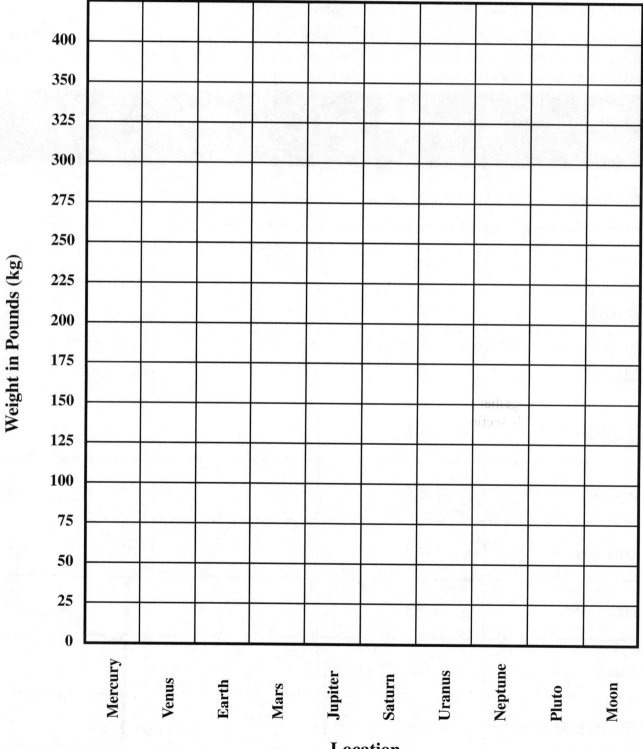

MY WEIGHT ON THE PLANETS AND THE MOON

Location

Weight in Pounds (kg)

400 · 350 · 325 · 300 · 275 · 250 · 225 · 200 · 175 · 150 · 125 · 100 · 75 · 50 · 25 · 0

Mercury · Venus · Earth · Mars · Jupiter · Saturn · Uranus · Neptune · Pluto · Moon

Accessing Interpersonal Intelligence Through Logical/Mathematical Intelligence

Group Problem Solving:

Any activity where students work on solving a problem or think logically in pairs, groups, or teams fits into this category. Working on math assignments together, completing a puzzle together, playing logic games together, and combining efforts on a scientific experiment are all excellent activities.

Code Clues:

Ask your students to create a code language that they can write down. Have them write a note to a classmate, using the code. A key should be included in the note. Then each recipient may respond to the note, using the same code.

This activity might be simplified by making up a class code first. Have the students write notes to each other using the class code and have the key easily visible. Once students have the hang of code writing, they might move on to develop their own codes.

Charting Individual Differences:

Have a discussion in which you point out that every person is special and different in his or her own way. Remind your students about some of the positive individual differences that are apparent in your classroom. Ask the students to interview classmates (lower grades might interview four classmates, while higher grade levels may interview as many as ten classmates).

Ask students to chart their classmates' names, hobbies, likes, and dislikes. When they are all done, you might incorporate the information into a classwide chart showing individual differences.

Math Simulations:

Students can work together in a variety of ways in this section. Younger students might play shop where they work together in figuring prices and making sure they have enough money to buy the things that they need. Older students might do the same but add complexity by using checkbooks and balancing these at the end of every month (or week). They might also work on minibudgets together.

Let students start small businesses in the classroom (in partnerships or corporations) and think of all the problems they might have to overcome. (Minisociety curriculum works very well in the third and fourth grades).

Fraction Quilts

Materials:

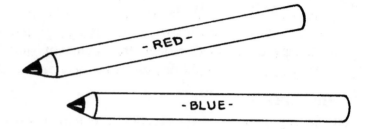

- construction paper in various colors (abundant supply)
- 8" (20 cm) square white paper
- rubber cement
- personal record sheets (following pages)
- colored pencils
- bulletin board paper
- 9" (23 cm) square white paper (optional)

Directions:

1. A discussion on fractions in general terms should occur. The points covered should include the fact that an object (or number) can be divided into equal parts, and these are sometimes called fractional parts. Fractional parts can equal the same amount but be called by different names (e.g., $^2/_4 = ^4/_8 = ^1/_2$). The terms numerator and denominator can be introduced at this time, if appropriate.

2. Tell the students that for the next few days, you will be exploring fractions. Tell them that, as a result, the class will be creating a paper quilt. Explain that this quilt will represent the fraction $^1/_2$ in many different ways and that it will be their job to see how many different quilt squares they can create.

3. Divide the class into groups of four students each. This number seems to work best but feel free to use other sized groups.

4. Give each group two 4" x 8" (10 cm x 20 cm) rectangles of colored paper. Each group should be given two different colors, and each group's colors should be different from those of the other groups. This is so that the groups' work can be differentiated. Each group should also be given one 8" (20 cm) square white paper. Each student in the group should also be given a corresponding personal record sheet.

5. When all material has been handed out, tell the students that they should use the next few minutes (whatever period you choose) to move the colored rectangles around on the white square. The two colored sheets should completely cover the square. As they move the colored sheets, they should record their designs (using matching colored pencils) on their record sheets. (This step should not take long since there are only two combinations, horizontal and vertical.)

6. After the groups have completed their designs, they should glue their pieces, creating two fraction quilt squares.

7. Discuss with the students what they have discovered about the pieces and talk about the term one-half ($^1/_2$).

8. Begin keeping a running experience chart about the students' discoveries. Allow them to write on it. This will be used to create a bulletin board at the conclusion of the activity.

Fraction Quilts *(cont.)*

9. For the next session, explain that you will be giving each group four pieces of colored paper (two each of the same colors as before), and they will again be covering the square. This time, the paper should be cut to 4" (10 cm) squares. As before, they should move the pieces around, recording their findings. When all combinations have been made, distribute more pieces so all patterns can be glued. Tell the students that they should only glue each design one time and not glue the same design repeatedly. They can color the designs on their corresponding record sheets. They can also write about their experiences on the experience chart after you have discussed it as a class.

10. During the next session, student groups will work with eight pieces (four each of two colors). Tell them that this time they must decide how to cut the pieces. (Do not tell them that there are several ways to do this, including triangles, rectangles, or squares. Let them discuss the problem and arrive at a decision.) After they have decided, cut the paper into the specified shapes or have the students do it. (You might also discuss any other possible shapes for halves and quarters and allow the students to add them to their record sheets and experience chart.)

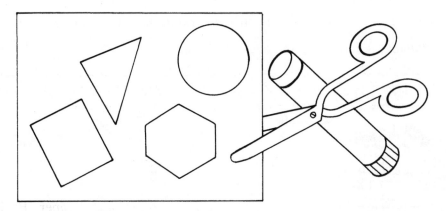

Proceed as before, allowing more time for experimentation since more patterns are possible. They may need more than one period to complete all arrangements and corresponding record sheets. When they feel they have made all possible arrangements, provide enough pieces for gluing. Fill in the experience chart.

11. At this point, the project can be brought to its conclusion, or you can go to sixteenths. This can continue until you feel the students have discovered the infinite number of ways $\frac{1}{2}$ can be shown.

12. At the conclusion of each exploration period, all the squares should be glued (or stapled) onto the bulletin board paper. Arrange the various designs and colors in a pleasing pattern. Next to the completed quilt, you can hang the experience chart, including the students' conclusions about fractions. It is also a good idea to display and label a sample of each fraction used in the quilt as well as the next fraction which would be used were you to continue subdividing. For example, if you ended using $\frac{1}{16}$, show what $\frac{1}{32}$ would look like.

Variations:

1. Each student can make his or her own quilt.

2. Other fractional pieces can be used, such as $\frac{1}{3}$ and its subdivisions.

Underground Place Value

Tunnel through place value with the following cooperative group activity.

Directions:

1. Reproduce the place value card (one per group of three to four children) on page 221 on tagboard or construction paper.

2. Cut out and laminate the cards.

3. Provide each cooperative group with a tunnel card, 40 one-ounce (28.5 g) cups and a large handful of raisins.

4. Call out a number. (**Note:** Using 40 cups, the numeral may not exceed 399.) Each group shows the number's place value by placing raisins in the cups to represent the numeral.

Example:

The numeral 127 is represented by the following arrangement of raisins and cups:

—ten stacked cups with ten raisins in each cup in the hundreds chamber

—two stacked cups with ten raisins in each cup in the tens chamber

—seven raisins spread out in the ones chamber

5. Allow children to take turns calling out numerals and working in groups to check each other's results.

Underground Place Value *(cont.)*

Place Value Card: See page 220 for directions.

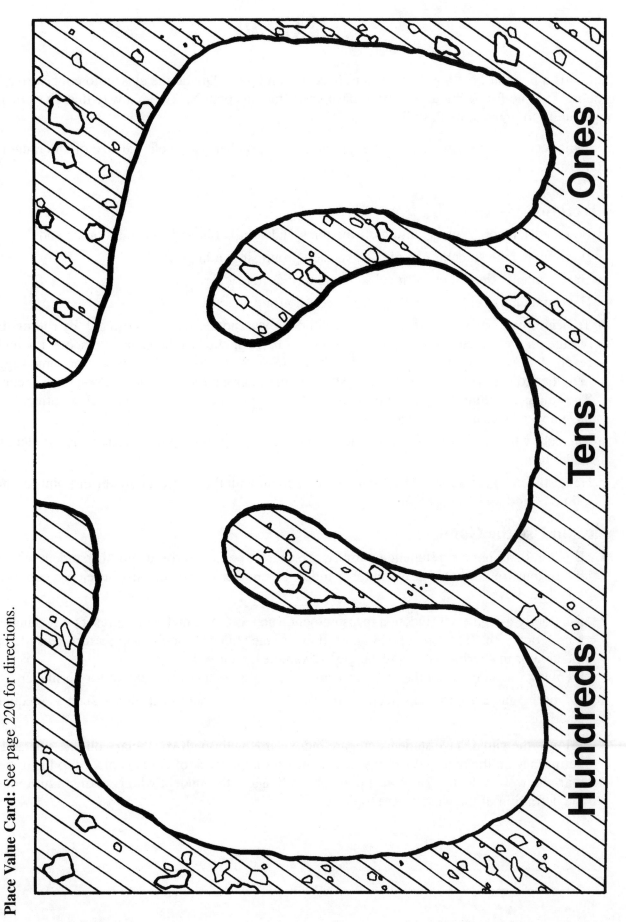

Ones

Tens

Hundreds

Nsikwi

Nsikwi is a popular bowling game among Nigerian children. Divide the class into cooperative learning groups. Use the following directions to have your students play Nsikwi in a way that gives them the opportunity to practice math skills.

You will need the following materials: one orange (or a rubber ball about the size of an orange) for each group, and a dry corn cob for each student.

Directions

- Prepare each corn cob by cutting off the thick end so it is flat and can stand on its end.
- If possible, take students outside. Have each group sit in a large circle.
- Have students stand their corn cobs on end to their left.
- Have students decide who will go first in each group.
- To begin play, have the first student try to knock over another player's corn cob by rolling the orange on the ground. If the student is successful, he or she has the chance to score a point by responding correctly during a specific activity. (See "Ways to Use the Game" for some suggested activities to use with students.) Other students in the group confirm that the response is correct. The student continues to play until he or she misses the question, fails to knock a corn cob down, or has knocked down all of the corn cobs.
- The corn cobs are reset. Play continues as the orange is passed to the left and each student takes his or her turn.
- Have students keep score. The winner is the person with the greatest number of points at the end of a time period that you specify.

Ways to Use the Game

1. Randomly assign each student a number. To score a point and roll again, the student who is taking a turn must multiply his or her number times the number of the person whose corn cob was knocked down.

2. Randomly assign each student a measurement, such as 6 cm, that will represent a rectangle's length or width. To score a point and roll again, the student who is taking a turn must determine the area or the perimeter of a rectangle. (Examples: 6 cm x 8 cm = 48 square cm for the area, or 6 cm + 6 cm + 8 cm + 8 cm = 28 cm for perimeter.)

   Adapt the game to provide students with practice in other math skills areas, such as inequalities or fractions.

3. Prior to the game, have students prepare index cards with math vocabulary on one side and definitions on the other. When it is a student's turn, the stack of cards is placed to his or her right with the word side up. To score a point and roll again, the student who is taking a turn must say the definition of the word on the top card.

A Game of Nim

This is a problem-solving activity that uses strategy. Originating thousands of years ago in the Orient it is still played with many variations throughout the world.

It can be used in cooperative learning groups or by paris of students. There are many variations of games which involve picking up markers (coins) according to specific rules. Try the simple rules first. They try to play the game with the more difficult variation. Duplicate the coins on page 224. Then have each pair use one set of 15 coins to play.

**Place coins right side up
in random order.**

First variation

1. Two players take turns.

2. At each turn a player may pick up 1 or 2 coins.

3. Whoever has to pick up the last coin loses the game.

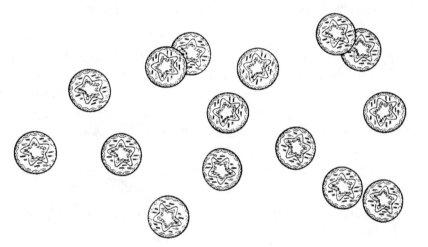

**Place 15 coins in 3
rows as shown.**

Second variation

1. Two players take turns.

2. At each turn a player picks up one or more coins from one row only.

3. Whoever has to pick up the last marker loses the game.

Nim Game Pieces

Copy these coins for every two players.

Mankala

Arabs call this game Kalah. They took it to Africa, where it has many different names. In East Africa, it is called Mankala. In West Africa, it is called Owara. In South Africa, it is known as Ohara. No matter which version of the game is used, you and your students will enjoy playing Mankala.

Materials

- clean egg carton
- tape or glue
- bean seeds
- 2 red markers, one for each player

Preparing the Game

You can make this game out of an empty egg carton. Look at the picture on this page. Build the game by separating the top and bottom of the egg carton. Cut the top section in half and attach each half to a side of the bottom section, as shown in the illustration. Each of the two end cups becomes a player's cup, where he or she collects beans (points). The player's cup is on his or her right.

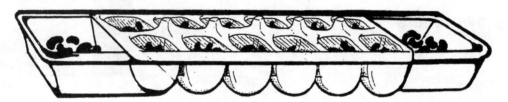

Game Directions

1. Have students pick a partner and sit across from each other. Tell them to put three beans in each of the twelve cups in the egg carton.
2. Have students decide which player goes first. The first player picks out the beans in the cup immediately on his or her left. This player should then put his or her red marker in the empty cup.
3. Going counterclockwise away from the red marker, have the first player place one bean in each cup until all three beans have been used.
4. Look in the cup opposite the cup where the last bean was dropped. Have the first player take those beans out and place them in the end cup to his or her right. These beans are now the first player's points.
5. Tell the second player to do the same thing that the first player just did by repeating the third and fourth steps.
6. When it is the first player's turn again, he or she finds his or her red marker and takes the beans from the cup to the right. That player distributes those beans as described in step 3. If there are no beans in the cup to the right, that player puts his or her red marker into the empty cup, and it becomes the other player's turn. It is important to remember to move the red marker so that you know which cup to start with for your next move.
7. Continue to play until there is only one bean left. The last player to put any beans in his or her end cup gets the last bean.
8. Both players count their beans. The player with the greatest number of beans in his or her cup wins the game.

Graph It!

How many students in your school know how to swim? Divide your class into groups and assign each group the task of discovering how many students at each grade level can swim and how many cannot. When all the data is collected, compile the information for the purpose of using it to make a graph. Each group can create its own graph or create one as a whole class activity. Explore different types of graphing possibilities with your students. Below are some examples of graphs you may want to use.

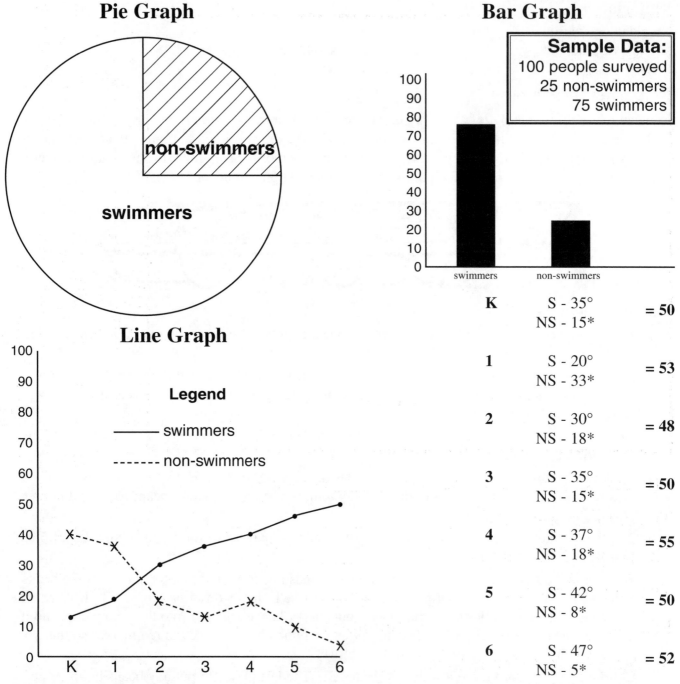

K	S - 35° NS - 15*	**= 50**
1	S - 20° NS - 33*	**= 53**
2	S - 30° NS - 18*	**= 48**
3	S - 35° NS - 15*	**= 50**
4	S - 37° NS - 18*	**= 55**
5	S - 42° NS - 8*	**= 50**
6	S - 47° NS - 5*	**= 52**

*It is helpful to assign a symbol designating swimmers versus non-swimmers when collecting data to facilitate the graphing. This type of graph will allow students to observe trends (i.e. as grade level increases, the number of non-swimmers decreases).

Goin' on a Leaf Hunt

You need to find 3 to 5 different types of leaves. They need to be fresh. Do no pick them off bushes and trees without permission.

In the box make a rubbing of your favorite leaf. (Your teacher will show you how to do this.)

MY LEAF

My leaf is _____ cm long and _____ cm wide.

The color of my leaf is_____.

The shape of my leaf is _____.

The edge of my leaf is _____.

I can see _____(number) of veins in my leaf.

My leaf is/is not symmetrical. _____

My leaf is from a _____tree.

Rain Forest Facts

Solve each problem. Write the answer in the box and then read the amazing rain forest facts.

1. 11 − 3 =   A tropical rain forest receives 4 to ☐ meters of rain per year. That's higher than a two-story building.

2. 7 − 5 =   Trees in a rain forest grow roots above ground because only ☐ inches of soil have food for plants.

3. 9 − 3 =   Hercules beetles can grow to 5 or ☐ inches long. They look like knights in armor with their large pincers and heavy shells.

4. 11 − 8 =   This sloth has only ☐ toes. It crawls upside down on tree branches.

5. 10 − 5 =   Toucans have ☐ -inch beaks which are almost as long as their bodies!

6. 9 − 5 =   Rain forests have ☐ main layers. Different animals live in each layer.

7. 8 − 6 =   A spider monkey's body is only ☐ feet long, but its tail is even longer!

8. 12 − 2 =   Some trees grow to be ☐ meters thick. That's as wide as 6 cars placed side by side.

The Plant World

The study of plants requires the use of math-oriented skills. The ability to measure, compare, and graph are just a few of the skills that can bring mathematics into your plant lessons.

- Teach or review the use of measuring tools (such as rulers and centimeters and inches to measure length.)

- Have students practice reading and making charts and graphs.

- Provide opportunities for students to record data on a variety of graphs and charts. Teach the skills necessary for success.

- Encourage students to devise their own ways to show the data they have gathered.

- On an appropriate level, teach how to average test results.

- Challenge students to find mathematical connections as they study plants.

Science Concept: *The plants world is full of recurring patterns.*

- Have students study the patterns on these cards. Have them cut the cards out and take them into nature. Can they find the same patterns in plants? How many? The use of a hand-held magnifying lens would be helpful.

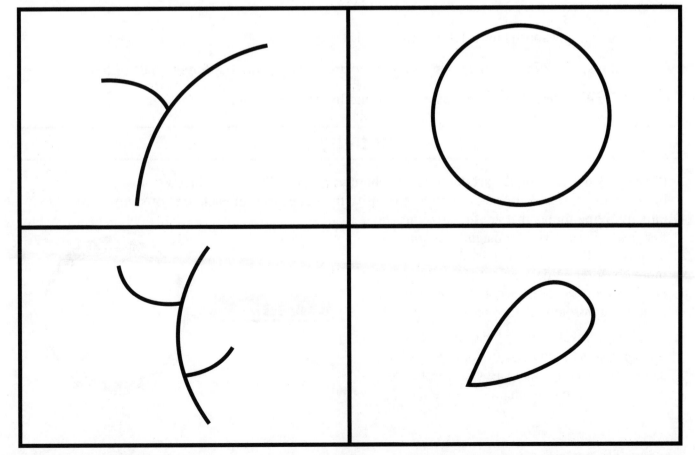

Biodiversity

Biodiversity refers to the differences that exist among all living things. Nowhere else on Earth, except for the tropical coral reefs, is life more abundant than in tropical rain forests. If you combined all of the tropical rain forests that still exist, they would contain at least half of the world's species, even though the rain forests cover less than six percent of the land's surface.

There is a greater diversity of plant and animal species found in the rain forests of Panama than found on the entire continent of Europe. More species of fish can be found in the Amazon River of Brazil than in all of the rivers of the United States combined.

Research in the tropical jungles has given us new information concerning the number of species found on Earth. A few years ago scientists believed that there were between five and ten million species globally. Now, after scientific exploration of the tropical canopy, the total number of species is believed to be closer to 30 million!

Why is there so much diversity found in the jungle? The varied layers of the rain forest provide a great variety of habitats for diverse species. Between the forest floor and the towering emergent layer, there is a vast difference in rainfall, temperature, and sunlight. It is these varying conditions between the layers which enable the many different species to flourish.

Believe It or Not...

- Two-thirds of all flowering plants are found in tropical rain forests.

- There are 103 different types of bats found in Costa Rica.

- Columbian rain forests have 1,400 different bird species.

- In just one acre of the Borneo rain forest, there are seven hundred different kinds of trees.

- Forty-three different kinds of ants can be found living on one rain forest tree in Peru.

Activity I

Choose a small area on the school grounds where you would like to conduct a study of biodiversity. Use either chalk or string to identify the boundaries of each area of study. List and tally all living things that are found within the assigned space. Use of a magnifying glass is suggested. Repeat this activity at least twice more on different days and at different times to obtain a more accurate account of the biodiversity of your chosen area.

Graph your results, using a bar graph or a pictograph and then classify your results into categories. Finally, compare your results from each day on a line graph.

Biodiversity (cont.)

Activity II

The purpose of this activity is to provide an understanding that the destruction of even a small section of a rain forest can result in the extinction of many species.

Materials:

- one biodiversity chart for each group (page 232)
- one bag of jelly beans (various colors) for each group
- pencils

Directions:

The biodiversity chart on page 232 represents the rain forest. The different colors of jelly beans represent the many species found there. Each color of jelly bean will represent one species found in the rain forest.

1. Divide the class into groups of three to four students. Give each group a small bag of different colored jelly beans.

2. Have each group randomly pour its bag of jelly beans onto the chart on page 232. Any jelly beans that fall outside the grids are not counted.

3. Choose one member of each group to count the number of species (jelly beans) in its rain forest. Record this number.

4. Destroy part of the rain forest by removing the jelly beans in grid number one. Count and record the number of different species left in the rain forest. Have any species become endangered or extinct yet?

5. Take turns destroying the rain forest (removing the jelly beans) one grid at a time. Count and record the number of different species still remaining after the destruction of each section.

6. How much rain forest was destroyed before the first species became extinct? Record the number of sections destroyed on the chart.

7. How much rain forest was destroyed before one half of the species became extinct? Record the number of sections destroyed on the chart. Have groups compare results.

8. What does this activity teach us about the importance of preserving the rain forest? Even if a small area of rain forest is destroyed, an entire species might become extinct.

9. This activity can be repeated using different grid sizes. Does this change the results?

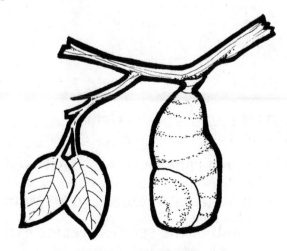

Biodiversity *(cont.)*

1	2	3	4
5	6	7	8
9	10	11	12
13	14	15	16

Total number of species in the rain forest: _____

Species remaining after destroying . . .

Grid 1 _____   Grid 5 _____   Grid 9 _____   Grid 13_____

Grid 2 _____   Grid 6 _____   Grid 10_____   Grid 14_____

Grid 3 _____   Grid 7 _____   Grid 11_____   Grid 15_____

Grid 4 _____   Grid 8 _____   Grid 12_____   Grid 16_____

How much rain forest was destroyed before the first species became extinct?

_____ **grids were destroyed.**

When half of the species became extinct, _____ **grids (sections of the rain forest) were destroyed.**

Ocean Plant Facts

To find out about some unusual plants that live in the ocean, solve the problems below. Write the letter that's beside each answer every time you find it in the puzzle below

38 x 24 = A	752 8 = B	26 x 18 = C	624 12 = D	14 x 49 = E	645 x 49 = F	385 15 = G	25 x 34 = H	38 x 16 = K
380 20 = L	700 28 = N	27 x 35 = O	29 x 17 = P	37 x 11 = R	784 16 = S	594 22 = T	15 x 14 = U	962 13 = W

1. Its stem has wavy edges that divide into fanglike fronds.

__ __ __ __ __ __ __ __ __
43 210 407 94 686 19 945 74 49

2. This brown, leathery, straplike seaweed is found in low waters.

__ __ __ - __ __ __ __ __
49 686 912   27 850 945 25 11

3. Sea otters make their home in this giant seaweed.

__ __ __ __
608 686 19 493

4. It looks a lot like a plant we put in our salads!

__ __ __ __ __ __ __ __ __
49 686 912   19 686 27 27 210 468 686

5. This seaweed contains air pockets which help it stay afloat.

__ __ __ __ __ __ __ __ __ __ __ __
94 19 912 52 52 686 407   74 407 912 468 608

6. It can be eaten raw or cooked as a vegetable.

__ __ __ __ __
52 210 19 49 686

7. This red seaweed can be found anchored to rocks in the shade.

__ __ __ __ __ __ __ __ __ __ __
43 686 912 27 850 686 407 74 686 686 52

8. A gel for jellies is made from this red seaweed.

__ __ __ __ __ __ __ __ __
468 912 407 407 912 11 686 686 25

Recycled Problems

Waste and pollution are taking place on our planet at a staggering rate. Solving the ecology problems below may help you realize the magnitude of this situation and why it has become a major concern.

1. In a 1988 beach cleanup along Texas' shoreline, 15,600 plastic six-pack rings were found in three hours. How many rings were found in one hour?	7. A small drip from a leaky faucet can wastes over 50 gallons of water per day. Approximately how many gallons of water are wasted per hour?
2. One 15-year old tree makes enough paper for only 700 grocery bags. How many 15-year old trees will it take to make 9800 grocery bags?	8. It takes 26 recyclable plastic soda bottles to make one polyester suit. How many bottles will be needed to make a dozen suits?
3. Approximately 240 million tires are discarded annually in the U.S. How many tires is that per month?	9. One hundred fifty-four million tons of garbage is produced in the U.S. in one year. Half of this trash is recyclable. How many tons is that?
4. Ten years ago there were 1.5 million elephants in Africa. Since then, 750,000 have been slaughtered for ivory. How many are left?	10. Every hour Americans throw away 2.5 million plastic bottles. How many plastic bottles are thrown away in one day?
5. If a five-minute shower can consume 35 gallons of water, how many gallons of water will be consumed during a nine-minute shower?	11. Two thousand six hundred seven dollars of water are needed to produce one steak. How many gallons of water are needed to produce eight steaks?
6. About 70 billion beverage cans were used in 1985. 94% of those cans were aluminum. How many cans is that?	12. Americans throw away 18 billion disposable diapers a year. How many diapers is that each month?

Teaching Science Through the Multiple Intelligences

Animal Journal

Animal journals are an effective way to integrate science and language arts. Students are to record their observations, thoughts, and questions about science experiences in a journal to be kept in the science area. The observations may be recorded in sentences or sketches which keep track of changes both in the science item or in the thoughts and discussions of the students.

Animal journal entries can be completed as a team effort or an individual activity. Be sure to model the making and recording of observations several times when introducing the journals to the science area.

Use the student recordings in the animal journals as a focus for class science discussions. You should lead these discussions and guide students with probing questions, but it is usually not necessary for your to give any explanation. Students come to accurate conclusions as a result of classmates' comments and your questioning. Animal journals can also become part of the student's portfolios and overall assessment program. Journals are also valuable assessment tools for parent and student conferences.

How to Make an Animal Journal

1. Cut two pieces of 8 ½" x 11" (22 cm x 28 cm) construction paper to create a cover. Make a creative front cover to glue on the front of the journal. Allow students to draw pictures in the box on the cover.

2. Insert several animal journal pages.

3. Staple together and cover staples edge with book tape.

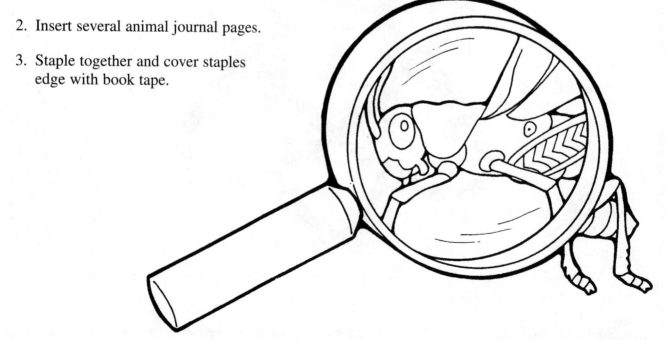

Language Arts

The Language Arts—reading, writing, listening, and speaking can be easily used to teach and reinforce science concepts.

Focus exciting activities involving poems, stories, writing assignments, and dramatic oral presentations around the area of science called chemistry.

Science Concept: Chemicals have physical properties such as phase, size, color, and smell which are used to help identify them.

Procedure

1. Have students write a creative story entitled, "I Am a Chemical." Each student should include a detailed description of his or her appearance.

2. Have students read their stories aloud in class.

3. Next, ask each student to exchange his or her paper with a friend. The friend should read the student's story and then draw and color a picture of that chemical.

4. Display the sets of stories and pictures on a bulletin board.

Science Concept: Water is a chemical that surrounds us and allows us to exist.

Procedure

1. Tell students that a drop of water falls from the sky.

2. Ask them to develop that statement into a short rhyming poem. See the following example:

The Drop
A drop of water falls from the sky.
It lands in a pond, why?
At this point the drop seems to die.
Sadness for the vanished drop makes me cry.
by Dana M. Barry

3. Have students read their poems in class.

Language Arts

Reading, writing, listening, and speaking experiences blend easily with the teaching and reinforcement of science concepts. In fact, science can be a focal point as you guide your students through poems and stories, stimulating writing assignments, and dramatic oral presentations. If carefully chosen, language arts materials can serve as a springboard to an animal lesson, the lesson itself, or an entertaining review.

There is a wealth of good literature to help you connect your curriculum.

Science Concept: *the complexity of food chains*

Read *Over the Steamy Swamp* (Harcourt Brace Jovanovich, 1988) to your class. Have volunteers retell the story using pictures of the characters. Discuss how food chains work. Help your class create a food chain of their own. Have students write a class big book based on their food chain. Students may also choose to create their own food chains and display them as mobiles.

Science Concept: *helping the environment*

If weather permits, take your class outside to a comfortable spot. Brainstorm and record ways to help the environment with your class. Read *It's My Earth, Too* (Doubleday, 1992) to the class. Discuss the book and allow students to add to their list of ways to help the environment. Have students make posters encouraging others to help the environment. Hang the posters around the school. Help students design a pamphlet to be sent home that encourages environmentally aware actions. As a class, choose at least two things on the list to do at school.

Science Concept: *ecosystems*

Talk about different ecosystems (e.g. deserts, mountains, oceans, plains, swamps, tundra, etc.) with your class. Read to the class a description of an ecosystem, such as *Mojave* (Thomas Y. Crowell, 1988) or *Sierra* (Harper Collins, 1991). List the elements of the ecosystem described. Ask your class to describe the ecosystem in which they live and to list its elements. Have students write their own descriptions of the local ecosystem. Create a class mural of the ecosystem in which they live. Display their descriptions around the edges of the mural.

Language Arts

Science Concept: A variety of minerals make up the Earth's crust.

The Magic School Bus Inside the Earth by Joanna Cole (Scholastic Books, 1987).

Ms. Frizzle takes her class on another unique field trip, this time to the center of the Earth. Students learn about soil, rock formation, the rock cycle, and the use of rocks.

- Have students find out the uses of the eight minerals used in this lesson, as well as other minerals.
- Have students locate minerals which are used at school and home.
- Have students make a mineral collection, including labels for each mineral.
- Have students write descriptions of various minerals, including gems, so someone can "guess" what each is.

Examples:

- My mineral is soft and smooth. I can easily scratch it with my fingernail. When it is ground into a powder, it is soft enough to put on your skin.

  What is my mineral? (talc)
- My mineral is a shiny, green jewel. People like to wear this mineral around their necks or on their fingers. It is rare and very expensive.
- What is my mineral? (emerald)

Myths About Weather

Long ago when people didn't understand something, they made up an imaginary tale to explain it. In The Cloud Book, the author talks about weather myths.

Write a myth of your own.

1. Read *The Hammer of Thunder* retold by Ann Pyk.

2. Reread the myth in *The Cloud Book*.

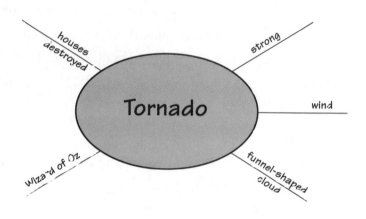

3. Imagine you lived long before there were meteorologists to help explain the weather. Now imagine that suddenly there was a terrible tornado. After it was over, all your friends and family tried to figure out what had happened and why. Put your ideas into a web. Now use your ideas to write a story.

Use the blank web to collect your ideas to write a story. Make your story into a book by adding a cover. Share it with friends.

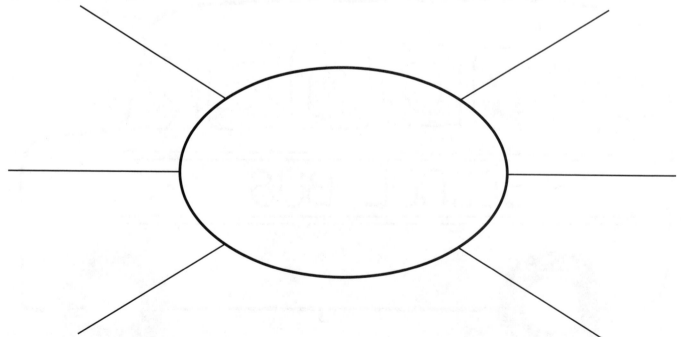

Some topics for weather myths include: lightning, hail, rainbows, hurricanes, and snow.

The Environment from A to Z

Name _____**Date** _____

Directions: Create an A-to-Z list of things you can do to help save the environment. For example:

A - Always turn water off when not using it.
B - Be sure to throw trash in trash cans provided.
C - Collect newspapers to recycle.

A - _____
B - _____
C - _____
D - _____
E - _____
F - _____
G - _____
H - _____
I - _____
J - _____
K - _____
L - _____
M - _____
N - _____
O - _____
P - _____
Q - _____
R - _____
S - _____
T - _____
U - _____
V - _____
W - _____
X - _____
Y - _____
Z - _____

Language Arts

Communication skills will be needed to convey information between space travelers and Earth in the future, just as early explorers had to be able to describe their journeys. Students can develop a variety of ways to communicate via letters, drawings, and code. These messages may be directed at Earth or for intelligent life in other planetary systems.

Science Concept: A variety of techniques will be needed to communicate with Earth and intelligent life in other planetary systems in the future.

Letters From a Lunar Base

- Have students write a letter to someone on Earth describing their adventures as members of a science team working at Tranquility Base on the moon in the year 2021. Have them gather information about future lunar bases that can be used in their letters.
- Have students write to NASA to request material that describes the *Apollo* landings.
- Have students include drawings of their spacecraft, the lunar base, and views of Earth.
- Tell students to describe how it feels to walk about on the moon.

Letters to Another Planet

- Have students design a message that would communicate information about our planetary system and Earth to intelligent life on a planet that is not in our solar system.
- Explain to them they may wish to use pictures or diagrams that could be interpreted easily by someone who does not know about our solar system and cannot read any of our languages.

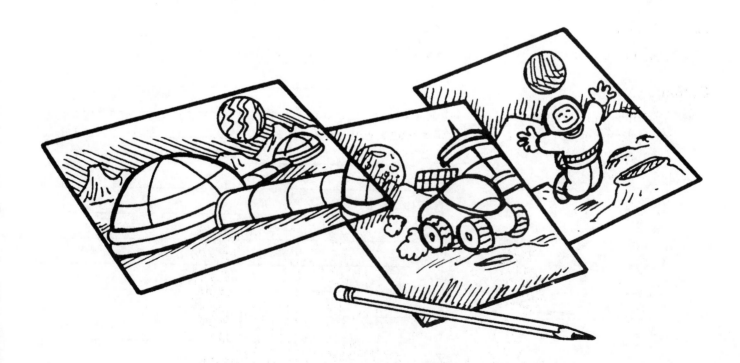

Major Divisions of Science

Students can research the divisions of science and present their information to the class.

Duration:

- 1 class period for research
- 1 or 2 class periods (per student or group) for creating presentations
- 1 class period for sharing presentations with the class

Materials:

- worksheet on the major divisions of science on page 244
  - biology—the study of living things
  - oceanography—the study of oceans and the seashore
  - geology—the study of Earth, its composition and properties
  - meteorology—the study of weather, climate, and atmosphere
  - physics—the study of how matter and energy are related
  - chemistry—the study of matter and energy
- multimedia planning sheet on page 245 (if students will be creating multimedia presentations)
- reference materials for research (science books, encyclopedias, electronic encyclopedias, online access)
- presentation software (*The Print Shop*, *HyperStudio*, etc.)

Before the computer:

- Allow students time to research the divisions.

On the computer:

- Students will create signs or multimedia stacks to explain their divisions and illustrate examples.

Option:

- Students could be grouped in teams of six with each student being responsible for one division, or the classroom could be divided into six teams with each team being responsible for one division. This will depend on how many computers you have available for students to use to create presentations.

Major Divisions of Science *(cont.)*

Name: _____   Date: _____

BIOLOGY

CHEMISTRY   OCEANOGRAPHY

SCIENCE

PHYSICS   GEOLOGY

METEOROLOGY

1. Pick one division of science and use all available reference materials to find out what it is and to find some examples of what that type of scientist might be studying.

2. Using available software, create a brief presentation of the information you found.

Note: You may use the back of this work sheet to take notes.

Multimedia Planning Sheet

Title Card

Buttons/Links: _____

Notes (Text/Sounds/Animations): _____

Card 1

Buttons/Links: _____

Notes (Text/Sounds/Animations): _____

Card 2

Buttons/Links: _____

Notes (Text/Sounds/Animations): _____

Card 3

Buttons/Links: _____

Notes (Text/Sounds/Animations): _____

Card 4

Buttons/Links: _____

Notes (Text/Sounds/Animations): _____

Card 5

Buttons/Links: _____

Notes (Text/Sounds/Animations): _____

Daily Writing Topics

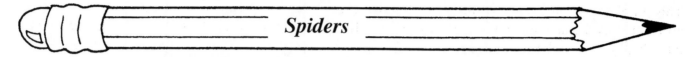

Spiders

1. Write a report on the different parts of a spider and their functions.

2. Make a list of the different types of webs that spiders weave.

3. Choose a web type. Describe how it is built and its function.

4. Write a comparison of how a garden spider and a crab spider catch their food.

5. Write a report about parasites that are enemies of spiders.

6. Write a report about spider wasps.

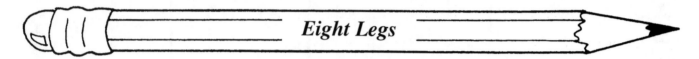

Eight Legs

1. Write a report on the differences between arachnids and insects.

2. Write an article on the eyes of spiders. Tell why you think some have 8, 6, 4, or 2.

3. Pretend you are an eye specialist. Write a report on your development of glasses for nearsighted spiders. Include illustrations.

4. Explain the molting process you are familiar with (human, animal, insect, etc.). Emphasize metamorphosis.

5. Choose an arachnid to write a report on. Include birth, habitat, prey, enemies, and life span.

6. Write an instruction manual on how to weave an orb web. Include illustrations and step-by-step procedures.

7. Explain in a paragraph the purpose of ballooning.

8. Explain the differences between web weavers and hunters. List pros and cons.

9. Do some spiders raise their babies? Explain your answer in a paragraph.

10. Write an interview with someone who has been bitten by a black widow spider (fact or fiction).

11. Use your imagination to interview Orion, the hunter, from the Greek myth. Interview him before he is bitten by the scorpion. Then interview him shortly after.

12. Interview the scorpion-goddess Selquet of Ancient Egypt. Find out why she chose the scorpion as her symbol.

13. Write a report on the similarities and differences between mites and ticks.

Animal Brain Strain

This problem has only one solution. To fill in the chart, mark an "X" in each square which is eliminated by a clue. When there is only one blank square left in a row or column within a category, put a happy face in that square.

Activity

A sloth, a spider monkey, a tree frog, and a toucan are named Fred, Harvey, Melissa, and Jana. Read the clues below to find each animal's name.

Clues:

1. Melissa is a different color than both the spider monkey and Jana.
2. The frog is younger than Fred.
3. Harvey is the oldest and is a good friend of the spider monkey.
4. Harvey and the toucan share the same tree.
5. Jana is not an amphibian.

Animal Brain Strain Chart

	Fred	**Harvey**	**Melissa**	**Jana**
Tree Frog				
Spider Monkey				
Sloth				
Toucan				

Order

Before beginning your investigation, write your group members' names by their jobs below.

_____Team Leader   _____Stenographer

_____Biologist   _____Transcriber

In the food pyramid below, organize each level according to its particular function or role. Begin by arranging, in order, the list of species provided. Complete by drawing and labeling each species in its appropriate placement or level on the food pyramid.

> hawk, mosquito larvae, plankton, minnows, algae, turtle, bass, worm, green plant leaves, spider, aphid, duck, mouse, lettuce, humans

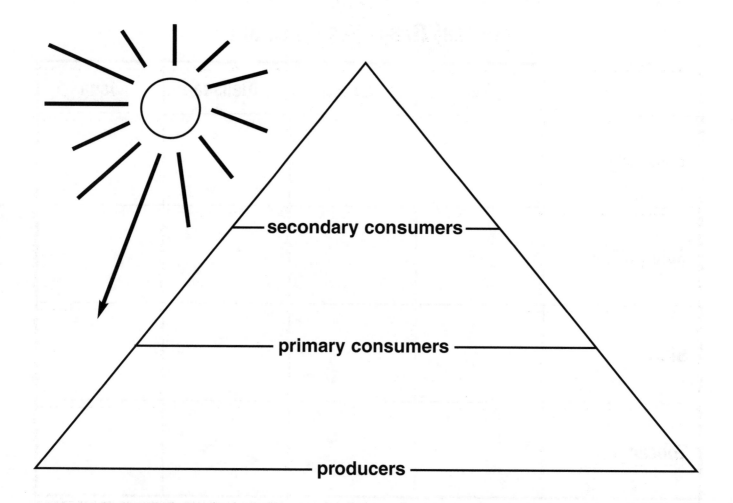

Plant Brain Strain

This problem has only one solution. To fill in the chart, mark an "X" in each square which is eliminated by a clue. When there is only one blank square left in a row or column within a category, put a happy face in that square.

Activity

The favorite rain forest trees and plants of David, Adam, Bianca, and Chelsey are bromeliads, orchids, ferns, and kapok trees. Read the clues below to find each person's favorite rain forest tree or plant.

Clues:

1. No person's name has the same number of letters as his or her favorite rain forest tree or plant.

2. David and the boy who likes orchids are from different tribes.

3. The kapok tree is the favorite of one of the girls.

4. Chelsey's favorite plant is a member of the pineapple family.

Chart
Plant Brain Strain

	David	Adam	Bianca	Chelsey
Bromeliad				
Orchid				
Fern				
Kapok Tree				

Categorize

Before beginning your investigation, write your group members' names by their jobs below.

_____Team Leader   _____Stenographer

_____Biologist   _____Transcriber

There are living and nonliving things in this world. Living things are plants, animals, insects, and bacteria. These living organisms are all made up of cells. They require food, water, and air to survive. Most living things are able to move or get around. Some accomplish this with limbs, fins, or wings. Most living organisms also must obtain food. Some catch their food, some make their own food using light energy from the sun, and some get their food by absorbing nutrients from the earth or decaying things.

Nonliving things are things that do not need food, water, or air to survive. These things are made from atoms. They are solids, liquids, or gases. Examples include rocks, soil, plastic, glass, cement, and metals.

As you take a tour of your schoolyard or your own backyard, look for examples of living and nonliving things. List them below and describe why you think they are one or the other.

LIVING

_____ _____ _____	_____ _____ _____

NONLIVING

_____ _____ _____	_____ _____ _____

What Is the Temperature?

You will need several weather thermometers for this activity.

Directions:

1. Find a safe place outside to put your thermometer.
2. Note the temperature at the same time each day.
3. Put a dot on the graph to show the temperature for the day.
4. Connect the dots for a line graph.

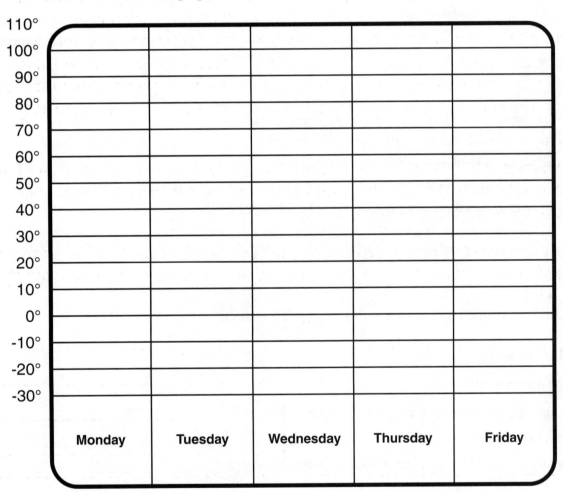

Extensions:

Compare temperatures in the morning, at lunchtime, and in the afternoon.

Compare your findings with local weather forecasts.

Put several thermometers in various settings. Compare readings.

Use subtraction skills to find how much hotter/cooler temperatures are when making the comparisons below. Mark bar graphs to show the comparisons.

How Much Water Is in Popcorn?

Popcorn pops because the water inside the hard kernel of corn is heated to boiling temperatures and literally bursts through the shell. The following activity is designed to measure how much water is inside a kernel of popcorn.

Materials

popcorn kernels, air popper (if possible), balance

Questions Before You Begin

1. Do you know what makes popcorn pop?

2. How would you use the materials for this activity to determine the amount of water in a kernel of popcorn?

Procedure

1. Using the balance, find the mass of 100 popcorn kernels.
2. Record their mass on the data table on page 253.
3. Place the popcorn kernels into the popcorn popper.
4. Pour some extra kernels into the popcorn popper as all 100 kernels may not pop.
5. When the popcorn is done popping, count out 100 popped pieces.
6. Find the mass of these popped pieces and record that number on the table on page 253.
7. Compare the mass of the popped pieces to the mass of the unpopped pieces.

Results

You should find the popped pieces have considerably less mass than the unpopped pieces.

Closure/Assessment

Complete the chart on page 253.

1. How many grams of water were in the unpopped kernels? _____

2. How did you figure this out? _____

3. How many grams of water were in each unpopped kernel? _____

4. How did you figure this out? _____

5. Using information about your body (from reference books), determine how much of your weight is not water. _____

6. How did you figure this out? _____

> **Fun Fact:** *Did you know that a popcorn kernel is about 13% water? When the kernels are heated to about 400° Fahrenheit (200° Celsius), the pressure inside each kernel forces it to pop. Popcorn kernels can pop to over 35 times their original size.*

Popcorn Chart

Instructions: Write the mass of 100 unpopped kernels of popcorn in the first space. After popping the popcorn, write the mass of 100 pieces of popped popcorn in the second space. By subtracting the two, you will find the mass of water which was in the unpopped kernels. Why? Because the water is what makes popcorn pop! When the kernels pop, they release the water trapped inside. The popped kernels are quite dry.

Mass of 100 Unpopped Kernels (grams)		Mass of 100 Popped Kernels (grams)		Mass of Water in Unpopped Kernels (grams)
_____ g	−	_____ g	=	_____ g

To find the amount of water in *each* kernel, divide your answer by 100. Do you know why?

Mass of Water in Unpopped Kernels (grams)			Mass of Water in Each Kernel (grams)
_____ g	÷ 100	=	_____ g

_____ g ÷ 100 = _____ g

Measuring Acceleration

Question
What amount of acceleration does a falling object experience?

Setting the Stage
- Discuss with students the force of gravity and the acceleration it produces.
- Drop an object and ask the students to observe the change in speed of the object. (The object drops too fast for easy observation.) Have the students brainstorm ways to slow down the acceleration of gravity so that observations can be made. Explain how Galileo "slowed down" the acceleration of gravity by rolling balls down inclined planes. In this manner he could observe the balls and their reaction to gravity easier than dropping them.

Materials Needed for Each Group
- a sink or other device to observe and regulate the speed of water droplets (A buret attached to a ring stand and hanging over the edge of a table with a pie pan to catch the droplets works best.)
- a measuring stick
- a stopwatch
- data-capture sheet (page 255), one per student

Procedure *(Student Instructions)*
1. Measure the distance in centimeters from where the water droplets begin to where they hit the bottom of the sink (or catch pan).
2. Adjust the drip rate so that one drop leaves the faucet (or buret) just as the previous drop hits bottom.
3. Measure the amount of time it takes for 20 drops to fall.
4. Repeat step 3 at least 4 times.
5. Record all data and calculate the acceleration using your data-capture sheet.

Extensions
- Have students research the life of Galileo.
- Have students do Galileo's experiments with rolling balls. (See any reference book on Galileo and his experiments.)

Closure
- In their force and motion journals, have students write a brief description of the experience. Tell them that the correct answer is 980 cm/sec. Have them describe why they think their calculation of acceleration was not exactly the same.

The Big Why
- Like speed, acceleration is a change. It is a change in speed measured over a time period. This often presents confusion when looking at the units—meters per second per second, or meters/second. It helps to explain that units can be multiplied together as well as divided. Technically, acceleration has a direction attached to it (similar to velocity). We include this direction when we use the terms acceleration and deceleration.

Measuring Acceleration *(cont.)*

Fill in the chart below.

Data:

Distance the drops fall: _____ inches(cm)

Trial	Time for 20 Drops to Fall
1	
2	
3	
4	
5	

The average time for 20 drops to fall:_____seconds

Calculation of Acceleration *(Use a calculator):*

1. Calculate the time for 1 drop to fall:

Average time 20 = seconds for one drop

2. Calculate acceleration using the formula:

$$a = \frac{2D}{T^2}$$

$$\text{acceleration} = \frac{2 \times \text{distance drops fall}}{\text{time} \times \text{time}}$$

My Calculation:

$$\text{acceleration} = \frac{2 \times \underline{\quad} \text{ Inches (cm)}}{\underline{\quad} \text{ seconds} \times \underline{\quad} \text{ seconds}}$$

acceleration = centimeters ÷ seconds^2

How High Is the Sun?

Science Concept:

> In the northern hemisphere, the sun is highest in the sky on the first day of summer (June 21) and lowest in the sky on the first day of winter (December 21).

Measurements can be made with a shadow stick to determine how high the sun is above the horizon. By measuring and recording this once a month at noon (using daylight standard time), students will realize that the sun's position changes throughout the year. The measurement should be done as close to the 21st of each month as possible to coincide with the first days of summer and winter. Two or three days before or after the 21st will still provide adequate data.

Setting the Stage

- Familiarize students with protractors so they can measure angles.

Materials Needed for Each Group

- protractors (These may be copied on overhead transparencies to make sturdy and inexpensive copies for each student to use. Cut off the ruler portion of the protractor before copying it to make measuring angles more accurate.)
- shadow stick
- length of string that can reach from the tip of the shadow to the top of the stick
- data-capture sheet (page 257), one per student

Procedure

1. Have students become familiar with learning how to measure angles.
2. Divide students into eight groups and demonstrate where to place the string and protractor to measure the sun's angular height above the horizon:

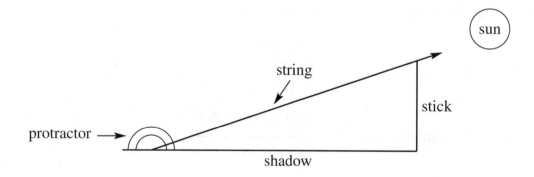

3. Distribute and have students complete a data-capture sheet.
4. Have students collect data over an eight- or ten-month period.

Closure

Have students place their completed data-capture sheets in their space journals.

How High Is the Sun? *(cont.)*

Make your measurements as close to the 21st of each month as possible. You should also measure the angle as close to noon as you can. Remember, if you are on daylight savings time (April–October), you will need to subtract an hour to determine when noon occurs.

DATE	TIME	ANGLE OF SUN ABOVE HORIZON
_____	_____	_____ °
_____	_____	_____ °
_____	_____	_____ °
_____	_____	_____ °
_____	_____	_____ °
_____	_____	_____ °
_____	_____	_____ °
_____	_____	_____ °
_____	_____	_____ °

Use the data you have collected to make a graph showing the changing position of the sun at noon through the months you recorded. An example of what this graph might look like is shown below:

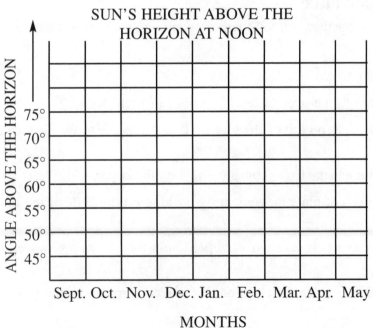

SUN'S HEIGHT ABOVE THE HORIZON AT NOON

Look at your graph and write a description of what it shows you about the sun's location in the sky through these months. Find the hours of daylight for each of these dates in an almanac.

The Earth Can Shake

Science Concepts: Sometimes, the Earth's plates push together.

Sometimes, when the plates push together, the ground shakes.

This shaking is called an earthquake.

An earthquake can cause the ground to break.

Concept Literature: *Earthquakes* by Semyour Simon and *Earthquakes* by Franklyn M. Branley

Question

What is an earthquake?

Materials Needed for the Class

- two pieces of wood, at least 6" x 12" x 2" (15 cm x 30 cm x 5 cm)
- wood or paper glue
- 12 thumbtacks
- one piece of paper, at least 12" x 12" (30 cm x 30 cm), or big enough to fit over both boards

Materials Needed for Each Child

- copy of page 260

Discovery Experience

Gather your children together and tell them they are going to learn what causes earthquakes to happen.

1. Place the blocks of wood side by side.

2. Put a thin layer of glue over the entire surface of both.

3. Lay a piece of paper on top of the glue so that it adheres to the surface of both pieces of wood.

4. Stand some thumbtacks (trees) upside down on the paper.

5. Imitate the actions of plate movement by pushing on the ends of the blocks in opposite directions.

6. Ask your children to observe what happens after the blocks are moved back and forth several times.

7. The paper will rip. Tell your children this is what happens to the ground during an earthquake.

8. After you have completed the activity, review page 260 with your children. See if a volunteer can explain what is happening.

The Earth Can Shake *(cont.)*

What Scientists Know

Earthquakes are among the most destructive and terrifying of all natural events. Some are just minor tremors, while others are so violent that they topple buildings and open up huge cracks in the ground. Earthquakes occur when two plates push against each other under the pressure of continental drift. Rocks have elastic qualities, and they can absorb pressure for hundreds or even thousands of years. Eventually, however, the stress becomes too great, and the rocks break and move into new positions, releasing all the stored up energy in the form of an earthquake. Earthquake tremors are caused by shock waves travelling swiftly through the ground. The vibrations spread out from the center of the earthquake, causing the ground to shake violently. The point on the surface immediately above the center point of an earthquake is called the *epicenter.*

Real Life Application

Take your children outside and line them up in two rows, one facing one direction and the other the opposite direction. Have them put their left arms on the persons in front of them and their right arms on the persons next to them. Then have each row move forward two or three steps. Ask your children what happened to the arms that were on the persons next to them. Explain that the reason they could not hang on to the other person is the same reason that causes earthquakes—in this case, your children were acting as plates, shifting in opposite directions. Just as the paper ripped, their arms were pulled from the other persons' shoulders.

The Earth Can Shake *(cont.)*

The place where two plates meet is called a *faultline*. These plates move in opposite directions because of forces within the Earth.

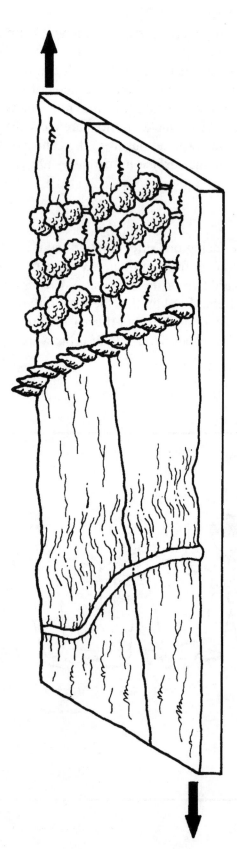

Pressure builds until . . . suddenly it is released causing an *earthquake*.

Physical Education

What can be more fun for primary students then imagining they are part of an ecosystem, subject to the forces that make ecosystems grow, thrive, and move? Here is an opportunity to let your students develop their knowledge of ecosystems in a physical way.

Science Concept: *the interdependence of all things in an ecosystem*

Have students stand front-to-back in a very tight circle, all facing one direction. The goal is to have everyone sit down on the knees of the person behind, without falling down. Instruct the students to sit on the count of three. Give it a try. With practice the class should be able to sit on one another's knees without the circle collapsing. Warn students to be still while sitting, as their movements will affect the rest of their classmates, just as changes in one part of the ecosystem can disrupt the entire ecosystem. Remove one of the students while the group is sitting. What happens? This is what happens when part of an ecosystem is removed.

Science Concept: *carrying capacity*

Draw a 4' x 6' (1.2 m x 1.8 m) rectangle on the playground with chalk. Tell your class that this is the ecosystem and they are the various plants and animals that live there. Have three students sit in the rectangle. Is there enough room for them? Have three more students sit in the rectangle. Is it as comfortable as it was before? Keep adding students to the rectangle until it can no longer hold anyone. How many students can the rectangle hold? This is the carrying capacity of the ecosystem. Explain to students what carrying capacity means. Ask them what factors, besides size, may affect the carrying capacity of an ecosystem (food and water availability).

Send a Message

Science Concept: Nerves carry messages between the body and the brain.

Question

How does my brain know if the water I touch with my finger is warm or cold?

Materials Needed for Each Group

- container of warm water
- container of cold water

Discovery Experience

1. Divide your class into small groups. Give each group one container of cold water and one container of warm water. Ask your children if they can tell by looking, which container has the warm water and which container has the cold water.

2. Pose a silly question to introduce the nervous system. If your brain is the part of your body that decides which container has the hot and cold water, should you stick your brain (head) in the water so that it can decide which is the warm water and which is the cold water?

3. Ask your children to explain an easier way to test the water temperature. Encourage them to try to explain how the brain can know the temperature of the water if it is the finger that will actually be in the water.

4. Encourage each child to test the water by sticking one finger in each container. Allow each group to report its findings.

What Scientists Know

Your brain and your finger each have an important job to do today. Your brain made the decision, but your finger did the water test. What makes the connection between the finger and the brain? Inside your finger there are nerves that run from your finger and up your arm to your brain. Just like the mail carrier or telephone wires, nerves carry messages from the finger to the brain. Nerves, however, are much faster than mail carriers or telephone wires. You did not need to get your head wet for your brain to quickly know which water was warm and which was cold.

Send a Message *(cont.)*

Real Life Application

How quickly can a message get from your brain to your hands? Play "Slap It" to find out. Find a partner and stand face to face. Hold out your hands, palms down. Your partner must try to slap the back of your hands before you move them out of the way. What is happening in this game? Your eyes sense when your partner is about to slap your hands, and so they flash a signal to your brain, "Here comes a slap!" When your brain becomes aware of the situation, it sends a message to the muscles in your hands. Flash! You are able to move your hands out of the way.

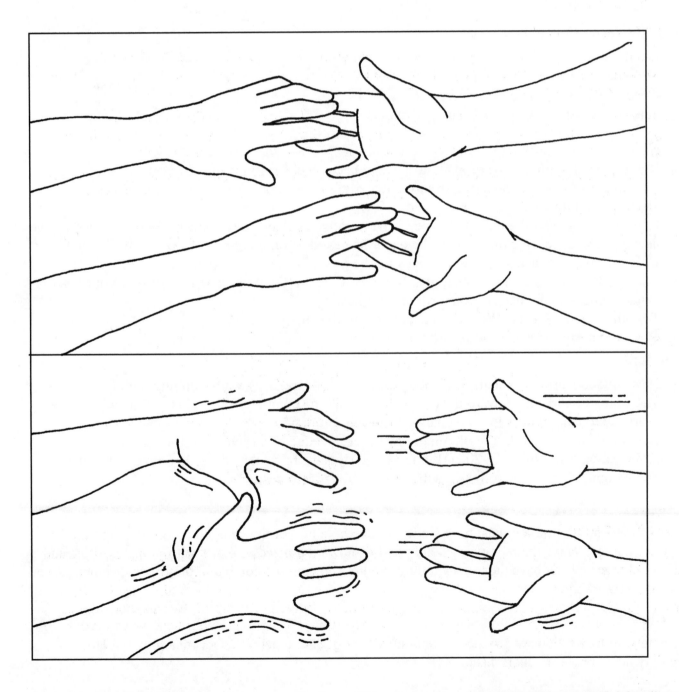

Electrostatic Forces

Question

Which force is greater—electrostatic force or the force of gravity?

Setting the Stage

- Explain to students that electrostatic forces are the forces between charged particles. We experience this force on a dry day when we get "shocked" or when we take clothes out of the dryer and they stick to each other. We often call this force "static electricity."
- Rub a balloon with a piece of wool, flannel, or felt and stick it to the blackboard. Ask students why this happens.

Materials Needed for Each Group

- plastic comb
- piece of wool, flannel, or felt
- piece of paper torn into dime-sized bits
- data-capture sheet (page 265), one per student

Procedure *(Student Instructions)*

1. Rub the comb with a piece of material. It will become electrostatically charged. The rubbing cause electrons to be transferred from the material to the comb. The comb has an excess of electrons and now is negatively charged.
2. Hold the comb near the pieces of paper. The negative charges on the paper will be repelled by the negative comb, causing the edge of the paper nearest the comb to become positively charged. Unlike charges attract, so the comb picks up the paper, overcoming gravity in the process.
3. Charge the comb again by rubbing it with the material. Hold it close to your arm or your head. What happens to the hair on your arm or your head?
4. Try other small objects. What can be attracted to the charged comb?
5. Observe each experience and record information on your data-capture sheet.

Extensions

- Have students bring the charged comb close to a small stream of water running out of a faucet. The water should bend toward the comb. Do not let the comb get wet. This will neutralize the charge and make it difficult to recharge the comb.
- Have students hang a strip of aluminum foil over the edge of a ruler. The foil should be about 1" (2.5 cm) wide and 6-8" (15-20 cm) long. Have students bring the charged comb close to the foil. The hanging ends of the foil strip will separate from each other.

Closure

In their force and motion journals, have students draw a picture of the charged comb, showing the negative charges. Have them draw a second picture showing a piece of paper with mixed positive and negative charges. Then have them draw a third picture showing the comb and the paper together. What happens to the charges now?

The Big Why

The magnetic forces that are produced from unlike charges are much stronger than gravity. However, they only act over a very short distance.

Electrostatic Forces *(cont.)*

Answer the questions below.

Observations:

What is happening to the comb as you rub it with the piece of material?

_____

What happened to the paper when you brought the comb close to it? What else were you able to find that was also attracted to the comb?

_____

Analysis and Conclusions:

Why was the paper attracted to the comb?

_____

_____

What else will attract the paper in a similar way to the comb?
Hypothesis: Why are some things attracted to the comb and others not?

_____

_____

How are electrostatic forces both similar to and different from magnetic forces?

_____

_____

Which forces are greater—electrostatic forces or gravitational forces? Why?

_____

_____

Delicious Combination

Question

In what ways do chemicals react?

Setting the Stage

Discuss with students the following ways that chemicals react: *synthesis, decomposition,* and *replacement.* Synthesis occurs when chemicals combine to form one or more new substances. For example, hydrogen (H) and oxygen (O) combine to form water (H_2O). Decomposition occurs when a chemical breaks down into its component parts. For example, water (H_2O) breaks down into hydrogen (H) and oxygen (O). A replacement reaction occurs when at least one part of one chemical switches places with a corresponding part of another chemical. For example, if one has sodium (Na) and water (H_2O), the sodium (Na) trades places with a hydrogen (H) of water (H_2O) to give sodium hydroxide (NaOH) and hydrogen gas (H).

Materials Needed for Each Group

- recipe for cookies
- ingredients (chemicals) required to make cookies
- bowls, pans, etc., needed to prepare and bake cookies
- data-capture sheet (page 267), one per student

Procedure *(Student Instructions)*

1. Each group should be given a copy of a simple recipe to make cookies. The baking of cookies demonstrates a synthesis reaction. Chemicals are combined to form a new substance. It makes science fun and rewards the students with tasty treats.

2. If possible, do this activity in the school's home economics room where cooking supplies and equipment are available. If that room is not available, do the activity in the school cafeteria.

3. Complete your data-capture sheet.

Extensions

- Obtain a mini-generator and have the students take turns decomposing water by the use of an electric current. This is called *electrolysis* of water. The students should collect twice as much hydrogen as compared to the amount of oxygen gas collected.

- Perform a demonstration for the class. Using a Bunsen burner and a pair of tongs, heat up a piece of magnesium ribbon (Mg). (Wear approved safety glasses.) The magnesium metal in the presence of heat and air gives off light and forms a new substance, a white powder called magnesium oxide (MgO). Have the students compare the appearances of the starting material and the final product.

Closure

In their chemistry journals, have students explain in a few sentences why the baking of cookies is a synthesis reaction. Also have them name and describe the type of energy used to carry out this reaction.

The Big Why

In this activity the students perform a synthesis reaction. Here they combine various ingredients (chemicals) to form a tasty treat (a new substance).

Delicious Combination (cont.)

In the space provided, list and describe the ingredients used. Draw a picture of the final product and briefly describe it. (Include taste, appearance, etc.)

Ingredients (Chemicals)	Appearance	State of Matter
1.		
2.		
3.		
4.		
5.		
6.		
7.		

Making a Balloon Rocket

Rockets were sent to the moon between 1966 and 1972. The American *Apollo* missions made six landings on the moon, the first coming in July, 1969. Trips to the moon required rockets with several stages to provide enough thrust to get away from Earth's gravity and send the rocket to the moon.

See if you can experiment with an inflated balloon to make a rocket engine and then explain how this demonstrates Newton's three laws of motion.

Materials: one balloon, ½ drinking straw, 15 ft. (4.5 m) heavy string, scissors, clear tape

Procedure: Work with a partner to thread the string through the straw. Attach the string to the backs of two chairs and then separate the chairs to stretch the string as tight as possible. Inflate the balloon only part way. Hold the balloon closed while your partner tapes it to the straw. Be sure the straw is at the beginning of the string and the opening of the balloon faces away from the direction you want your rocket to go. Release the balloon to let the air escape. How far did the balloon go?

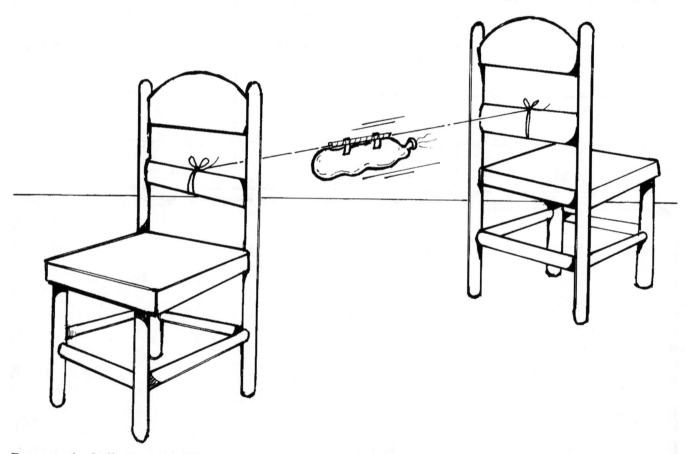

Remove the balloon and inflate it with more air this time to see if it goes the same distance. Mark where it stopped on the string.

Closure: On another paper, make a drawing of what happened in your experiment. Do some research about the laws of motion. Describe which laws of motion were being demonstrated in each step.

Challenge: Try balloons of different sizes and shapes to see if you can perfect your rocket, just as real scientists do. Make a lightweight spaceship to fasten to your balloon rocket.

Assessment Strategies

Science Artwork

Young children love to draw. "Pictures speak a thousand words." It is appropriate, and acceptable, to utilize children's artwork as a means of assessment. An excellent year-long science artwork assessment tool is a Science Art Journal which will contain artwork from all topics learned during science time.

To make an artwork journal, begin by punching three holes on the short left side of two 12" x 18" (30 cm x 45 cm) pieces of tagboard and ten to fifteen sheets of cut 12" x 18" (30 cm x 45 cm) chart/butcher paper. Create a book by sandwiching the chart/butcher sheets between the tagboard cover sheets. Line up the left short side and punch three holes (top, middle, bottom) through the entire thickness. Thread a short piece of string through each hole and tie in a knot or bow (make certain that the pages can turn easily before knotting tightly), or alternatively, open three small metal clasp rings and place through the three holes and shut rings. Write "The 'Art' of Science" and the child's name on the cover. When the child has completed the first piece of artwork you want to place in the journal, simply glue or tape the artwork to the first sheet of chart/butcher paper. Then place the date in the top corner and write any comments you and/or the child desires to make pertaining to the piece of artwork.

This is an excellent tool to use during parent-teacher conferences. It is also a great resource for the child's next teacher. This type of visual log can follow the growth that took place during a number of years if the continuing teacher simply adds more pages to the back of the book.

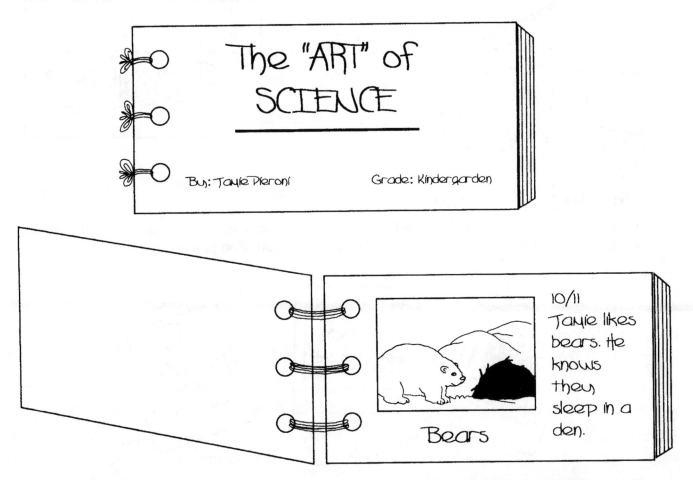

Assessment Strategies *(cont.)*

Science Projects

Provide opportunities throughout the year for children to create projects based on their science topics or themes. Among the most popular for the young learner are these:

Posters

Dioramas

Mobiles

Student-Created Bulletin Boards

Scientist at Work (Photographs)

Keep a camera in the classroom and regularly take pictures of "learning in progress." Keep the pictures in a photographic time line to refer to during assessment and evaluation processing.

A Magnetic Masterpiece

Science Concept: Magnets can be used doing everyday tasks.

Have children try using magnets to paint.

1. Put a few objects made of iron or steel in some tempera paint.
2. Have children cut a piece of white paper to fit the bottom of a shallow glass baking dish.
3. Tell children to put the paper in the bottom of the glass dish.
4. Have children put the paint-coated objects into the dish.
5. Have each child takes a turn being a magnet artist and move a magnet under the dish to pull the paint-coated iron and steel objects around on the paper to make a painting.

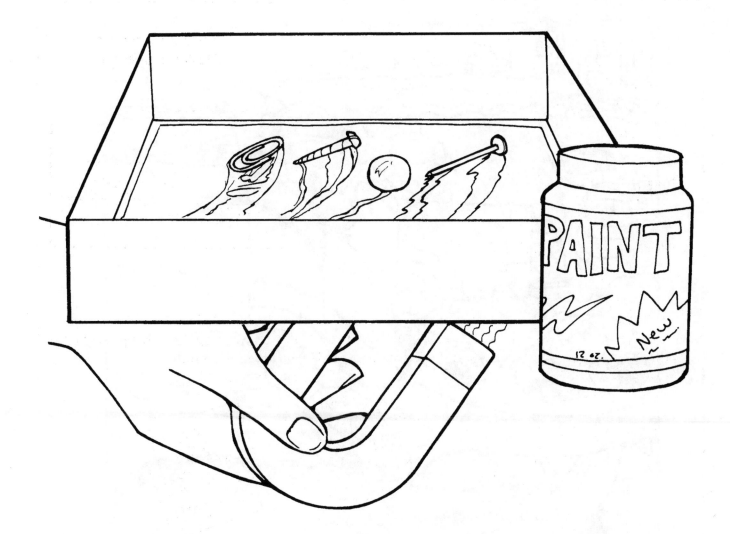

Hidden Pollution

Color the picture below. You will find two common causes of pollution. Write them here.

_____   _____

My Seed Book

Directions: Cut the seed book along the dashed lines. Fold down along the solid line, so that pages 2 and 3 are behind pages 1 and 4. Fold on the line between pages 1 and 4 to make a book. Tape or glue some real seeds (bean, corn, pea, cucumber, etc.) to page 1 of the seed book. Read and complete the sentences in the seed book. Draw pictures to go with the sentences.

3

My
seeds need _____ rain.

2

My
seeds need _____ sunshine.

Soon my _____ seeds will look like this.

4

These are _____ seeds. I will plant them in my garden.

1

Worm Report

Worms fall into a special category of animals called invertebrates. Invertebrates are animals without backbones. Using a real worm, conduct the following experiments.

Locate the following parts of the worm. As you find the part on your worm, draw a picture of it in the space below. Be sure to label each part. Color your drawing the same color as your worm.

Be careful! Some parts listed below cannot be found on a worm! You may want to use an encyclopedia to help you.

eyes mouth	legs head	tail segments or rings	bristles clitellum

Conduct the following extra experiments with your worm.

1. Place the worm on a piece of clear plastic or glass. Can you see through the worm's body? Can you see its blood vessels or its beating heart?

2. Turn the worm onto its back. Watch how it flips itself over.

3. Place the worm on a damp paper towel. Find the pairs of small bristles and gently touch them. What do they feel like?

4. Write several sentences summarizing your experiences with the worm.

Create an Environmental Flyer

Directions: Select a topic or problem such as the greenhouse effect, air pollution, acid rain, hazardous waste, etc. Use that topic or problem as the basis of a flyer to create awareness and generate solutions for your community.

Topic or Problem to Identify

_____

_____

_____

_____

Solutions to Suggest

_____

_____

_____

_____

Draw a draft of your flyer here and then draw it on art paper. If possible, duplicate the flyers and distribute them in your community (but do not create waste).

By the Moons of Jupiter

Teacher Information: When Galileo Galilei pointed his homemade telescope at the moon, sun, planets and Milky Way, he could see things invisible to the naked eye. Most people of his time believed that the moon, sun, and planets were smooth spheres revolving around the Earth. Through his telescope, Galileo could see the moon was pockmarked with craters and had mountains on it. He also pointed the telescope at the planets and discovered that Jupiter had four moons. After observing these for several nights, he concluded they were orbiting the planet. Thus the accepted theory of his day that everything orbited Earth was proven wrong.

Materials: 12 file cards 3" x 5" (7.6 cm x 12.7 cm) and a copy of Flipbook of Jupiter's Moons (page 277) for each student, scissors, glue, wide clear packing tape.

Procedure:

1. Distribute 12 file cards and a copy of page 277 to each student. Tell them to carefully cut out each picture. Show them how to glue each picture to the lower left corner of a card. Place the cards in order with #1 on top.

2. Stack the cards so the edges are offset about ¼ inch (4 mm). On the back of the cards, use clear packing tape across the top edges both vertically and horizontally to hold the cards in place.

3. Have students flip through the book to see Jupiter's moons move back and forth on either side of the planet, sometimes passing in front (#5, #6, #7, and #12).

1. Single Card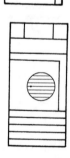

2. Two Cards

3. Stacked Cards

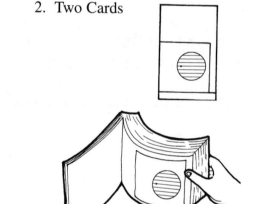

4. Flipbook

4. Explain that as Galileo made drawings of these moons each evening, he noticed they changed positions on either side of Jupiter. He concluded they were in orbit around the planet. This would make them appear at times on one side, then the other, even passing in front of the planet.

5. Tell students today these moons are called the *Galilean moons,* and we use the names Galileo gave to them.

6. Write on the board the names of the moons and the number of days each takes to orbit Jupiter.

Io—1.77 days   *Ganymede*—7.166 days
Europa—3.55 days   *Callisto*—16.75 days

Closure:

Ask students which of these moons is most distant from Jupiter and how they know. (*Callisto*—it takes the longest time to complete its orbit). Have them tell you which moon is closest and how they know this. (*Io*—it moves the fastest around the planet.)

By the Moons of Jupiter *(cont.)*

Flipbook of Jupiter's Moons

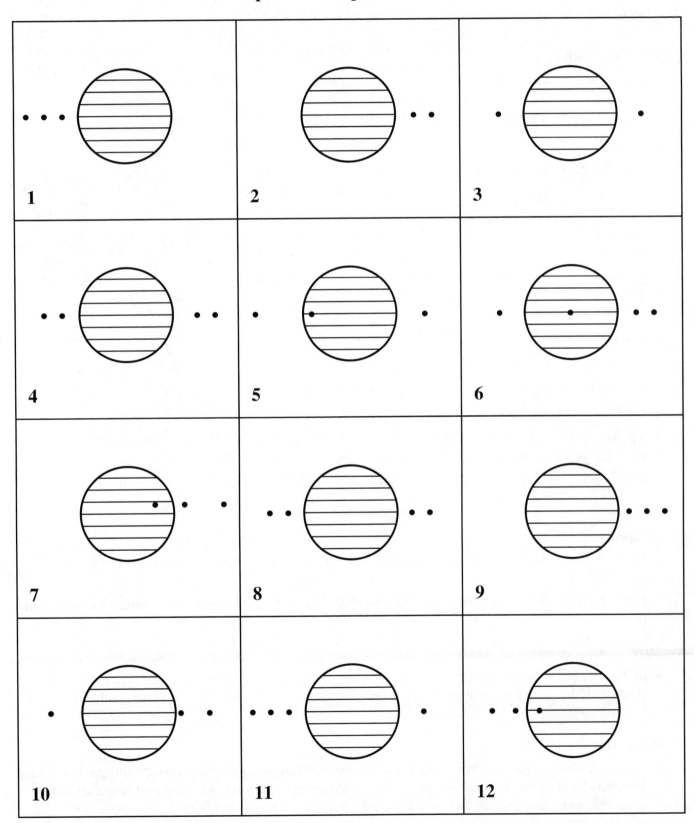

Balancing Butterflies

Question

How can you resist (or at least seem to resist) the force of gravity?

Setting the Stage

- Find videos of circus acts that show people juggling a number of object (plates on poles, etc.). Discuss with students how the jugglers might use some "tricks" to make balancing the objects slightly easier. (Twirling objects balance better. Use a bicycle as an example.)
- Review with students the earlier activities using the center of gravity.

Materials Needed for Each Individual

- heavy paper or card stock
- reproducible butterfly design
- scissors
- new pencil
- small ball of clay to use as a base
- two pennies
- rubber cement
- markers or crayons for decorating the butterfly

Procedure (*Student Instructions*)

1. Trace the butterfly pattern onto heavy paper. Cut out the design.
2. Decorate the butterfly.
3. Use the clay to form a sturdy base for the pencil. Be sure the pencil is perfectly straight.
4. Glue the pennies on the butterfly where indicated.
5. Balance the butterfly on the eraser of the pencil. The butterfly should balance at its "nose." It might take a little adjustment of the pennies to obtain a stable balance.

Extensions

- Have students make other shapes—spaceship, bird, superhero—and balance them in the same manner.
- Have students research the animal kingdom. Have them find out how many animals use their tails for balance.

Closure

- In their force and motion journals, have students trace their butterflies and mark the center of gravity. Have students write short paragraphs explaining how they know that this is the center of gravity.

The Big Why

- Artists use the center of gravity concept to create interesting effects. By manipulating where the weight is located (in this case by using coins), we change the point where the center of gravity lies. This can cause the illusion of a balancing act that seems to defy gravity.

Balancing Butterflies *(cont.)*

Use this pattern for making your Balancing Butterfly.

Why Is My Body Special?

What Scientists Know

Each body part has a job. To do its job well it has to be in its proper place on your body. Your hands would become very tired if you had to walk around on them all day, but your feet do the job just fine. It would be tricky to brush your teeth with your foot holding a toothbrush, but your hand can brush really well. Your body is designed to help you get the job done.

Real Life Application

You may be familiar with the song "Head and Shoulders, Knees and Toes:"

Head and shoulders, knees and toes, knees and toes

Head and shoulders, knees and toes, knees and toes

Eyes and ears and mouth and nose

Head and shoulders, knees and toes, knees and toes!

Invite your students to sing this song and point to their body parts as they sing their names and then add this verse:

Fingers, hands, and elbows and elbows

Fingers, hands, and elbows and elbows

And legs, knees, feet, don't forget about my toes!

Fingers, hands, and elbows and elbows

Animal Sounds

Singing songs about animals, selecting orchestral numbers to "promote" the importance of animals and making animal sounds in groups are just a few of the ways to integrate music into your animal-based lessons.

Science Concept: *Animal make sounds for many reasons*

- Have you ever been outside a night when all you can hear are the animals? Almost everyone has heard crickets and howling dogs. Animals can make such interesting sounds. Each is like a musical instrument.

- Create your own classroom symphony orchestra of animals. Decide which animal sounds you want in the orchestra. Assign students to make those sounds. You can have a symphony depicting the sounds of any type of animal environment you like. For example, the desert, the forest, or the rain forest can be depicted by your animal symphony.

- "Animals" making the same sounds should be in the same group. Let the students take turns conducting the orchestra. They can make any kind of rhythm they want.

Music

Music and chemistry are closely related fields. Musical instruments are made of chemicals. Brass instruments such as trumpets and trombones are made of a copper (Cu) and zinc (Zn) alloy. (An alloy is a substance with metallic properties and consists of two or more elements.) A number of songs have been written about chemicals. "The Blue Danube," by Johann Strauss and "Waves of the Danube," by J. Ivanovici are about the chemical water (H_2O). The waltz, "Gold and Silver," by Franz Lehar contains chemicals in its title. Musical sounds can be produced by the vibration of chemicals. Stringed instruments produce sounds by vibrating strings of different metals, and brass instruments produce sounds as a result of vibrating columns of air (mixture of chemicals known as gases).

Science Concept: Vibrating chemicals produce musical sounds.

- Have students produce musical sounds by blowing. Have them note the sounds produced when they blow across the top of a glass soda bottle that is first empty, then half-full of water and finally three-fourths full of water. Discuss the sounds in class. **Note:** The sounds are produced by vibrating columns of air (a mixture of gases).

- Have students produce musical sounds by hitting. Using a metal teaspoon, have them hit the center of a glass soda bottle that is half-full of water and one that is three-fourths full of water. Discuss the produced sounds in class. **Note:** The sounds are produced by vibrating columns of water. Have students note the sounds produced by hitting other items such as empty metal cans and wood.

- Have students produce musical sounds by plucking. Provide them with boards containing pairs of nails, at various distances apart with rubber bands stretched over them. Have students pluck the rubber bands with their fingers. Discuss the produced sounds in class. Repeat this activity using metal strings in place of the rubber bands.

Jubil*ant* Songs

I've Been Working in an Anthill

(Sing this song to the tune of *I've Been Working on the Railroad*)

I've been working in an anthill.
All the livelong day.
I've been working in an anthill.
I have no time to play.
Lots of dirt to move around here,
Lots of food to find and store.
We must get our city ready
Before winter comes once more.
Tunnel through the ground,
Tunnel through the ground,
Tunnel through the ground,
To make a new chamber.
Tunnel through the ground,
Tunnel through the ground,
Let's dig a new room for the queen.

There's a Little Anthill

(Sing this song to the tune of *Twinkle, Twinkle, Little Star*)

There's an anthill over there.
Ants are crawling everywhere.
They live in groups called colonies.
They feast on insects, plants, and seeds.
Queen ants, worker ants, together will be.
They learn to work cooperatively.

Digging Tunnels

(Sing this song to the tune of *Frére Jacques*)

Digging Tunnels, Digging Tunnels,
In the ground, In the ground.
Storing food for winter, Storing food for winter,
All around, All around.

Brilli*ant* Idea: Have children make up hand movements or full-body movements to these Jubil*ant* songs. Children may also want to make up their own ant lyrics to add to the list of Jubil*ant* songs.

Perfect Pitch

Background

If we talk about making a high sound, are we referring to pitch or volume? (pitch) The concept of pitch is something that many young children do not understand. Even if they understand that there are different musical notes, they have trouble identifying which ones are higher in pitch. This experiment gives them the opportunity to explore what pitch is.

Objectives

- to understand the concept of pitch
- to make and then test predictions

Student Instruction

Explain the difference between volume and pitch. Demonstrate higher and lower volumes, using louder and softer sounds and then demonstrate different pitches. This could be done with a musical instrument such as a piano or recorder, by singing different notes, or by using examples from the animal kingdom. For example, a mouse makes a high-pitched squeak while a lion has a low-pitched roar. Point out that these two animals also have different volumes because a lion's roar is louder than a mouse's squeak.

If you are going to have students fill the bottles themselves, introduce the funnel, what it is used for, and how to use it.

Center Preparation

Materials: 3 identical glass bottles, 12-16 ounce (360-500 mL) size; 1 metal teaspoon (5 mL); water; pitcher; 1 funnel; a 12" (30 cm) ruler; bath towel

Directions: Cover the table in the center with a bath towel. This helps absorb the spills and keeps the glass bottles from slipping off the table. Provide a metal teaspoon and three identical bottles from juice or soft drinks with lids. Label them *A, B,* and *C*. Pour water into each bottle, making sure there are different amounts in each. For younger students, fill the bottles ahead of time, and put on the lids to minimize spills. If you are going to have students fill the bottles, you will need a funnel and an easy-to-use pitcher.

Follow-Up Activities

Have students predict how the size and shape of a bottle will affect its pitch. Get several bottles and jars of different sizes, and allow students to try them out. Note that there are many variables in this follow-up experiment, so the results are likely to be different from what you would expect. In other words, this is not a controlled experiment. However, this type of follow-up still helps reinforce the basic concepts and motivates students toward doing their own explorations.

Relate the partially filled bottles to a flute, recorder, or clarinet. As you close more of the holes on these instruments, you effectively make the air column longer. This is analogous to taking water out of the bottles to achieve a lower pitch.

Perfect Pitch *(cont.)*

Lab Worksheet — Level A

Ask Yourself

How can I change the pitch of a sound?

What You Need

_____ 3 glass bottles

_____ water

_____ 1 metal spoon

What You Do

Use **Bottle A** and **Bottle B**.

_____ 1. Tap each bottle with the spoon.

_____ 2. Which has a lower pitch?   _____ Bottle A   _____ Bottle B

_____ 3. Which one has more air?   _____ Bottle A   _____ Bottle B

Use **Bottle A** and **Bottle C**.

_____ 4. Which has more air? _____ Bottle A _____ Bottle C

_____ 5. Predict: Which do you think has a lower pitch?
             _____ Bottle A _____ Bottle C

_____ 6. Tap each bottle with the spoon.

_____ 7. Which has a lower pitch? _____ Bottle A _____ Bottle C

Use **Bottle B** and **Bottle C**.

_____ 8. Which has more air? _____ Bottle B _____ Bottle C

_____ 9. Predict: Which do you think has a lower pitch?
             _____ Bottle B _____ Bottle C

_____ 10. Tap each bottle with the spoon.

_____ 11. Which has a lower pitch? _____ Bottle B _____ Bottle C

What You Learned

Does a bottle with more air have a higher or lower pitch? _____

Perfect Pitch *(cont.)*

Lab Worksheet — Level B

Ask Yourself

How can I change the pitch of the sound made by tapping a bottle with a spoon?

What You Need

_____ 3 glass bottles   _____ 1 metal spoon

_____ 1 ruler   _____ 1 funnel

_____ water

Height
of
Air

Height
of
Water

What You Do

_____ 1. Use the funnel to fill Bottle A with 1 inch (2.5 cm) of water. Measure how much air is in the bottle: _____ inches (_____ cm).

_____ 2. Use the funnel to fill Bottle B with 4 inches (11 cm) of water. Measure how much air is in the bottle: _____ inches (_____ cm).

_____ 3. Which bottle has more air in it? _____

_____ 4. Tap each bottle with the spoon.

_____ 5. Which bottle has a lower pitch? _____

_____ 6. Now use the funnel to put some water in Bottle C. You choose how much. Measure how much air is in the bottle: _____ inches (_____cm).

_____ 7. Does Bottle C have more or less air than Bottle A?

_____ 8. Does Bottle C have more or less air than Bottle B?

_____ 9. Predict: Do you think Bottle C will have a higher or lower pitch than Bottle A? _____

_____ 10. Predict: Do you think Bottle C will have a higher or lower pitch than Bottle B? _____

_____ 11. Tap each bottle with the spoon.

_____ 12. Does Bottle C have a higher or lower pitch than Bottle A? _____

_____ 13. Does Bottle C have a higher or lower pitch than Bottle B? _____

What You Learned

The bottle with more air has a _____ pitch.

Make a Violin and Bow

Use the following directions to make a violin and bow.

Materials:

- empty tissue box
- 5 wide rubber bands
- rubber bands of different widths
- pencil, unsharpened

Directions:

1. Place a rubber band on your pencil by stretching it from the eraser to the other end.

2. Place four rubber bands on the tissue box over the opening. Be sure they are about $1/2$ inch (1.25 cm) apart from one another.

3. Rub your bow (the pencil with the rubber band) across your violin (the tissue box with the rubber bands).

Now try using rubber bands of different widths. How does the width of the rubber bands change the sound they make?

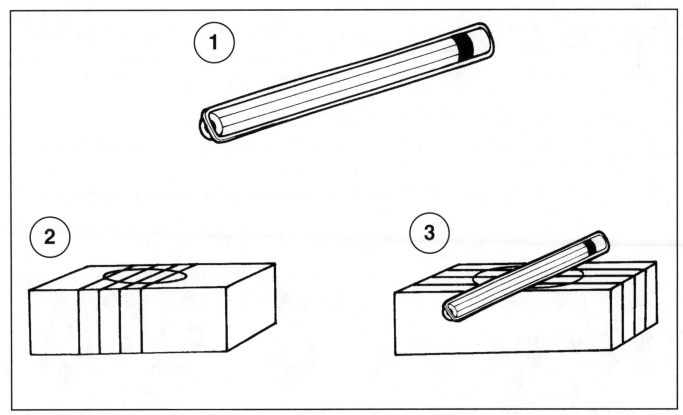

Musical Instruments

Students will gain an understanding of musical instruments through this project. Have students complete this activity after they have studied a unit on sound and have an understanding of how sound is produced in each of the musical instrument families. Music played an important role in the development of societies and cultures. Music is also thought to increase intelligence when introduced at an early age.

Grade level: six to eight

Duration: 30 to 40 minutes on the computer

Materials: information sheet, *ClarisWorks* planning sheets

Before the Computer:

- The teacher assigns groups or individual instruments for research.
- Using the information sheet, students will use available resources to research their topic.
- The *ClarisWorks* planning sheets will be used to plan at least four or five slides (or whatever the teacher feels necessary). The first slide will include the title and student/group name.
- If a scanner is available, students can scan pictures to be used in the presentation.
- If students have access to the Internet, locate and save pictures and photographs to be used in the presentation.

On the Computer:

- Students will use the *ClarisWorks* word processing module to type in their information, inserting graphics or pictures saved from the scanner or Internet.
- From View in the menu, select slide show. Students will choose background color, transitions, and other options.
- Save to disk.

Options:

Students could have local musicians demonstrate their instruments. The class could go on a field trip to a concert.

If your computer supports sound, you could download musical pieces through the Internet.

Musical Instruments *(cont.)*

Group/individual name(s): _____   Instrument:_____

What kind of instrument is this (example: string, wind, percussion)?_____

_____

When was the instrument first invented? _____

_____

When did it become popular?_____

_____

What historical musicians or composers have used this instrument in their compositions?

_____

_____

What modern musicians or composers have used this instrument in their compositions?

_____

_____

Find at least two musical compositions that were written specifically for this instrument. Who wrote them?_____

_____

When? _____

_____

Why do you think the composer chose this instrument over another? _____

_____

Instruments and Their Families

STRINGED INSTRUMENTS

Banjo	Classical Guitar	Mandolin
Bass	Harp	Viola
Cello	Lute	Violin

BRASS INSTRUMENTS

Bugle	French Horn	Trombone
Flugelhorn	Sousaphone	Trumpet

WOODWIND INSTRUMENTS

Bass Clarinet	English Horn	Piccolo
Bassoon	Flute	Soprano Saxophone
Clarinet	Oboe	Tenor Saxophone

PERCUSSION INSTRUMENTS

Bass Drum	Cymbals	Snare Drum
Bongo Drums	Gong	Triangle
Chimes	Kettle Drum	Vibraphone

KEYBOARD INSTRUMENTS

Harpsichord	Piano	Pipe Organ

Environmental Sounds

Purpose: to make students aware of the sounds in their environment

Skills: knowledge, comprehension, application, analysis, synthesis, and evaluation

Intelligences: Potentially all may be involved.

Materials:

- a recording of environmental sounds (Get one with a variety of types.)

- copies of Translating the Experience, one for each student (page 292)

Procedures:

- ◆ Have students review the definition of musical/rhythmic intelligence.

- ◆ Introduce this experience by discussing the two classes of environmental sounds and asking the students for input.

- ◆ Play the recording of environmental sounds. Ask students to identify them and decide which ones are pleasant and which ones cause stress.

- ◆ Next, without any further discussion, ask students to work individually on the sheet entitled "Translating the Experience sheet.

- ◆ Use the sheets for discussion during Evaluation and Processing and then place them in the students' folders.

To Simplify:

Allow students to work with aides or parent helpers.

To Expand:

Ask students to brainstorm for ideas to control unpleasant noises in the environment.

Evaluation and Processing:

Allow students to share and discuss their Translating the Experience sheets.

Environmental Sounds *(cont.)*

Translating the Experience

Think about the experience you just had. It was a musical/rhythmic experience. You listened to some of the sounds that occur in the environment.

Think about your reaction to the experience. Decide how you could translate your reaction by expressing it through another one of the intelligences. Do not express your reaction through your musical/rhythmic intelligence!

Which intelligence will you use to translate your experience?

_____

What materials, if any, will you need?

_____   _____

_____   _____

_____

Will you need time to prepare your translation? How much?

_____

How will you share your translation with the class?

_____

_____

_____

_____

_____

_____

Brain in Charge

Science Concept: The brain tells every part of my body what to do.

Concept Literature: *Thinking* by Kathie Billingslea Smith

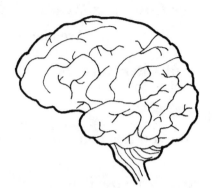

Question

Why is my brain important?

Discovery Experience

This game, a variation of Simon Says, will help your children to understand that the brain is the boss of the body.

1. Ask each child to point to his or her brain. Tell your children that their brains are hidden under a thick bone called the skull. Explain that the brain is the boss of the body because they need their brains to think, talk, read, run, dream, love, color, cry, breathe. . . They need their brains for everything they do.

2. Gather your children in a circle to play "The Brain Says." To play, explain that every command that is preceded by the phrase "the brain says" should be followed. Commands that are not preceded by this phrase should be ignored. Remember, if the brain does not tell you to do it, you cannot do it. A sample round may go something like this:

The brain says, "Scratch your head." The brain says, "Hop on one foot." The brain says, "Think of something good to eat." The brain says, "Say hi to your neighbor." The brain says, "Laugh." Raise your right hand. Whoops! If you raised your right hand, you should not have. Remember, the brain is the boss of the body and you cannot do anything until the brain tells you to.

What Scientists Know

Scientists have been using their brains to think about their brains for a long time, but there is still much about the brain that scientists do not know. The brain is very complicated, but scientists do know that your brain is busy working all the time, storing information and directing your body. Some people say the brain is like a computer, but it is much more powerful than the best computer in the world. Your brain is what makes you special and unique. Your brain is a very important part of your body.

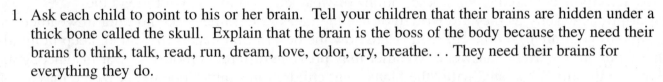

Real Life Application

The brain has many functions. Memory is but one of its functions. Cut out different body part pictures (two of each part) from magazines and glue them on index cards. Play concentration with the body cards. Place all the cards, pictures down, on a table. Children flip two cards over, hoping to get a match. When they do match two cards, they remove those cards from the table and put them in a pile to keep track of their scores. Give your brain the credit every time you remember and are able to make a match.

Today I Feel . . .

Science Concepts: Weather can affect the way we feel.

Weather can determine a day's activities.

Concept Literature: *In for Winter, Out for Spring* by Arnold Adoff and Jerry Pinkney

Question
How do you feel and what can you do on a rainy/sunny day?

Discovery Experience
This activity is centered around descriptions of weather. You may wish to read the descriptions exactly as they are written or use the ideas as a framework and plug in weather unique to your area. As the children relate how the description makes them feel, keep in mind that there are no "right" answers. Weather may provoke different emotions. For instance, gray days are usually associated with "the blahs," but children in sunny Phoenix, Arizona, may consider a rainy day to be exciting and fun. After you read each description, ask the children how it made them feel and why. Then ask what sort of activity they would choose to do on a day like this.

Gather the children around you. Give the class permission to stretch out and get comfortable. Begin the discussion:

When you woke up this morning and looked out the window, what kind of weather did you see? How did it make you feel? I'm going to describe some different types of weather to you. I want you to close your eyes and try to imagine the day and the weather. Think about how you would feel if you woke up to find a day like this:

1. Rainy Day

The day is cloudy and dark. Big, heavy raindrops are falling against your bedroom window. Splat, splat, splat, the raindrops fall. You draw back the curtains and look outside. Large puddles are everywhere! Bucketfuls of rain are filling the gutters and then gushing out from the downspout. The ground is wet and soggy. The street in front of your house looks more like a river than a street today. The smell of rain seeps into the house. Everything feels damp and clammy. It is a rainy day.

Can you picture a day like this? How does it make you feel? What would be a good activity to plan on a day like this? (Indoor games, reading a book, watching television)

2. Sunny Day

Bright, powerful sunlight comes streaming in through your bedroom window and wakes you up. You squint a little and look outside. It takes a moment for your eyes to adjust. Everywhere you look there is sunshine. Sunshine on the trees. Sunshine on the grass. Sunshine bouncing off the cars as they drive by. There is not a cloud to be seen, only warm, sunny, blue skies everywhere you look. It is a sunny day.

Today I Feel . . . *(cont.)*

3. Thunder Storm

Rumble! Rumble! The skies are complaining. Flash! Crash! A lightning bolt flies from the sky followed by another loud CRASH! You hide underneath the covers, but it does not seem to help. You can still feel the rumble of the clouds. It is dark outside, but when the lightning strikes, it lights up your entire room. Now it is dark again. The wind is blowing too. The whole house seems to move and sway as the heavy winds slam against the side of your house. You can hear the great oak tree creaking just outside the window as it is tossed about by the strong and powerful wind. It is a stormy day.

4. Snowy Day

Everything is still. Oh, so still. Something is strange. Something seems different. You jump out of bed and shiver as you run to the window. It is frightfully cold in your bedroom compared to your warm bed, but you pull back the curtain and peer outside. Snowflakes as big as quarters are drifting silently down from the sky. Already there is a thick blanket of snow on the ground. The first snow of the season came while you were asleep! The trees are white and the cars are white. The telephone wires are bending under the fresh, white snow. The whole world seems to stop as the first flakes fall silently from the sky.

What Scientists Know

We all know that bad weather can cause us to cancel outdoor activities, but did you know that weather can affect the way you feel too? There is a sickness that some people get if they do not get enough sunshine (Seasonal Affect Disorder). People usually get this in the wintertime in places where there is not very much sunshine. To help them feel better, doctors sometimes have the people sit underneath very bright lights. The lights, just like the sun, can help people to feel better.

Real Life Application

Teach weather safety and help the children to see that weather conditions can alter planned activities by completing the activity sheet, page 296. The children should use the pictures to tell the story and then decide what they would do next in each situation.

Today I Feel . . . *(cont.)*

What Would You Do?

Rain Forest Dictionary

Make your own rain forest dictionary. Cut out the boxes. In each box write what the word means.
Draw a picture. Put the pages in ABC order. Staple the pages together with the cover on top.

My Rain Forest Dictionary by_____	**equator**
rain forest	**understory**
canopy	**layers**

Planning a Fitness Program

By keeping yourself in good physical condition, you will have a better chance of surviving in any emergency situation. You can do this by developing a regular fitness program. A good fitness program has several components. Some of these components are regular exercise, a healthy diet, and adequate rest.

Exercise: Exercise strengthens your heart, lungs, and muscles. It also will often improve your mental attitude. Remember a time when you sat at your desk in school all day. How did it feel to get up, stretch, and walk around? Exercise reduces stress and usually feels good. Most people enjoy different forms of exercise. Some people like to run while others would rather do aerobics or play basketball. Of course, some exercises provide a greater workout than others. For example, swimming exerts more energy than walking, but both are good for you. When planning a fitness program, it is best to choose exercises you enjoy so that you will be more likely to stick with the program. It takes only 20–30 minutes for most exercises to provide some benefit.

*Make a list of exercises. Note which ones would provide you with the greatest workout and then mark the ones which you enjoy.

Healthy Diet: A healthy diet is based on the food pyramid. According to the pyramid, we should eat: 6–11 servings from the bread, cereal, and pasta group, 3–5 servings from the vegetable group, 2–4 servings from the fruit group, 2–3 servings from the milk, cheese, and yogurt group, and 2–3 servings from the meat, poultry, beans, eggs, and nut group. Fats, oils, and sweets should be eaten sparingly. By following this plan for a healthy diet, you will naturally receive the nutrients that your body needs to function.

*Design a week's menus which meet these requirements for a healthy diet. In your menus, try to incorporate the foods that you usually like to eat.

Rest: We all have mornings when we do not want to get out of bed and feel like we could use more sleep. This can be a result of several things. You may have gone to bed late, you may not have slept well, or you may be tired from an exceptionally busy activity on the previous day. It is important to try to schedule an adequate amount of time for sleep. Your body needs time to rest each night so it can recuperate from its exertions during the day. Although sleep needs vary from one individual to the next, most growing bodies need between eight and ten hours of sleep each night.

*Keep a sleep diary for several nights to record the number of hours that you slept and how you felt during the day. This will help you assess how much sleep you need to feel well.

Fitness Schedule

Use the information you gained from the activities on the previous page to help you fill out your own fitness schedule. Fill in the chart with activities that you do during the day. Briefly describe your meals and try to schedule at least one 20 to 30–minute exercise time each day. Remember to plan for adequate sleep time. While making the chart, also remember to allot times for responsibilities (like homework) and times for pleasure (like watching television).

Time	Sun.	Mon.	Tue.	Wed.	Thu.	Fri.	Sat.

Exercise Record

Exercise Record for _____

Use this chart to keep a record of your daily exercise habits. Record your exercise and sports activities and the amount of time you participated in each activity. Use the chart to determine if you are getting enough exercise each week. If you are not, try to increase the number of days or the length of time that you exercise.

Date	Type of Exercise/Sports	Amount of Time

My Science Project

Present science projects in a new way—on the computer. Use *HyperStudio* to create an impressive lab report.

Grade Level: four to five

Duration: 120–240 minutes on the computer

Materials: planned science project and Science Project Summary Sheet (page 302),

Procedure:

Before the Computer:

> As part of a science unit, your students will plan and perform their own science experiments. The experiments will be presented on a *HyperStudio* stack.

On the Computer:

- Your students can begin their *HyperStudio* stacks even before their science projects are complete. Once your students have chosen topics, they can set up the organization of their stacks, including the title pages and the cards that will support their experiments. Set the expectations about what must be included. It will be helpful to use the planning form provided, but some students may not be ready for a complete science project.

- Those who do research or have extensive graphs or supporting information may want to include an additional category called "Supporting Data." As they complete each portion, they can add the information on the cards.

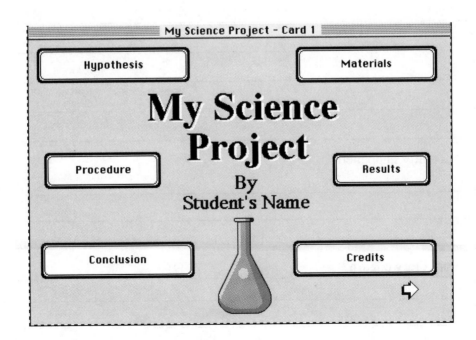

Options:

> For beginners or younger students, use *Kid Pix 2* Slide Show to present their science projects. Use one slide for each portion of the project (a hypothesis slide, a materials slide, etc.).

My Science Project *(cont.)*

SCIENCE PROJECT SUMMARY SHEET

Science Project Title: _____

Question: What do we want to find out?

_____

_____

Hypothesis: What do we think we will find out?

_____

_____

_____

Materials:

_____

_____

_____

_____

Procedure: How will we find out? List step-by-step instructions.

1. _____

2. _____

3. _____

4. _____

5. _____

Results: What actually happened?

_____

_____

_____

Conclusion: What did we learn?

_____

_____

_____

_____

Helpful as Can Be

Science Concepts: Animals help people work and provide transportation. Some animals help people stay safe.

Concept Literature: *Animals Helping People* by Suzanne Venino
Animals on the Job by Nancy Krulik

Question

Is it easy for two animals to work together?

Discovery Experience

Give children the opportunity to discover that animals have to work together (cooperate) when people use them in teams (dogs with snow sled, horses with wagon, oxen with plow). Show children a picture of two oxen in a yoke. Share that they are going to be teams of oxen and run an "Oxen Race" where they will need to pull and carry a "load." (**Note:** Do not mention the need to cooperate. They will discover on their own that cooperation is a must.) Take children outside or into a large, open room.

Oxen Races

Materials:

- 20" x 4" (50 cm x 10 cm) soft cloth strips (two strips per "team" of two oxen)
- toy wagon filled with dolls (to pull)
- pillowcase filled with small, soft objects to carry
  (with knotted or sealed end)
- yard stick (meter stick)/string or tape

Directions:

1. Have two children stand side-by-side. Gently wrap and tie one cloth strip around inner arms and other strip around inner legs. (Give teams a chance to simply walk in unison before race.)

2. Measure out two relay "go" lines 10 yards (10 m) apart.
   Mark with string or tape and label one string A, the other B. Place half the oxen teams behind "go" line A; half behind opposite "go" line B (opposing lines face each other, relay-race style).

3. Place filled wagon directly in front of "go" line A (and stuffed pillowcase off to side of "go" line A for present time).

4. Upon giving a signal, the race begins. The first oxen team behind "go" line A gets in front of wagon and pulls it (while trying to run) to "go" line B and hands first team behind "go" line B the wagon's handle. This oxen team must now turn wagon around and run back to "go" line A. Pattern continues until all teams have had a chance to pull the wagon.

5. Repeat race process, but this time oxen teams must be on "all fours" to carry the pillowcase "cargo" on their backs as they try to get to the opposite "go" line.

Helpful as Can Be *(cont.)*

What Scientists Know

Animals help people work and move objects by pulling (wagon/plow), pushing (logs), and carrying (people/cargo). Not all animals can pull, push, or carry because these animals have to move heavy things. Animals must be strong to do this. Sometimes people will put two (oxen) to ten (dog sled team) animals together because animals working together are stronger than one animal working by itself. (Ask children what it was like to have to work together when they had to work as a pulling and carrying team during the oxen races.)

The most common animals used around the world for work and transportation are the horse, donkey, camel, water buffalo, ox, elephant, and dog. (Read *Animals Helping People*). Some animals also help people stay safe and happy. These animals are specially trained to do special jobs. Some of the jobs are search and rescue (usually dogs who help find lost people), drug sniffing (usually dogs who help find hidden drugs so people won't use them), "hands" for disabled people (usually monkeys, but sometimes dogs, trained to open doors, answer phones, turn on lights/television/computer or anything electrical, and feed human owners), and leading visually impaired or fully blind people (guide dogs). (Read *Animals on the Job*.)

Science Simulation

When an animal helps a person stay safe, the person must trust the animal to do its job well. Have children experience a "need to trust" by taking turns being a seeing-eye dog for its "owner." Divide children into teams of two. Give each team a blindfold.

Explain that one child will be blind (wears blindfold) while the other child will be the seeing-eye dog. A seeing-eye dog will never let anything, or anyone, hurt its owner. If the owner is not safe or happy, the dog feels sad. Have the "blind" person hold the elbow area of "seeing-eye dog" person's left or right arm. Share the "path" you want teams to follow (e.g., go out of classroom door, down the hallway until you are out on the playground, go around the swing set or jungle gym, back inside the hallway to get a drink at the water fountain, back inside classroom, and return the blind person to his or her seat and have the blind person sit down).

After the first round, children change roles. When the simulation has been completed, have children share how it felt to trust (depend on) an animal to lead them around and keep them safe.

Extension

Invite someone visually impaired or fully blind who has a seeing-eye dog to come and talk with your children. They will be fascinated since they have had a hands-on experience of what it is like to be both a seeing-eye dog and a blind person.

Communications

Question

Why is it important to communicate accurately?

Setting the Stage

- Have students play the communications game "Telegraph." Whisper a message into someone's ear, and have him or her whisper the message into someone else's ear. The message may only be spoken once and not repeated. Continue telegraphing the message in whispers. Have the last person tell the class what the message was.
- Discuss with students the importance of making sure that what you say is understood.

Materials Needed for Each Group

- two sets of space shapes (page 306), one per student
- scissors

Note to the teacher: The children will work in pairs.

Procedure (Student Instructions)

1. Each pair will sit back-to-back so that they cannot see their partner's desk.
2. The Senders will arrange the shapes on their desks in any configuration desired. They will then communicate to the Receivers where each shape is located and the orientation of the shape.
3. The Receivers will arrange the shapes on their desks in the positions that they think correspond to the messages being received. The Receivers may not ask questions!
4. After all of the information has been sent and received, compare the two arrangements of figures.
5. Take turns being Senders and Receivers.

Extensions

- Have students repeat the experience allowing the Receivers to ask questions. Which method works best?
- Have students use the same process, only this time the Senders have drawn a simple picture and need to transmit the picture without saying what the picture is. They will only describe how to draw it. The Receivers will attempt to draw the same picture.

Closure

Have students compare experiences from each group. Ask them what kinds of directions produced the best results? Discuss applications to flight controllers. How Do Machines "Think" and Communicate?

The Big Why

This activity will point out the difficulty in communicating exact instructions. One method that works well is to use the hours of the clock as a reference for directions. Older children might use a coordinate grid method. The children were working on a flat desk —two dimensions. Imagine the problems involved when you are in an airplane and have to deal in three dimensions!

Communications *(cont.)*

Cut out shapes before beginning the activity.

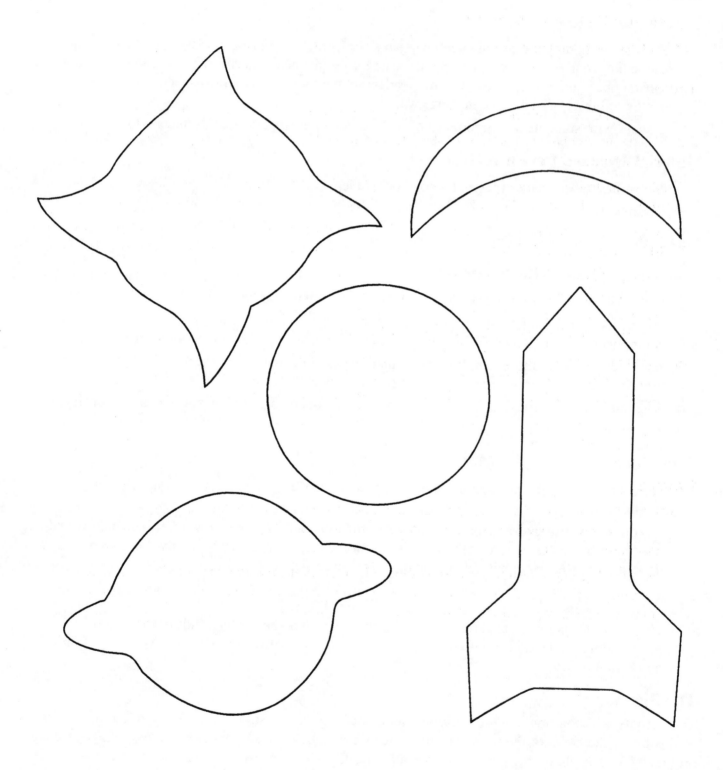

Match My Mineral

Overview: *Students will describe mineral specimens.*

Materials

- sets of eight mineral specimens
- transparency and copies of the worksheet Match the Minerals (page 308)

Activity

1. Review the list of mineral characteristics students discovered in the previous lesson.

2. Divide the students into groups of three or four students and distribute a set of minerals and the worksheet to each group.

3. Show the transparency of the worksheet. Explain the terms *luster* and *texture* and write examples of these on the board. Write examples of colors students see in the eight minerals on the board.

4. Select one of the mineral specimens and show it to the students. Place it on the worksheet in the #1 position. Have the students help you write a description of its color, luster, and texture.

5. Explain that each member of the group will pick one of the minerals and write a description of its color, luster, and texture on the worksheet. Tell the students that they may not choose the mineral that was used for the demonstration. Be sure they know that they are only to describe one mineral per group member, rather than describing all eight minerals.

6. Let students know that when all have finished their work they will go to another group's table, just as in the last class, to see if they can match their minerals with their descriptions. The group will be considered successful if the other group can match all of their minerals.

7. Monitor the students as they work, assisting when needed. Be sure the students are as specific as possible with their descriptions.

Closure

- When all students have finished describing their minerals, have them put the minerals in a pile next to the worksheet and move to another group's table. They should read the descriptions and match the minerals.

- Have each group return to their own table and check on the matching to see if it was done correctly. To help students see how they can improve on their descriptions, discuss any of the minerals which were not matched.

Match the Minerals

Names of Group Members: _____

Each member of the group should pick a different mineral to describe. Next to one of the numbers, write the color, luster, and texture of that mineral.

Mineral	Color	Luster	Texture
1			
2			
3			
4			

My Nose Knows

The sense of smell is also important in aiding our sense of taste. A study showed that over two million Americans had taste/smell disorders. One such disorder is anosmia—loss of the sense of smell. Use this activity to take the often-used smelling/tasting exercise one step farther and survey your class or school.

Duration:

- two class periods to do the lab activity and computer activity with one class
- more time for a school survey—perhaps during lunch periods, other science classes, etc.

Materials:

- plastic bags (for food samples)
- tiny paper cups (for drink samples)
- paper towels
- food samples (carrot, bread, raw potato, onion, apple, celery, green pepper, peanut, pear, mint candy)

    or

- several powdered drink flavors (orange, cherry, grape)

    or

- several jellybean flavors (Buy them as separate flavors at a candy store.)
- spreadsheet software

Before the computer:

- Have students work in pairs with sets of food samples or drink samples.
- Each student will close his or her eyes and try to guess the food or drink first by just smelling it (then by just tasting it, holding nose closed, as well as keeping eyes shut) and then by smelling and tasting it.
- Record correct and incorrect responses on a piece of paper.
- Create a spreadsheet for students to fill in their results.

On computer:

- Fill in a number 1 for each correct guess in the spreadsheet column.
- Have a student (or do this yourself) key in a function command for the spreadsheet program to count all the "ones" in each column.
- Use the totals to create a graph showing the results of the survey (students should see quickly that there were fewer correct responses when only one of the two senses was used).

Option:

- This could be used as an example of surveying techniques for possible science fair projects. Students need to learn how to collect survey data and how to present it so that it actually represents what they are trying to prove.

My Nose Knows *(cont.)*

Sample Spreadsheet for Entering Experiment Results

TASTE.WKS

	A	B	C	D	E	F	G	H	I	J
1		Cherry	Cherry	Cherry	Orange	Orange	Orange	Grape	Grape	Grape
2	Name	Smell	Taste	Smell & Taste	Smell	Taste	Smell & Taste	Smell	Taste	Smell & Taste
3										
4	Kim	1		1		1	1	1		1
5	Ed		1	1	1		1		1	1
6	Wayne		1	1	1				1	1
7	Bernadette		1	1					1	
8	Jacques	1		1	1		1	1		1
9	Mike			1		1	1		1	1
10										
11										
12	Totals									
13		Smell	Taste	Smell & Taste						
14	Cherry	2	3	6						
15	Orange	3	2	5						
16	Grape	2	4	6						
17										

Sample Graph to Present Experiment Results

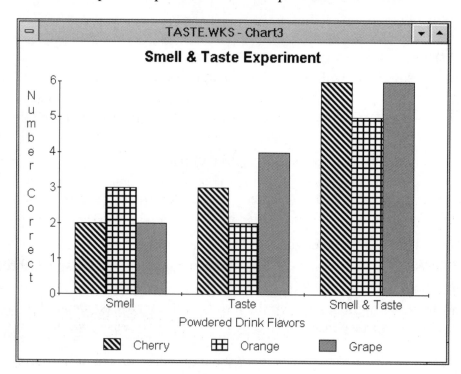

TASTE.WKS - Chart3

Smell & Taste Experiment

Number Correct / Powdered Drink Flavors (Smell, Taste, Smell & Taste)

Cherry — Orange — Grape

The Forest on Film

Research to find out more about the tropical rain forests and their plight. It is time to take action. It is necessary to teach others about the importance of saving our disappearing rain forests.

Activity

In cooperative groups, create a slide show or film strip presentation about the problems and solutions associated with the tropical rain forests of the world.

Materials for Slides:

- one sheet of thermal transparency film
- 2" x 2" (5 cm x 5 cm) Slide Grid Sheet (page 313)
- 2" x 2" (5 cm x 5 cm) super slide frames (available at your local camera store)
- permanent markers
- overhead markers
- scissors
- slide projector
- thermocopy machine

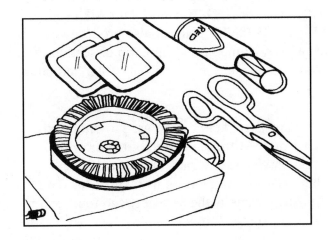

Directions for Slides:

1. Look at the 2" x 2" (5 cm x 5 cm) Slide Grid Sheet. The solid line portions of the squares are designed to be cut out and placed in the 2" x 2" super slide frame. The dotted portion of the square indicates the maximum area allowed for the message or picture that will be placed in the frame area.

2. Use a soft lead pencil to complete at least ten frames. You can use words and/or drawings on each frame. The pencil marks should be bold and clear. It may be necessary to darken the printing or drawing after the initial tracing.

3. When your frames are completed, use the thermocopy machine to produce a transparency.

4. Use permanent markers or overhead markers to color the completed frames.

5. Cut the transparency film on the solid lines of the grid and mount the printed material into a super slide frame. Load the slide frames into a projector and preview the product.

6. Show the slides to other classes to teach them about the plight of the disappearing rain forest.

Challenge:

Write a script for narrating each slide of your presentaion.

The Forest on Film *(cont.)*

Materials for Filmstrip:

- blank 35 mm film strip
- permanent markers

Directions for making filmstrips:

1. Since the filmstrip is a fixed sequence media, the images and words must be drawn in the proper sequence on the 35 mm film. A single length of 35 mm film must be used. This can be ordered from: Highsmith Co., Inc., W5527 Highway 106, P.O. Box 800, Fort Atkinson, WI, 53538-0800. You can also produce your own by washing an old filmstrip or section of film with a solution of one-half water and one-half bleach.

2. Permanent markers can be used to draw and write on the film. Location of the drawing area, known as the frame, is difficult since there are no frame divisions on the film The filmstrip frame is the area between four adjacent sprocket holes.

3. Make certain to leave enough empty frames to allow it to be loaded into the projector. Also, add a focus frame at the beginning.

Note the number of sprocket holes for each frame. There are no frame lines in blank 35 mm film.

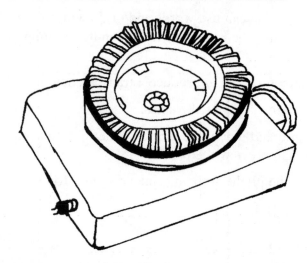

The Forest on Film *(cont.)*

Slide Grid Sheet

For the Love of Animals

Create a mini-zoo by adopting a class pet. Below is information on taking care of the three most common classroom pets. Read *Eye Openers: Pets* to children before selection process begins.

Goldfish

- 2-3 common or fantail goldfish
- large goldfish bowl
- aquarium gravel
- water (Make certain it is pure.)
- commercial fish food
- fish net

1. Place aquarium gravel in bottom of fishbowl approximately 1" (2.5 cm) thick.
2. Pour pure water (no chlorine) into fishbowl until 2" (5 cm) from rim.
3. Place purchased fish, still in purchased plastic bag of water, inside the bowl. (Bag will float near top.) Let float for 15 minutes, allowing the goldfish to become acclimated to water temperature in the fishbowl. Using a net, transfer the goldfish from bag to bowl. Feed fish a pinch of food once a day.
4. Change water once a week. (If fish are coming to the surface to breathe with mouths, change water immediately.) Pour small amount of current fish water into a plastic bag; add fish to bag with net; change water in bowl, including rinsing out gravel; then follow Step 3.

Gerbils

- two male or two female gerbils
- water bottle
- shallow, heavy dish for food
- exercise wheel
- gerbil litter
- commercial gerbil food*
- glass or plastic cage (An old aquarium with wire mesh "roof" works well.)
- hiding places (e.g., old baby shoe, empty tin can, etc.)

1. Line bottom of cage with thick layer of gerbil litter.
2. Place eating dish and drinking bottle in easy reach of gerbil's mouths.
3. Place exercise wheel and hiding place(s) in corners of cage.
4. Place gerbils in cage. Secure wire mesh or lid of cage well. (Gerbils like to get out.) Make sure gerbils always have water. Feed gerbils at the same time each day.
5. Change gerbil litter once a week, wiping out bottom of cage before adding fresh gerbil litter.

* Gerbils also like fresh carrots, sunflower seeds, lettuce, cabbage, apples, peas, and a little grass.

Rabbit

- newspaper
- hiding place (shoe box with opening)
- two heavy bowls (for food and water)
- rabbit and rabbit hutch (wire cage on wooden frame so cage is elevated off ground)
- commercial dry rabbit pellet food, piece of wood (for rabbit to gnaw on), fresh raw vegetables

1. Lay down newspaper (keep folded). Place frame on top of paper and cage on top of frame.
2. Place water/dry food in heavy bowls; put inside cage. Add hiding place and wood for gnawing.
3. Put rabbit in cage and secure door. Make certain rabbit always has water and dry pellets. Give fresh vegetables (favorites: carrots, lettuce, and dandelion greens) daily, but always take out leftovers at night. Change newspaper daily, too.

Insect or Not?

Background

Most students think that all bugs are insects. This experiment will help them realize that this is not true. They will start to appreciate the details that help to differentiate bugs and insects.

Objectives

- to learn the difference between bugs and insects
- to improve students' powers of observation and review the idea of classification

Student Instruction

Review the animal kingdoms, the general idea of classification, and how to put data in a table. Talk about the characteristics of insects: six legs, exoskeleton, and three body segments. Also discuss the characteristics of other closely related animals such as spiders, ticks, and centipedes. Talk about the differences between what we commonly refer to as bugs (any wingless or four-winged insect; mouthparts used for piercing and sucking) and insects (usually small invertebrates with an exoskeleton; adults have six legs, three body segments, and two pairs of wings).

Center Preparation

Materials: 8–12 plastic bugs

Directions: You will need to collect 8–12 small plastic bugs. Try to get an assortment of spiders, worms, ants, flies, beetles, centipedes, butterflies, and, if possible, a scorpion. These can often be purchased where novelties or party favors are sold or in the trinket machines found in grocery stores. Some students may own the toy that makes bugs by cooking liquid plastic and would be willing to make some for the class.

Label each specimen with a letter of the alphabet. To do the labeling, you can use a permanent marker and masking tape, or you can glue each plastic bug to an index card and label the card. Make sure all the legs are visible.

Follow-Up Activities

Talk about how to classify animals. Ask students what types of characteristics they could use to classify animals.

Let students develop their own classification systems by separating the set of bugs into groups that share common characteristics.

What Do Plants Need to Grow?

Once the children begin to plant and care for their own plants, they will begin to create hypotheses about the process. This activity uses controls to better help them form conclusions about how plants grow. If appropriate for the age group, they will then create multimedia slide shows telling what plants need to grow.

Materials:

- many books about plants
- seeds
- soil
- foam egg cartons or small containers to start seeds
- craft sticks
- watering can

Plant Reference Software
- Plants CD

Productivity Programs
- *Paint*
- *HyperStudio*
- *Kid Pix Studio*

Procedure:

Into: Before the Computer

- If students have not yet had the joy of planting, now is the time. Give each child a container, at least three seeds, some soil, and a craft stick.
- Help them put soil in the container, add the seeds, a little more soil, and water it well.
- Each child puts his name on the craft stick and inserts it into the soil.
- Put the containers into a dark room or closet until they germinate.
- Once the seedlings start to sprout, immediately bring them out of the closet and into a location where they will receive ample sunlight.
- At this point the children need to be sure to give the same amount of water to each plant every three days.

What Do Plants Need to Grow? *(cont.)*

Into: Before the Computer *(cont.)*

- There should be four extra containers for the controls:

    -One has no soil but receives same amount water and light as the rest.

    -One has soil and light but no water.

    -One has soil and water but is placed in a dark room or closet for the duration of the activity. (This one will germinate, but then it will wither and die.)

    -One has soil and water until germination; when taken out of the closet, it no longer receives any more water.

*For this example *HyperStudio* was used.

Through: On the Computer

- The children carefully care for their plants for about three weeks.
- After the children observe all of the plants, including the controls, generate some discussion as to what plants need to grow.
- The children will work in small groups to create a six-card stack telling what plants need to grow.
- The first card is the title card and has a bright, yellow sun drawn on it with the paintbrush tool. The title uses a text box which says, "Plants need light to grow," and the background is a light blue.
- The first card is the only one that has a button to click. It will play CNTRYSTP.WAV; this is a little song that will play throughout the entire six cards.
- The second card will have a mound of grass painted on it with a sun painted in a different position. (See the next page for a screen shot of all six cards.) The beginning of a stem can be painted in, as well as some brown soil around the stem. This card can then be copied four more times. The text box will say, ". . . and soil."
- The second through fifth cards will have invisible buttons and automatic timers to go to the next card after three seconds.
- Clouds and wind lines can be added to the third card with the words, ". . . and air."
- Add some darker blue spray can splotches for rain on the fourth card which says, ". . . and water."
- Just paint some leaves on the fifth card.
- And the sixth card finally gets the bright red, orange, or purple flower. This card's button will have applause and not go to any card.
- Naturally, there are many choices of buttons, paint colors, etc., when the children create their stacks. The above directions are merely suggestions.
- The children will probably want to share their stacks with parents and other classes. Sometimes the best part of creating is sharing with others.

What Do Plants Need to Grow? *(cont.)*

Beyond: Extra Activities

- If appropriate, plants can be planted on the school grounds.

- By integrating writing, the children could use the word processor to write "how to" paragraphs on what plants need to grow.

HyperStudio Stack

(*HyperStudio*, Roger Wagner Publishing)

Seeds

Question

Can plants be seriated?

Setting the Stage

- Show students a variety of fruits. Discuss similarities and differences in the fruits. Cut open the fruits to display their seeds. Observe the numbers of seeds in each fruit. In some fruits there may be only two seeds per fruit while in others there may be numerous seeds. Carrots produce only two seeds per fruit, while peas, beans, and citrus produce many. Tobacco, for example, produces as many as 40,000 seeds per fruit.

- Ask students to predict if the same type of fruit produces the identical number of seeds.

Materials Needed for Each Group

- a large bag of peas in the pod (If fresh peas are not in season in your area, then two large #303 cans of whole beans will provide enough beans for a class of thirty.)
- paper plate
- pencil
- sheet of notebook paper, one per student

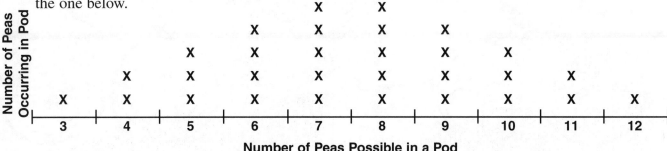

Procedure

1. After students make their predictions, pass out two pea pods to each student.
2. Instruct students to open each pod and count the number of peas in each.
3. Have students do this over a paper plate. It will prevent the peas from rolling off the table.
4. Ask students who found the most number of peas. Write the number on the board.
5. Ask students who found the least number of peas. Write that number on the board.
6. Have students record the range of peas found in their class, dividing the space into equal segments. For example, if the range of peas found was from 3-12, prepare a base line with equal segments labeled 3, 4, 5, 6, 7, 8, 9, 10, 11, 12.
7. After students have prepared their lines, open a pea pod and count the number of peas.
8. Have students put an X on their data-capture sheets above that number.
9. Have students repeat this for the second pea, the third, and so on.
10. When students have completed this, they will have constructed a bar graph with results similar to the one below.

```
                              X     X
                        X     X     X     X
                  X     X     X     X     X     X
            X     X     X     X     X     X     X     X
      X     X     X     X     X     X     X     X     X     X
    ──┼─────┼─────┼─────┼─────┼─────┼─────┼─────┼─────┼─────┼──
      3     4     5     6     7     8     9     10    11    12
```

Number of Peas Occurring in Pod (vertical axis)

Number of Peas Possible in a Pod

11. Tell students their results will lead to the following inductive thinking. If they were to pull another pod out of the bag, what is the most likely number of seeds you will find in the pod?

Seeds *(cont.)*

Extensions

- Have students repeat this activity with any other fruit that can be found in pods (e.g., apples, beans, citrus, or watermelon).
- Have students cut apples in half across the diameter, not from stem to blossom. Have them notice the star pattern of the seeds. Have them count the number of seeds. Ask them if all apples have the same number of seeds.

Closure

Have students bring seeds to school. Then in their plant journals, have them classify the seeds in as many ways as they can. Have them justify their classifications.

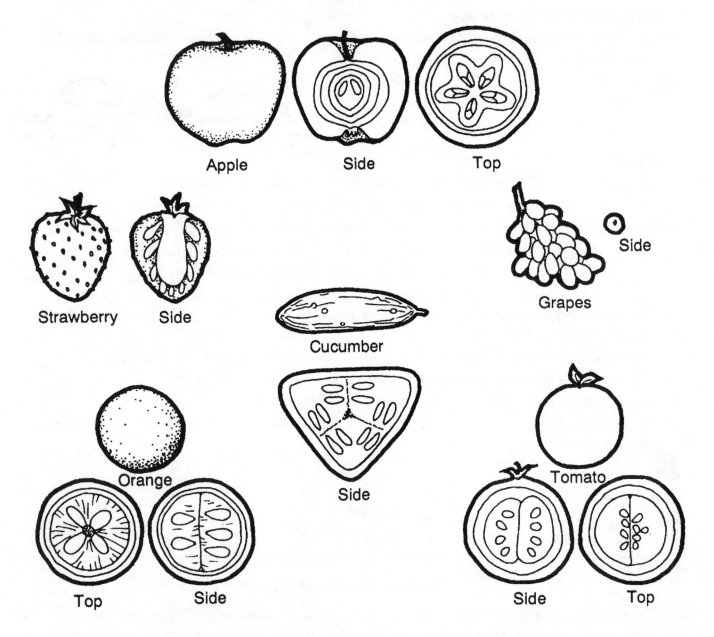

Apple   Side   Top

Strawberry   Side

Grapes   Side

Cucumber

Orange   Top   Side

Side

Tomato   Side   Top

Who Am I, and Why Am I Unique?

Question

Who am I, and why am I unique?

Setting the Stage

- In studying the aquatic environment, students become aware of the vast variety of animal life and the adaptations of each. Ask students to compile a list of their favorite sea animals.
- Ask students the following questions about their favorite animals. Why is it your favorite? Does it have any unusual characteristics? What does it feed on? What level of the sea does it live in?
- Play a guessing game called Who am I? Begin by giving students a few characteristics about a sea animal and letting them guess what the name of the animal is.

Materials Needed for Each Individual

- colored markers or crayons
- resource books for research
- sheet of notebook paper

Procedure

1. Conduct discussion suggested in Setting the Stage.
2. Have students research and complete information on their favorite sea animals.

Extensions

- Have the students play the guessing game using other animals from different environments. It is a quick assessment tool, and you can ascertain if further study is necessary.
- Have students draw underwater pictures with watercolors.

Closure

Have students make up their own guessing games, share them, and play them when they have extra time.

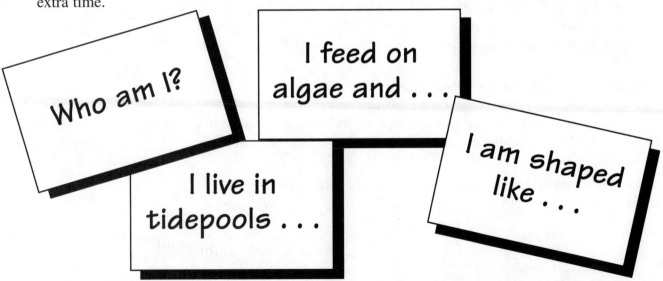

Designer Plant

Through a process called *photosynthesis*, green plants use sunlight to produce food. Trees and plants which are found in the canopy and emergent layers live in a sunnier and drier atmosphere than those found in the understory or forest floor. Plants found in the understory have adapted to less sunlight by developing broad flat leaves. Other plants absorb their food and nutrition directly from other plants. Therefore, they are not dependent on sunlight to survive.

Plants need nutrients to grow, and they receive these nutrients in a variety of ways. Many absorb them through their root systems; however, there are not many nutrients in tropical rain forest soil (they all wash away with the rain). Therefore, plants store most of the nutrients they need in their leaves and stems. Nutrients can also be found in a thin layer of decaying vegetation found on the forest floor. Epiphytes (ferns, bromeliads, orchids, etc.) trap falling bits of vegetation and water in their basket-like shapes.

Understory leaves stay wet, encouraging lichens, molds, and fungi to grow. Constantly wet leaves encourage this growth, which prevents the plants from getting their needed sunlight. To reduce this problem, many plants have drip tips (smooth leaves with points at the end where the water can drip off easily). Other plants have smooth, waxy leaves which help rid them of excess water.

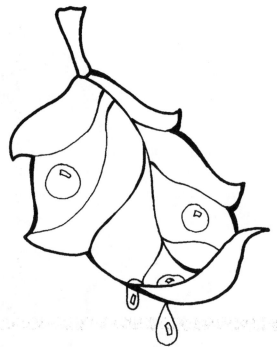

Due to the enormous height of many rain forest trees (65 feet/20 meters or taller), scientists believe that they have adapted a specialized root system. Special support-like buttress roots or stick-like stilt roots help keep the tree from being blown over by spreading the tree's ponderous weight.

Plants discourage leaf-eating insects and animals in unique ways. Some produce poisonous or foul tasting chemicals. Some have spines on their leaves or thorns on their stems, and some have developed symbiotic relationships with insects.

There are other ways to absorb water besides a plant's root system. An orchid's aerial roots can absorb moisture directly from the air around them. Bromeliad leaves grow in a basket-like shape where water can collect like a miniature pond. These miniature ponds provide an environment for a multitude of rain forest life.

Rain forest plants and trees depend upon animals, such as the fruit bat, for pollination. The wind also carries seeds for pollination.

Designer Plant *(cont.)*

Design and draw an original plant or tree that can survive in a tropical rain forest environment. As you create, consider the questions below. Label all of the parts. Then, on a separate piece of paper, answer the questions about your plant.

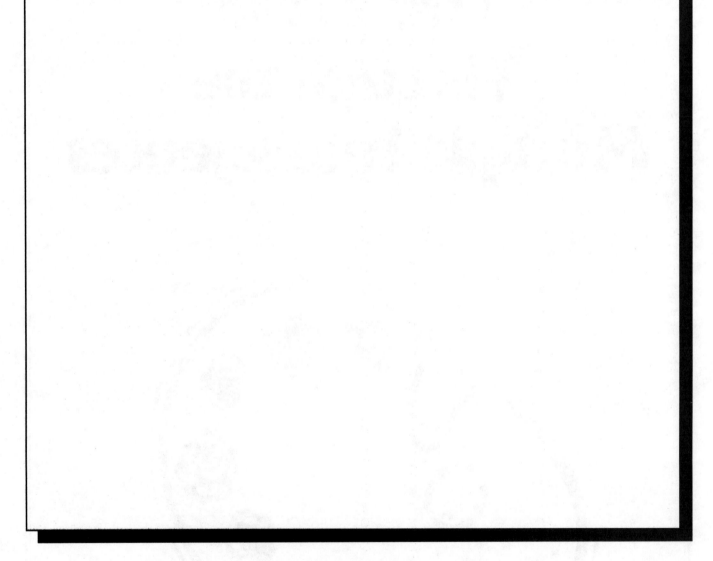

1. In which layer of the rain forest does your plant grow?

2. Tell about its leaves and root system.

3. How is it pollinated?

4. How does your plant receive its nutrients and water?

5. How does your plant get the sunlight it needs?

6. How does your plant defend itself from being eaten?

7. How does your plant defend itself against molds?

Teaching the Arts Through the Multiple Intelligences

Capital Art

Have you ever thought of letters as art? They are an art form. In the days before computers, artists would hand-letter advertisements. It was a careful and meticulous art form that required special skills. Today there are people who do *calligraphy*, a form of artistic lettering. This also requires special skill. You don't need to be a commercial artist or a calligrapher to enjoy letters as art. You can take the capital letters of your choice, maybe your initials, and see what you can do with them. Here are some ways:

- Perhaps the simplest thing you could do with your letters would be to write them next to each other and then see what kind of art you could form from the arrangement.

- In medieval times scholars created what was known as *illuminated manuscripts* where special letters were highly decorated. We don't often use such an ornate style today, but you can try something like the letter *F* shown here. Do you see why it might start the words for *Fourth of July*?

- Sometimes it's fun to form letters out of drawings of people bending, jumping, and joining hands, or animals might make interesting letters:

- You can also create doodle art using words or stringing the alphabet on a page:

Extension: Using a friend's name or a word like "Mommy" or "Grandpa," create art and frame it as a gift.

Capital Art *(cont.)*

Here are some letters that are waiting for a makeover. Can you turn them into a picture with your doodles?

Story Quilt

Purpose

After listening to *The Velveteen Rabbit* and other stories about favorite stuffed toys, each child will make a small piece of a story quilt. The story quilt will illustrate our most lovable stuffed toys.

Materials

- *The Velveteen Rabbit* or books about stuffed toys
- paste
- several stuffed animals
- 4" (10 cm) white construction paper squares
- crayons
- large banner – Our Favorite Stuffed Toys (pages 328 and 329)

Preparation

Using butcher paper or construction paper taped together, create an outline for children to put their quilt pieces together. At an area accessible to the children, place the quilt outline so children can glue their pieces to it. Use pages 328 and 329 to make a large banner. Enlarge it if possible. Color it. Display with the finished quilt.

Instructions

Each child takes a quilt piece. On it they draw and color their favorite stuffed toy. When finished, they paste it onto the large quilt in an outlined area.

Clean Up

Put all extra supplies away neatly and have children attach their quilt piece to the class quilt.

Helpful Hints

Story quilts can be made for any number of stories. They make an attractive bulletin board.

Story Quilt *(cont.)*

Story Quilt (cont.)

Quilt Stories

Goal: to share stories about quilts to see the roles they play in people's lives

Materials: a book that features quilts as part of the story (see list below), construction paper, crayons, tape

Directions: Choose a story that features quilts. Share it with the class. After reading the story, ask the children why the quilt was so important to the story. If possible, share a patchwork quilt with the students, pointing out the different squares. Many quilts have squares that are made from old items of clothing and may represent an important event in its creator's life.

Talk about story quilts and how they are made to tell a particular story. Let students know they will be making one. Have them, as a class, choose a favorite picture book. Read several stories to the children and then let them vote for the one they would like to create a story quilt for. Give each child an 8" (20 cm) construction-paper square. Have each child choose a scene to illustrate on the square, making sure to include his or her name on the square. Put the square together to create a quilt. An inch (2.5 cm) border of construction paper can be placed around the quilt. It can then be exhibited on the wall or can be displayed with the different quilt books and story it illustrates.

- *The Patchwork Quilt* by Valerie Flournoy. (Dial Books, 1985)
- *The Canada Geese Quilt* by Natalie Kinsey. (Dell, 1992)
- *Sam Johnson and the Blue Ribbon Quilt* by Lisa C. Ernst. (Lothrop, Lee and Shepard, 1983)
- *The Keeping Quilt* by Patricia Polacco. (Simon and Schuster, 1988)
- *The Quilt* by Ann Jonas. (Greenwillow, 1984)
- *The Quilt Story* by Tony Johnston. (Putnam, 1992)
- *The Josefina Story Quilt* by Eleanor Coerr. (Harper Collins, 1989)

Sensory Poems

Touching Hand Poems

Recreate on paper or the chalkboard the hand poem to the right. Read the poem with the students. Provide each student with a sheet of white construction paper on index paper. Have the students trace their hands on the construction paper with their fingers wide apart. Ask students to think of something special that their hands do, such as wave "hello" in friendship, paint a beautiful picture, help them to climb a tree, or play a sport, etc.

Next, have each student write a poem about his or her hand around the inside edges of the hand outline. Cut out the hand shapes. Display the hand poems along a classroom wall so that one hand touches another to form a border of "Touching Hand Poems."

Inside, Outside Sense Poems

Find a few poems that are rich in perceptual detail. After you read the poems to the class, have students discuss how each sense is used in the poems. Ask students to write poems based on their senses, using as the subject things that they hear, smell, taste, touch, and see inside the classroom, house, etc. Use the following "Inside Poem" example to demonstrate a sense poem.

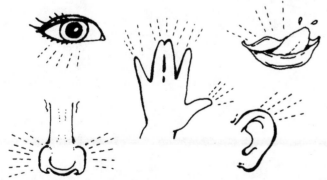

Inside Poem

Inside, I hear the thud of my brother's feet.

Inside, the smell of pizza floats across my desk.

Inside, I taste the sweetness of my gum.

Inside, I run my hand across my paper.

Inside, I see my mother going down the hall.

Read the poem and discuss how a different sense is introduced on each line. Have students write a few inside poems. Challenge them to write the poem without using the words "see," "hear," "feel," "touch," "taste," or "smell." When students have written some inside poems, ask them to write outside poems which express the use of their senses in an outdoor environment.

Assemble the students' sense poems into a class book.

The Language of Art

Aesthetic sensibility is the degree to which you are tuned into beauty and to its conditions, the degree to which you are aware of its principles—the concepts that help us define beauty. Aesthetic perception refers to learning to see the world metaphorically as well as directly. For example, a gun is a weapon for killing. It is also a symbol of brute power.

Aesthetic experience is an experience that you value for its sake alone. It can do nothing for you except please you for the duration of the experience. While it lasts, you are aware of the relationship between the form and content of the experience.

Have you ever heard anyone say, "I don't know much about art, but I know what I like?" The aesthetic experience is enhanced when you do know much about art, for in the knowing you become aware of principles of beauty and the relationship between form and content.

The following glossary of basic terms is printed on one side of your page so you can write, paraphrase, and draw the meaning of each term as it is used in visual art. Do not leave the space blank, for in responding to the terms, you learn to use them.

Basic Terms   ## Question, Paraphrase, Draw

Color is made up of hue, value, and intensity. When you see a color, your sensation depends on the reflection or absorption of light from a given surface.

Hue is determined by the specific wave length of the color in the ray of light. Every ray of light coming from the sun is composed of waves which vibrate at different speeds. The sensation of color which humans experience comes from the way our vision responds to different wave lengths. If a light beam passes through a triangular piece of glass (prism) onto a sheet of white paper, the rays of light will bend at different angles as they pass through the glass and will show up on the paper as color. Hue tells us the color's position in the spectrum.

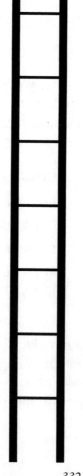

The Language of Art *(cont.)*

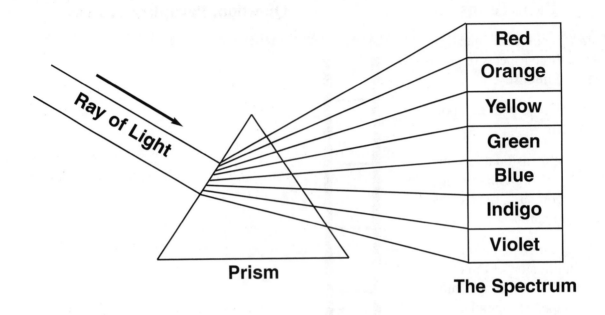

Prism

The Spectrum

Red
Orange
Yellow
Green
Blue
Indigo
Violet

Basic Terms

Value: the gradation of light and dark. It refers to the lightness or darkness of tone, the quantity of light, not the quality. In mixing colors we can produce a wide variety of tones by adding neutrals, black, or white.

Intensity: the saturation or strength of a color determined by the quality of light reflected from it. A vivid color is of high intensity. In the bright sunlight of the tropics, colors are intense. In the diffused light of northern climates, colors are less intense.

Analogous colors: those colors are closely related in hue, for analogies show relationships.

Question, Paraphrase, Draw

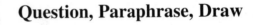

The Language of Art *(cont.)*

Basic Terms

Question, Paraphrase, Draw

Color Tonality: color schemes including the three aspects of color—hue, value, and intensity.

Line: an identifiable path of a point moving in space.

Shape: a two-dimensional area or plane that may be organic or inorganic, free-form or geometric, open or closed, natural or of human origin.

Form: a three-dimensional (or possessing the illusion of three dimensions) volume with the same qualities as shape. (Remember that volume has a lot more meanings than what you turn up for more sound.)

Form (another definition): the totality of the work of art; the organization (design) of all elements which make up the work; elements of form—line, shapes, values, textures, and colors.

Volume: any three-dimensional quantity that is bound or enclosed, whether solid or void.

Space: a volume available for occupation by form; an extent, measurable or infinite, that can be understood as an area or distance, one capable of being used negatively and positively.

Mass: the actual or implied physical bulk, weight, and density of three-dimensional forms occupying real or suggested spatial depth. How do you define mass in your science class?

The Language of Art *(cont.)*

Basic Terms

Question, Paraphrase, Draw

Texture: the surface quality of materials, either actual or visual.

Media, Medium: the materials and tools used by the artist.

Technique: the manner and skill with which the artist uses tools and materials—the ways that use of media affects aesthetic quality.

Representation: subject matter naturally presented; visual elements which look like actual forms.

Naturalism: all forms used by the artist appearing essentially representative.

Abstract, Abstraction: forms created by the artist abstracted, or "pulled out," from real objects; the essence of something. (There may be little or no resemblance to the original object.)

Balance: an equilibrium of similar, opposing, or contrasting elements that together create a unity.

Symmetry: a balance in which elements are alike and will appear to demand one another.

Asymmetry: a balance achieved through the use of unequal parts or elements.

Contrast: use of opposites in close proximity (light and dark, rough and smooth).

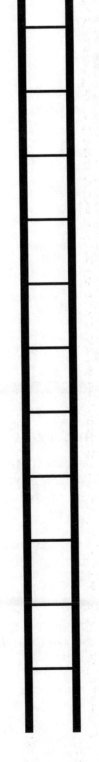

The Language of Art *(cont.)*

Basic Terms	**Question, Paraphrase, Draw**

Basic Terms

Dominance: the difference in importance of one aspect in relation to all other aspects.

Repetition: the recurrence of elements at regular intervals.

Rhythm: the regular repetition of particular forms or stresses and the suggestion of motion by recurrent forms.

Style: individual mode of expression and, in its genus, a family of characteristics when applied to a period of time or particular school of art.

Content (or form-meaning)**:** the final statement, mood, or spectator experience with a work of art; the significance of the art form.

Art Vocabulary Bee

1. Because your understanding of the words your teachers use in any field of learning has a direct effect on what or whether you learn, take a look now at your questions, drawings, or paraphrases and compare what you have with other members of your group. Discuss the meaning of each term. Come up with examples for each.

2. You can make a word yours for life if you use it three times—twice in speaking and once in writing. Take some time to use the art terms in meaningful ways in your speech and in another way in a written sentence.

3. Divide your class in two. Line up on both sides of the room. Appoint a scorekeeper. Have members of each team draw basic terms from a hat and attempt to explain them. Let your teacher be the final judge on whether or not you came close enough to stay in line.

Color by Number

Color this picture using the color key in the box.

1 = yellow	3 = blue	5 = green	7 = pink	9 = gray
2 = red	4 = orange	6 = purple	8 = brown	10 = black

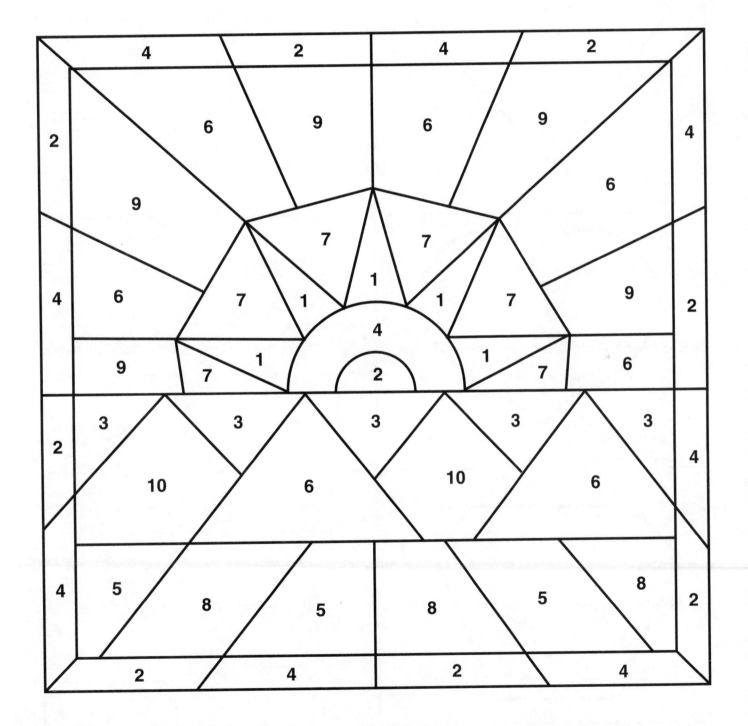

Shape Animals

Turn each of these shapes into an animal by adding more lines and shapes. Color the animals. Write a brief description of your newly created animal.

Animal Drawing　　　　　　　　　　　　**Animal Description**

Hidden Picture

Find the hidden picture.

Use the following colors for the numbers used in the picture puzzle: 1 = purple, 2 = yellow, 3 = green, 4 = blue, and 5 = black.

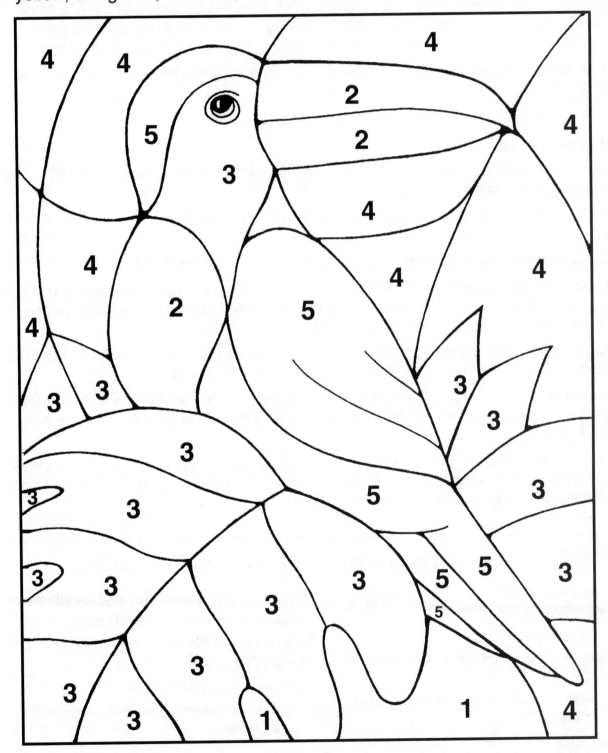

Mathematical Grid Egyptian Portraits

The painters of the famous temples and tombs in Egypt followed a strict set of rules to create their works of art. Have your students create colorful Egyptian portraits following these same guidelines.

Preparing for the lesson:

1. Gather for each student a sheet of graph paper with half-inch (1 cm) grids, a fine-point black marker, colored markers (including flesh colors), and gold and silver fine-point paint pens, available at art or office supply stores. You may wish to ask students to provide their own.

2. Make an overhead transparency of the seated and standing portrait example (page 341), showing the dimensions.

3. Gather other examples of portraits.

Teaching the lesson:

1. Tell students that they will be creating an Egyptian portrait, using the same methods and guidelines as the Ancient Egyptians.

2. Display portrait examples with dimensions. Point out the specific dimensions and copy the chart below onto the chalkboard for reference.

3. Have students review many different samples to get ideas for their portraits.

4. Distribute the graph paper. Have students decide to each make a seated or standing figure. (The standing figure is easiest!) Have students mark and label their graph papers with the proper dimensions as shown on the overhead transparency.

5. Check to make sure students' graph paper is properly labeled and then have students sketch their figures in pencil. Circulate around the room and offer help as needed.

6. When students have completed their sketches, check them. If they are okay, have them outline the sketches in permanent black marker. Have students trace their outlines onto white copy paper before coloring.

7. Have students add details, an Egyptian-design border, and color their drawings. Have students choose color schemes that use no more than five colors on their entire portraits. The background color will need to be a contrasting color not used on the figure.

Egyptian Portrait Grid Chart

1 square = the width of the fist of the figure

18 squares = wig line/forehead to the soles of the feet

3 squares = sole of the foot to the middle of the calf

3 squares = middle of the calf to just above the knee

3 squares = just above the knee to the wrist

3 squares = wrist or mid-figure to the elbow

3 squares = elbow to the shoulders

3 squares = shoulders to the wig line/forehead

2 squares = the face

3 squares = length of the foot

5 squares = shoulders to approximately the waistline

Mathematical Grid Egyptian Portraits *(cont.)*

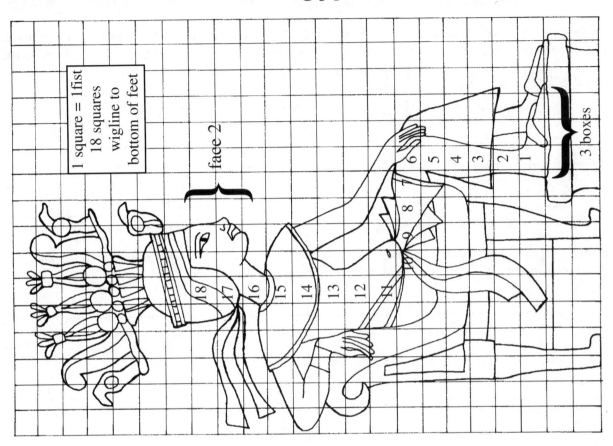

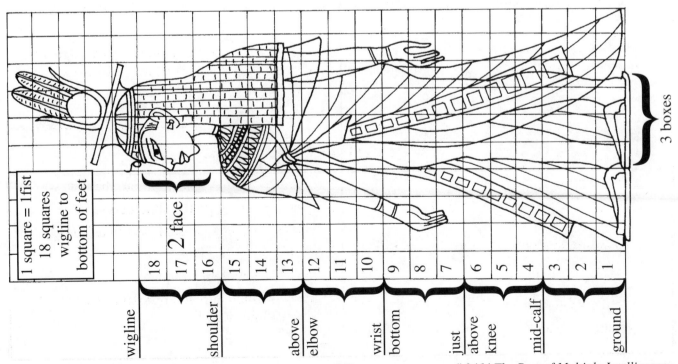

Tessellations

A tessellation is a design that uses interlocking shapes to fill a plane, as in a mosaic. Tessellations cover a plane and have no gaps or overlaps in the design. When a design is created in this way, the process is referred to as "tessellating" or "tiling" the plane. Tessellations can be made using various geometric shapes, block letters, or organic shapes.

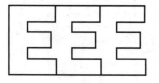 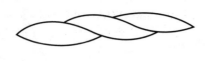 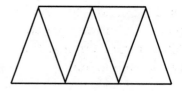

Directions: In each space below, create a tessellation. Use geometric figures in the first space, a block letter in the second space, and your own ideas in the other four blocks.

geometric figure	block letter

Dream Catchers

Dream catchers are special objects created by Native Americans to catch good dreams. Many dream catchers are circles woven with yarn or string to create a net inside. Special beads, shells, rocks, and feathers can be added to the net. Here is an example of a dream catcher.

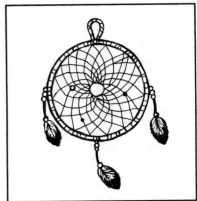

Design a dream catcher pattern in the circle below. Use an interesting geometric pattern that could be used as a template for an actual dream catcher. Follow the pattern you designed to make your own dream catcher using a circular frame, string or yarn, and decorative materials to give it a unique look.

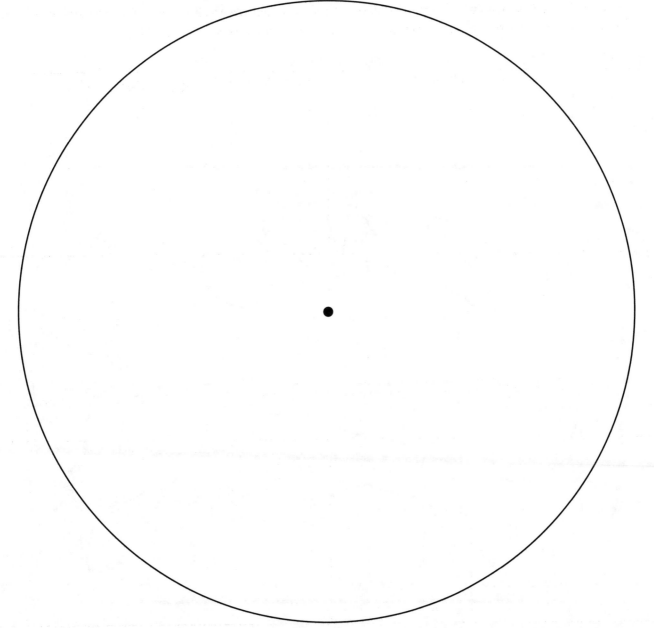

Limbo-Dancing: A West Indies Dance

Goal: to challenge children to move in an awkward but fun way to perform a task (moving under the bar)

Materials: two high-jump standards, a bamboo pole or high jump crossbar, music is optional

Directions: The limbo is a challenging dance-type activity that comes from the West Indies. The object is to bend/lean backwards from the waist and move under the bar pole. The bar is then lowered. Students are eliminated for not making it underneath, touching the pole, having parts of the body touch the floor, or not going under the bar the correct way. The unacceptable ways to do the limbo-bending are going under, ducking under, and touching the ground. Adding lively music, preferably from the West Indies, will keep the game moving.

Extensions: Set up two limbo poles and form two teams. The team who has the most members still playing at the end is the winner.

The Tarantella

Goal: to help children develop an appreciation for the dance and music of another country—Italy; to dance the tarantella

Materials: recording of the tarantella (The cassette or compact disk of *All the Best from Italy*, *Volume 3* features "La Danza Tarantella." It is available at record stores.) tape or compact disc players, tambourine (optional)

Directions: Share the story behind the tarantella. It gets its name from the city of Taranto in Italy. It is believed that the people danced this dance as a cure for a tarantula bite. Therefore the dance is very light and lively.

Teach the basic step. Begin by stepping to the right on your right foot. Hop on it. Repeat this basic step on your left side. Practice this. When it feels comfortable, do the step-hop on the right, and then swing your left foot over the right. Repeat on the other side. Now add arm movements. Hold arms straight up over the head. When moving to the left, bend them a little to the left; when moving to the right, bend a little to the right. There are many variations for performing this dance. Let children try these with partners. They may move forward and backward of hop on one foot. Let them try some heel-toe movements, runs, or skips.

Tambourines can be used while dancing the tarantella. Shake them and then bang them in rhythm to the movement.

Puppetry

Here are some easy puppets you can make!

Materials:

- old socks
- cardboard
- white glue
- newspaper
- rubber bands
- pieces of felt
- fabric scraps

- handkerchiefs, bandanas, scarves
- googly eyes
- markers, paint (tempera)
- cardboard tubes (from toilet paper and paper towels)
- scissors
- paper towels (plain white or tan colored)

You can make almost any kind of puppet from an old sock. Here's how to make a funny dragon:

1. Cut a circle about 4–6 inches (10–15 cm) in diameter out of cardboard and fold it in half.

2. Apply glue in a circle around the outer edge.

3. Push the circle into the sock, all the way to the end, with the glued edges facing the toe.

4. Push in the toe of the sock so it sticks to the glued circle and let dry. This will form the dragon's mouth.

5. Roll up two balls from newspaper, about one inch (2.54 cm) across, and push them into the heel of the sock. These will form the dragon's eyes.

6. Wrap rubber bands around the base of the newspaper balls to form eyes that stick up. Glue on googly eyes.

7. Cut felt scales and glue them on the dragon's back.

8. Cut a red tongue and put it in the dragon's mouth.

Puppetry *(cont.)*

Paper tubes are also good for making lots of different kinds of puppets. Here's how to make a wizard.

1. Cut a piece of cardboard tube about 2–3 inches (5–8 cm), depending on what you will make.
2. Tear a paper towel into pieces.
3. Mix together 3 tablespoons of white glue and 3 tablespoons of water.
4. Dip the paper towel pieces into the glue mixture and cover the outside of the tube with them.
5. Dip some more pieces of paper towel to make shapes like a nose and ears.
6. After it dries, use markers to draw the eyes, eyebrows, and mouth.
7. Out of cardboard, cut a cone-shaped hat, curl it into shape and tape it. Then glue it to the top of your wizard's head.
8. If you wish, you can decorate the hat with star stickers.
9. Drape a colorful handkerchief, bandana, or scarf over your hand. Put a rubber band around your little finger and the fabric and another rubber band around your thumb and the fabric. These will be the wizard's hands. Your middle three fingers, covered by fabric, go into the tube for the wizard's head.

To make a puppet stage:

1. Drape a sheet from a tabletop to the floor.
2. Puppeteers sit behind the table, hidden by the sheet.
3. Puppeteers raise hands to move puppets across the stage floor (tabletop).
4. Pin or attach stage decorations to the wall behind the table.

Once you have a set and some puppets, it's time to write a puppet play. Brainstorm for ideas and, if you want, you can outline your script by making Roman numeral I the beginning, II the middle, and III the end. Fill in the details of your outline and you'll have a basic script; you just need to add dialogue. Be sure to speak loudly and clearly when your puppet is speaking. You'll be hidden behind the stage so it will be harder to hear you. Also be sure to move your puppet when it is speaking.

At the library you will find books that tell how to make many more kinds of puppets and marionettes, too. Just about any story will make a good puppet show, but you can also find books in the library that have plays written especially for puppet presentation.

Pantomime

Pantomime is acting without speaking. All the information, the emotion, and the action have to be seen in your silent movements. When you pantomime, you must pay particular attention to your body motions and facial expressions. You might want to exaggerate your expressions, and you definitely want to have fun. Choose several ideas to pantomime from the following list.

◆ You are peeling onions.

◆ Your shoes are too tight.

◆ You ate much too much.

◆ You are washing a very large window.

◆ You are outside, and it is very hot.

◆ You are walking through mud.

◆ You see someone walk by, and you instantly fall in love.

◆ You feel a bug crawling down your back.

◆ You are going horseback riding for the first time.

◆ You are eating a very sour lemon.

◆ You just ate a large spoonful of peanut butter.

◆ You have a piece of cellophane stuck on your finger (and later stuck on your foot).

◆ You are walking across the room on a tightrope.

◆ You are chewing about six pieces of bubble gum.

◆ You are trying to start your motorcycle.

◆ You are just getting settled into your favorite chair after a hard day, and a fly lands on your nose.

◆ You are eating a watermelon on a hot day.

◆ You are making a snowman.

◆ You are at one end of the rope in a tug-of-war contest.

◆ You are in a small room with a skunk.

◆ You are sleeping and having a really good dream when your alarm goes off.

◆ You are sitting on a park bench enjoying your lunch when you realize that a snake is resting on the same bench.

◆ You are in-line skating through a crowd.

◆ You are the passenger in a car, and the driver is driving recklessly.

Work in groups of 2 to 3 students to list more pantomime activities to perform for the class.

Mystery Animal

Draw exactly what you see from the numbered boxes above into the same numbered boxes below to form this picture.

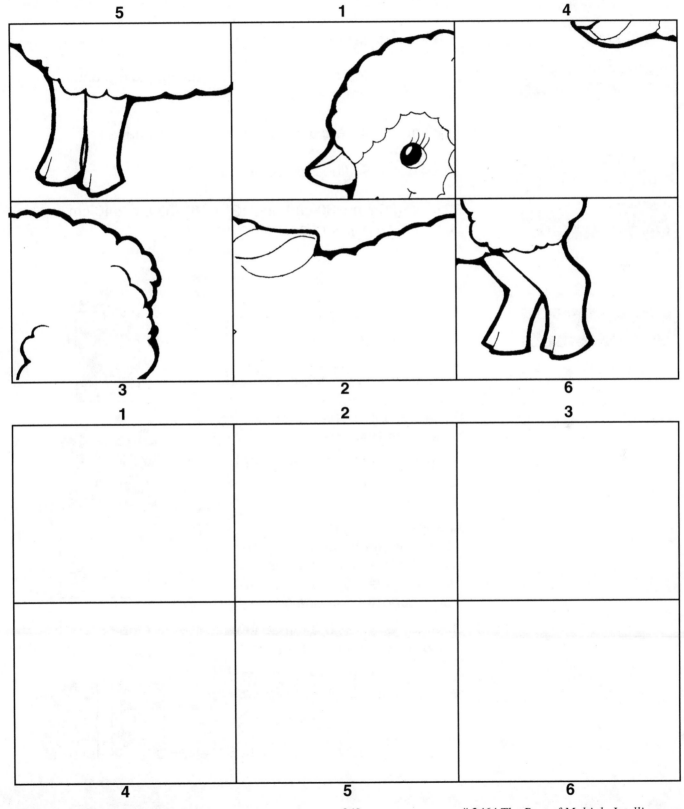

Masterpiece: *Beasts of the Sea* by Henri Matisse

Concept: **Shape**

Grade: **Second**

Lesson: **Cut out paper patterns**

Objectives:

1. Students will increase their skills in cutting, gluing, and arranging a composition.

2. Students will create a design using organic shapes.

Vocabulary: organic, curved lines, diagonal

Materials: 9" x 12" (23 cm x 30 cm) and 12" x 18" (30 cm x 46 cm) construction paper of contrasting colors
glue
scissors
pencil

Process:

1. Fold the 9" x 12" (23 cm x 30 cm) paper in half like a book.

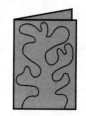

2. Draw a curved line that starts on the bottom edge of the paper and winds around and curves upward to the top half of the paper and back to the bottom edge.

3. Cut on this line while the paper is still folded into the double thickness. Save all pieces.

4. Arrange the two pieces that are cut out into the large paper which has been folded into fourths. Place one piece in each corner that is opposite diagonally.

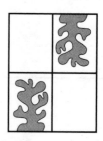

5. Open the 9" x 12" (23 cm 30 cm) folded paper and cut on the fold.

6. Arrange these two pieces in the remaining two diagonal corners.

7. Glue desired arrangements in place.

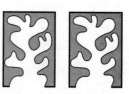

Masterpiece: *Beasts of the Sea* by Henri Matisse (cont.)

Evaluation:

A. Did the student understand the concept introduced?

B. Did the student show creativity in creating their organic shape?

C. Did the student arrange shapes to create a successful composition?

Quilt Puzzles

Materials:

- white paper
- scissors
- crayons or markers
- plastic zipper bags
- glue
- oaktag

Directions:

1. Make several quilt blocks, each about 8" (20 cm) square. Create several designs for the class. Draw only the black outlines of these blocks, leaving the interior of each space blank. Duplicate these quilt block patterns in sets of two so that each student will have two of the same kind.

2. Give each student two blank quilt blocks. Although you will use a variety of blocks within the class, be sure that each student works on two duplicate blocks.

3. Tell the students that they may use markers or crayons to color their blocks, but the blocks must be colored symmetrically. Both quilt blocks should be colored in the exact same way.

4. When the blocks have been colored, mount one of each onto oaktag for durability. The students' names should be written on the backs of these blocks.

5. Put the mounted blocks into a file folder for safekeeping. These will become answer keys for the students.

6. Cut the remaining quilt blocks into puzzles. Your cuts can be random or straight across panels. Make your cuts as intricate as you feel your class can manage. Put the puzzle pieces that go together into plastic zipper bags for safekeeping.

7. Allow the students to exchange bags and to reassemble the blocks to look like the originals. Students can go to the file when finished to see if they are correct in their placement of pieces.

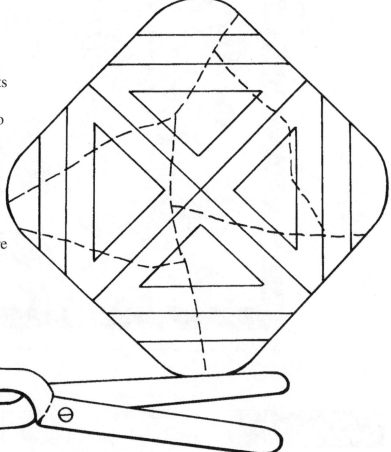

Scribble Art

In the space below draw a scribble pattern. Look in your scribble pattern and see if you spot any shapes of people, animals, or other objects. Turn your paper to help find an object or objects. Color in the objects and add details to help others see them too.

King Tut's Mummy Mask

Draw the other half of the mummy mask. Outline the mask with permanent black marker and color it with markers and paint pens. Cut out your mask and glue it onto black construction paper to display. Write your name on the back.

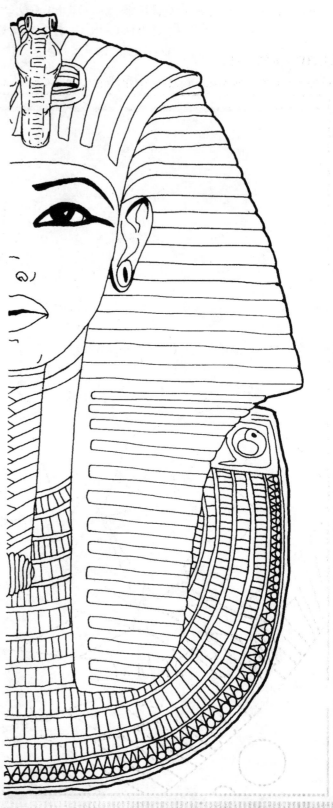

Rhapsody in Color

One of George Gershwin's most famous compositions is "Rhapsody in Blue." Create your own "Rhapsody in Color" with the illustration on this page. Use only one color and its various tints and shades to complete the picture. Share your creative "rhapsody" with the class.

Rhapsody in _____

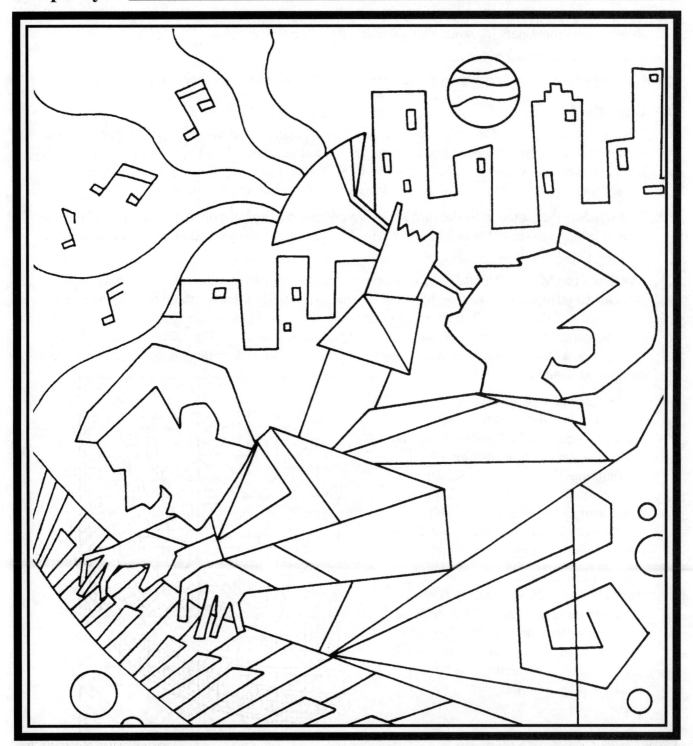

Make a Mosaic

Have students create paper mosaics using techniques developed by the Romans. Students will create individual mosaic panels that combine to form a large mosaic to display on a bulletin board.

Preparing for the lesson:

1. Reproduce a Mosaic Panel (page 357) for each student onto gray construction paper. Trim the edges so that each panel is a square.

2. Cut $\frac{1}{2}$" (1 cm) squares of white and at least four other colors of construction paper. Place the squares into containers for students to share.

3. Gather glue and scissors for each student.

4. Gather pictures of mosaics from books, and make a sample mosaic panel yourself as a sample.

Teaching the lesson:

1. Display the examples of mosaics. Note that many Roman mosaics were intricate portraits and scenes created on the floors of homes, temples, and other public buildings. Ask students if they have ever seen a mosaic and what it looked like. Today, most mosaics are created from pieces of tile set into mortar to form pictures and designs. This technique is similar to the Roman mosaics.

2. Tell students that sometimes the mosaics were created on smaller panels and then combined to form a larger mosaic. This is what they will do as a class, only instead of tile and mortar they will use paper and glue.

3. Distribute the Mosaic Panels, glue, scissors, and paper squares to students. (You may want students to push their desks together to share materials easily.) Have students write their names on the back of the panel. Tell students to use only white squares on the sections labeled "white" on their patterns. They may use any color and pattern on the rest. The white border will help incorporate all of the panels so that it looks like one large mosaic when completed. Show your completed sample.

4. Encourage students to cover only a small area with glue, then cover the glue with colored squares. The squares should be close together but not touching or overlapping. They may use scissors to cut the squares to a different shape to make it fit the pattern outline. All portions of the mosaic panel should be covered with paper when finished.

5. Let the mosaic panels dry. Then arrange them all on a bulletin board to form a large square or rectangle. Use strips of white paper to make a border around the entire mosaic. If bulletin board space is not available, line them above the chalkboard as a border.

Make a Mosaic *(cont.)*

Mosaic Panel

Three Little Pigs Rap

by Lynn DiDominicis

Once upon a time in a land far away
There were three little pigs   *three little pigs*
They went to seek their fortune and soon they found
They had to find a way to build a house.
Had to find a way to build a house.

The first little pig just scratched his jaw
And found a man selling a load of straw
Found a man selling a load of straw
Worked real hard to build his house
When the wolf came by and said, "Let me in!"
Wolf came by and said, "Let me in!"
"No, no, no," said the little pig,
"Not by the hair of my chinny chin chin."
"Not by the hair of my chinny chin chin."
So he huffed   *so he huffed*
And he puffed   *and he puffed*
And he blew the house in.

And he blew the house in.
The second little pig was in a fix
Until he found a man with a bundle of sticks
Until he found a man with a bundle of sticks
Worked real hard to build his house
When the wolf came by and said, "Let me in!"
Wolf came by and said, "Let me in!"

Three Little Pigs Rap *(cont.)*

"No, no, no," said the little pig,
"Not by the hair of my chinny chin chin."
"Not by the hair of my chinny chin chin."
So he huffed　　　*So he huffed*
And he puffed　　　*And he puffed*
And he blew the house in.
And he blew the house in.

The third little pig was out of tricks
When he met a man selling a pile of bricks
Met a man selling a pile of bricks
Worked real hard to build his house
When the wolf came by and said, "Let me in!"
Wolf came by and said, "Let me in!"
"No, no, no," said the little pig,
"Not by the hair on my chinny chin chin."
"Not by the hair on my chinny chin chin."
So he huffed　　　*So he huffed*
And he puffed　　　*And he puffed*
And he couldn't blow the house in.
Couldn't blow the house in.

Into the chimney　　　*Into the chimney*
Wolf went in a flash　　　*Wolf went in a flash*
Ended his life　　　*Ended his life*
With a thud and a splash　　　*With a thud and a splash*

The moral of the story is clear to see
The moral of the story is clear to see
Build your house of bricks, you'll never have to flee.
Build your house of bricks, you'll never have to flee.
Oh, yeah Oh, yeah
Oh, yeah Oh, yeah
Oh, yeah Oh, yeah

Using Sound to Create a Classroom Band

Blowing Instruments

Straw Flute and Trumpet

Materials: drinking straw; paper cup, scissors

Directions: Flatten the first 2 inches (5 cm) on the straw. Snip off the corners of the flattened end with scissors.

To Play: Blow into straw to make a flute-like sound. The pitch of the flute will depend on the length of the straw.

To make a straw trumpet, prepare the straw the same way, but insert the straw into the bottom of a paper cup.

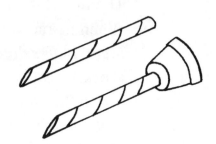

Comb Kazoo

Materials: hair comb, rubber band, wax paper, scissors

Directions: Wrap wax paper around a comb and fasten it with a rubber band.

To Play: Hold the kazoo up to your lips and hum gently while pursing your lips and letting them vibrate against the paper.

Tube Kazoo

Materials: toilet tissue or paper towel tube; scissors; wax paper; rubber band

Directions: Cover one end of the tube with a 4" (10 cm) square of wax paper. Use rubber band to hold paper in place. Punch three holes in a row, about 1" (2.5 cm) apart, lengthwise along one side of the tube.

To Play: Blow into tube. Change notes by covering and uncovering the holes with fingers.

Design Your Own Instrument

Design a new instrument. It should make sound when you strike it, blow through it, or pluck it. Draw a picture of your instrument. Label its parts. Write directions on how to make your musical instrument. Describe the sound your instrument makes. Explain why it works.

Do-It-Yourself Sing Along

Materials:

- blank tape for each child
- tape recorder
- your own class's favorite songs

What to Do:

This transition activity allows you to use the songs you sing every day in your classroom in a taped format. This will make sing-alongs possible in which you do not always have to lead. It will also provide a transition activity that will give the children in your class a chance to take a break between activities, singing some of their favorite songs. Also, this tape makes an excellent way to get parents involved with what is happening at school and gives parents and children a great at-home activity that helps to create a bond between home and school.

Before this activity, think about how you want to make this tape. You can make the singing tape very informally, or rehearse, as you wish. You can simply flip on a tape recorder every time your class sings a song, or you can have someone play a piano and sing the tunes into the recorder in a rehearsed fashion. Do whatever you feel comfortable with and whatever will be most enjoyable for you. One idea is to teach songs to children and let them make the tape. Not only is it fun for the children, but it will make a wonderful keepsake for parents once they have used it as an activity at home with their children.

What to Say:

Today we are going to make a tape of ourselves singing our favorite songs. Then, after we are done with it, we will hear ourselves sing. Now, if we really like it, we can make extra copies of this tape and give them to your mommies and daddies. This will be a really neat way to be able to sing our favorite songs whenever we want to. What song shall we try first? (Teacher models the process with children and records songs, etc.)

Variations:

1. Use completed tapes for a fundraiser. Many parents would love to support your school by buying a live taped version of their children singing.

2. Present tapes to a convalescent home or a retirement home. It is a great way to build a relationship between some seniors and the children in your class, and the seniors will love it.

Keeping the Beat

Stravinsky's use of dissonance and rhythms in pieces such as *The Rite of Spring,* helped make him one of the most influential composers of the 20th century. In his works, percussion instruments often drove the pace and created the excitement.

The percussion instruments are a family of instruments that usually make their sound by being struck, shaken, or scraped. These instruments had their beginning thousands and thousands of years ago in the Stong Age. Through the centuries, more and more percussion instruments were developed. Today, we have a growing family of percussion instruments.

Activity

You can create many simple percussion instruments out of supplies you have at home or at school. Here are just a few.

Sand Block (Scrape)

Sand blocks can be made from the following materials: 2 small blocks of wood (about 2" x 3" x 1" or 5 cm x 8 cm x 2.5 cm); sandpaper; tacks or staples; scissors; empty thread spools; glue. Measure and cut the sandpaper to fit each block so that it almost wraps around the block. Staple or tack the sandpaper to the block as shown. Glue a thread spool to each block to from handles. Allow the glue to dry thoroughly. To use the sand blocks, rub the blocks together to the rhythm of the music.

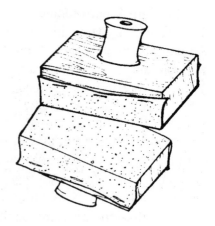

Maracas (Shake)

Make a pair of maracas from these materials: 2 clean and dry soda pop can; 2 unsharpened pencils; tape; markers; glue; a hammer; a large nail. Have an adult use a hammer and nail to punch a hole in the center of the bottom of each soda pop can. Poke the end of the pencil through the hole in the top of the can so that the end of the pencil sticks out no more than 1/2" (1.2 cm). To prevent the ends of the pencil from slipping out of the can, secure them with tape. Decorate the maracas with markers.

Drum (Strike)

To make a drum, you will need to the following materials: oatmeal or ice cream container (with lid); paint or markers; glue; scissors; string or heavy yarn; wooden spoon. Decorate the container with paint or markers. Punch two holes near the tope of the container. To make a strap for carrying the drum, cut a three-foot (1 meter) length of yarn or string and thread it through the holes. Tie the ends together inside the drum. Place the lid on the drum and you are ready to use it. A wooden spoon can serve as a drumstick.

Move With the Music

In Munich in 1924, Carl Orff began a school that mirrored what he thought possible and necessary for the musical education of children. In his school music was combined with the motion of dance and gymnastics.

Activity

One of the most enjoyable ways to experience music is to move with it.

Here are some ideas to put you in motion! Remember, of course, that when you move to music, people and property are not to be harmed!

- Explore the movements that come naturally to you as you hear a selected piece of music and do what the music makes you feel like doing.

- Listen to music with different tempos and moods. Create a movement reaction to each piece. Try to tell the story of the music in the way you move.

- If you are in a safe place, dance barefoot! Your complete range of movement will not be limited by shoes.

- Dance in groups, working together to create movements that are in unison (the same) and individualistic (different) to communicate the feeling of the music.

- Combine movements from gymnastics (such as forward rolls and cartwheels) or dance (such as pirouettes and leaps) with music. Move only with the strongest beats of the music, creating a type of "freeze" dancing.

- Add a scarf or ribbon to your movements.

See how many composers and their pieces you can remember with more ease because you move to them! Most of all, have fun!

Instruments

Mardi Gras, or Carnival as it is called in South America, is a very loud, raucous event. Laughing and talking are everywhere, as are the sounds of music.

Create your own Mardi Gras instruments by following the directions here and on the next page.

Drum

Materials:

- coffee can with plastic lid
- construction paper
- glitter
- glue or tape
- scissors
- drumstick (See step # 5.)

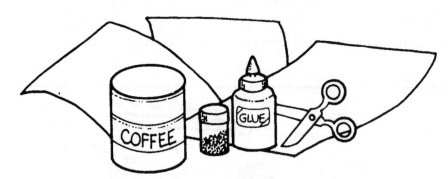

Directions:

1. Cut the paper so that it fits around the can. Glue it in place.
2. Draw designs with glue on the paper. **(Hint:** Do not make your lines of glue too thick because the glue will run.)
3. Sprinkle glitter over the wet glue and let the drum dry.
4. Put the lid on the can. Strike either end of the drum with your hand or a drumstick (see next step).
5. To make a drumstick, use one of the following:

    pencil with a large eraser
    pencil with a metal nut on the end
    coat hanger section with a cork on the end
    dowel with a wooden bead on the end

Shaker

Materials:

- two paper plates
- hole punch
- yarn
- crayons
- dry macaroni, beans, or peas

Directions:

1. Place the plates on top of one another.
2. Make holes ¹/₂" (1 cm) apart around the plate edges. Be sure to punch holes in both plates at the same time.
3. Decorate the outside of each plate.
4. Put 2 tablespoons (30 mL) of the dry food in one of the plates.
5. To sew the plates together, tape one end of the yarn to form a point. This will make the sewing easier.
6. Place the plates on top of each other, tops facing inward. Sew them together by going around from the bottom up on every stitch.
7. After sewing around the plates, tie a sturdy knot between the two yarn ends and trim any excess

Sectional Activities

1. Franz Schubert often drew inspiration for his music from poems. Poems became the lyrics, or words, for his songs. Have students examine the lyrics to familiar songs. Note that some, like "The Sidewalks of New York" or "Arkansas Traveler," tell stories, while others, like "Black Is the Color," create a mood. Yet these and many other songs have one thing in common: their verses are written in poetic form. Have the class write a poem and set it to music with a simple but familiar song or ask students to create their own melodies for the new lyrics!

2. Johannes Brahms was inspired to write the *Liebeslieder Waltzes* by the waltzes he heard in Vienna. The waltz is a dance form that goes back hundreds of years, originating in southern Germany and Austria. A number of composers, such as Johann Strauss, Richard Strauss, and Brahms, honor it in their music.

   Although it is still quite popular today, many students are probably unfamiliar with the waltz. Students can experience this dance form as they listen to some of the waltzes of the romantic era. If students are not amenable to dancing in pairs, have them form rows to learn the waltz steps (similar to a "line dance" arrangement). If possible, show segments from classic movies which feature the Viennese waltz or give students "a taste of the times."

   Unlike most other types of dance music, the waltz reflects triple time and is easy to recognize when we hear it. Have students count in they rhythm:

   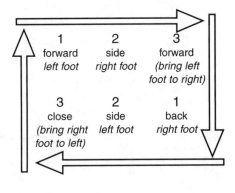

1 - 2 - 3, 1 - 2 - 3, 1 - 2 - 3

   There are several popular versions of the waltz. On the right is the basic pattern of the box waltz. Enlarge the pattern on a chart or chalk board. Have the students practice the box waltz as they listen to *Liebeslieder Waltzes* by Brahms or *The Blue Danube* by Johann Strauss.

3. Introduce students to music for the ballet with Tchaikovsky's *Swan Lake, Sleeping Beauty,* and *The Nutcracker*. If possible, obtain videotapes of the actual ballet so that students can see the relationship of the dance movement to the music.

Suggested Listening

Composer Franz Schubert: *The Winter Journey; Hark, Hark, the Lark!; Symphony in B Minor* (The Unfinished Symphony); *Trout Quintet; Ninth Symphony in C Major* (The Great)

Composer Robert Schumann: *Papillons* (Butterflies); *Carnaval; Piano Concerto in A Minor;* any of his *lieder,* such as *Widmung* ("Dedication")

Composer Clara Wieck Schumann: *Piano Concerto; Theme and Variations; Completely Clara* (a collection of Clara's most popular pieces)

Composer Franz Liszt: *Hungarian Rhapsodies; Les Preludes; Concerto in E-flat Major*

Composer Johannes Brahms: "How Lovely Is Thy Dwelling Place" from *A German Requiem; Academic Festival Overture; Symphony Number One; Liebeslieder Waltzes*

Composer Peter Ilich Tchaikovsky: *1812 Overture; The Nutcracker; Swan Lake; Children's Album; Sleeping Beauty; Piano Concerto in B-flat Minor*

Making Masks

Goal: to give children the opportunity to create their own masks

Materials: paper bag, paper or aluminum plates, paint, scissors, glue or tape, bits of foil, yarn or other decorative materials, hole punch, pencil

Directions: Have each child choose the kind of mask they would like to make, such as a Native American or African, or one that he or she feels represents him or her. Masks may be made out of paper bags or paper or aluminum plates. Decorations might include wool, shells, yarn, or feathers. Have children draw on the mask or cut out and glue or tape the decorations onto it. If children are going to wear the masks, help them determine where the eye holes will go. To wear the masks, have them poke a hole using a hole punch or pencil and tie yarn around their heads.

Making Masks *(cont.)*

Mask Pattern

Photo Album

Materials:

- 12" x 18" (30 cm x 45 cm) colored construction paper (2–3 sheets)

- scissors

- stapler or hole punch and yarn

- crayons or markers

- glue and/or photo corners

Directions:

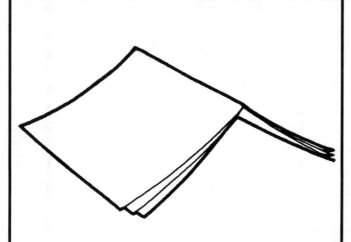

1. Stack the paper and fold it in half.

2. Staple down the fold or punch holes and string yarn.

3. Decorate the front, including your name. Write something important about yourself.

4. Fill in the album with photos or drawings that say something special about you. You may include a few sentences with each photo or drawing that explain its importance.

Your Favorite Instrument

Which instrument do you like best? Use the space below to draw a picture of yourself playing that instrument.

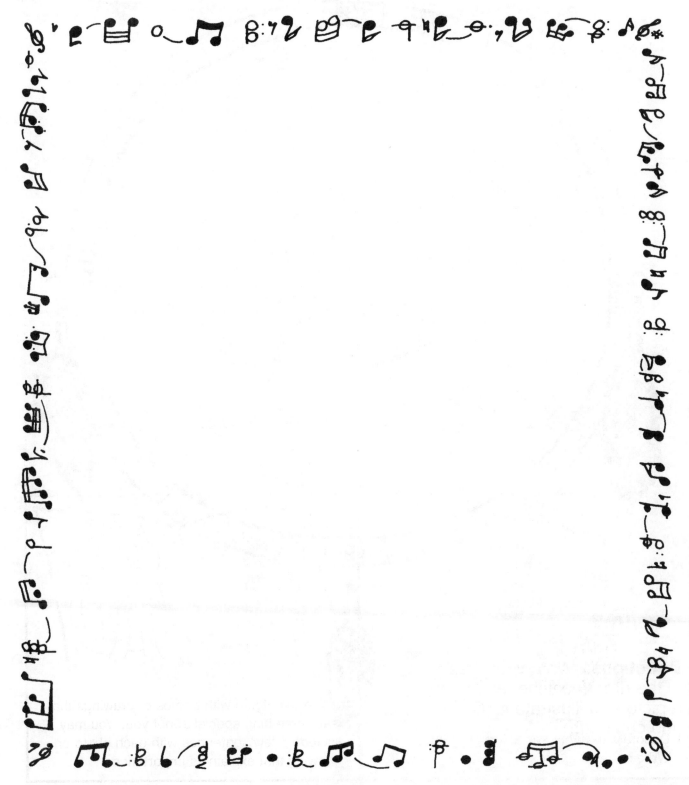

My Dream

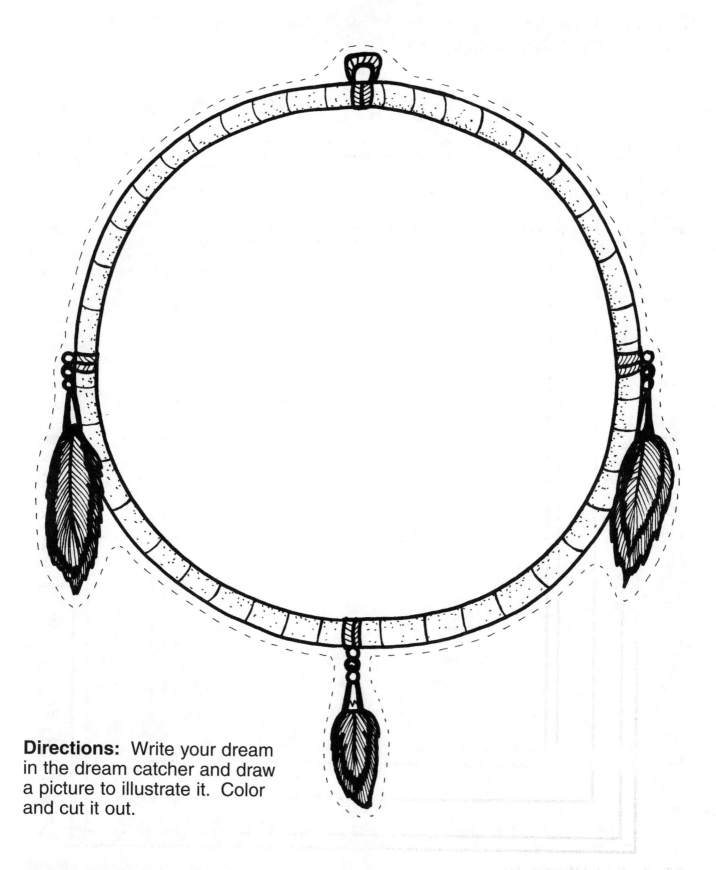

Directions: Write your dream in the dream catcher and draw a picture to illustrate it. Color and cut it out.

Who I Am

Cut out magazine pictures that would help others know you better (think of things and activities you like). Glue them onto this page.

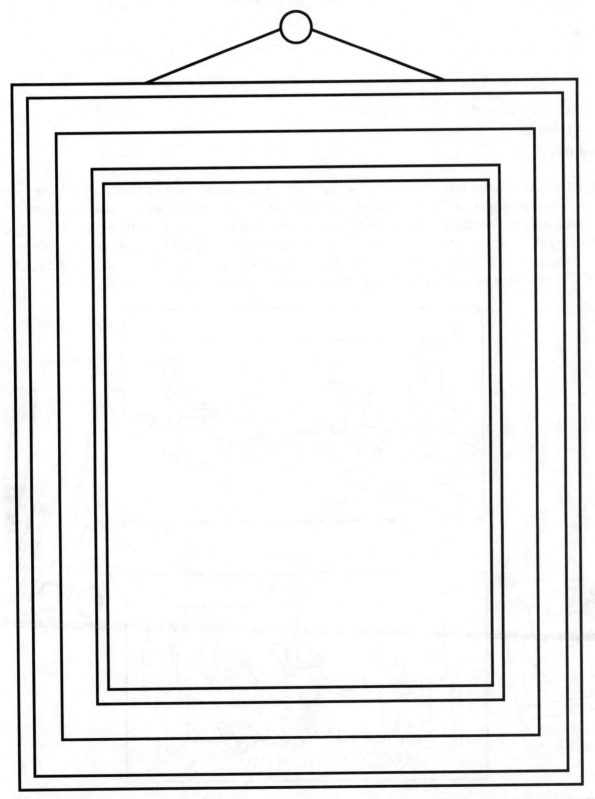

Favorite Sport Diorama

A diorama is a scene that is recreated inside a box. In this activity, you will be creating a diorama of your favorite sport. You may want your scene to be about something that actually happened to you or someone else, or you may want to create a totally new scene.

Materials

- empty boxes of assorted sizes
- glue and scissors
- construction paper of assorted sizes, colors, and shapes
- markers, crayons, colored pencils
- assorted craft materials

Procedures

Make a diorama of your favorite sport. Use the materials above to create a scene replicating your favorite sport being played. You will want to give some of your characters a three-dimensional appearance by standing them up in or on your diorama. You may want to draw a picture on paper before beginning the diorama to help you brainstorm an idea for your scene. Be sure to give your scene a title. When you are finished, display your diorama in your classroom. Some sample dioramas have been drawn below to help you get started. *Remember:* be original and be creative!

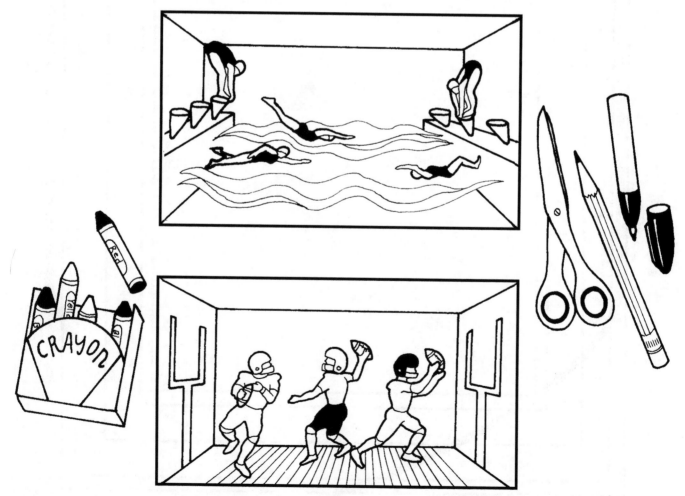

My Coat of Arms

Use the shield below to create your own coat of arms. Divide your shield into sections. Use symbols to show what is special about you.

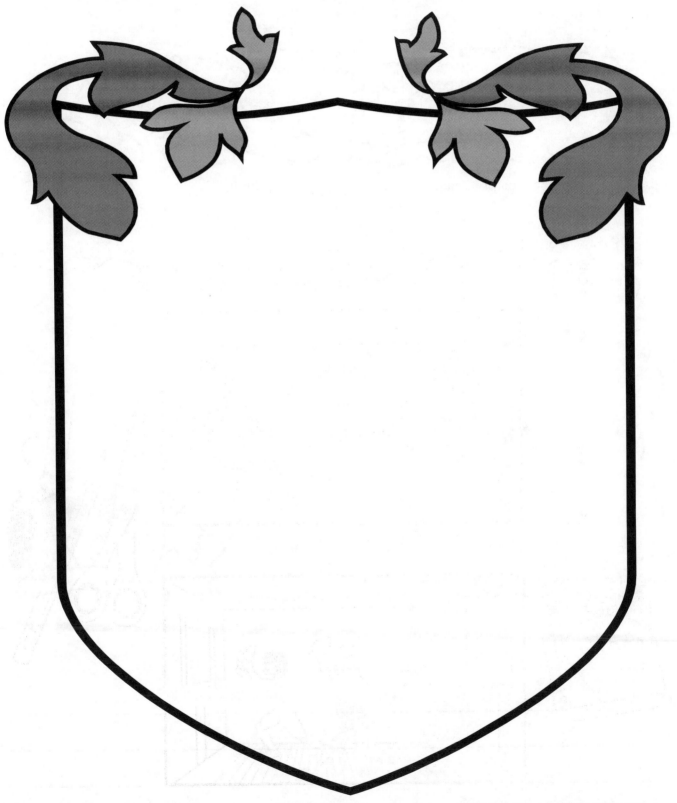

Dream On!

Once I dreamed that I rode on the back of a hippopotamus. Its skin was smooth and slick. The ride was bumpy across land. All of a sudden, the hippo walked right into the water and I got wet!

Describe a dream that you once had, and draw a picture to go with it.

_____

_____

_____

"Me" Collage

Day 1:   Collect or draw pictures about yourself below.

Day 2:   Cut the pictures. Add additional pictures and/or words that describe you. Arrange all in an interesting and appealing collage. Mount on construction paper.

Me	**My Home**
How I Get to School	**A Chore I Do**
My Family	**Something I'm Learning to Do**
A Time When I Did Something I Shouldn't Have Done	**Animals I Have**

Frida Kahlo

Frida Kahlo was born on July 6, 1907, in Coyoacan, Mexico, a small town near Mexico City. Her father, Guillermo, was a professional photographer and an amateur painter. He taught Frida about all the wonderful things in nature such as rocks, birds, insects, animals, and shells. In addition, he gave her lessons in photography and Mexican archaeology and art. From her mother, Matilde, Frida learned how to cook, sew, embroider, and keep a clean house.

When she was six years old, Frida contracted polio and was bedridden for nine months. During this time, she created an imaginary friend to help her through this lonely period in her life. With the encouragement of her father, Frida began to swim, skate, bicycle, and play ball to help strengthen her right leg which remained shorter than the other one. Some of her playmates made fun of her and called her "peg leg."

At age 15, Frida entered prep school where she planned to study to become a doctor. A tragic accident a few years later changed her life dramatically. When a trolley car hit her school bus, she was thrown into the street. Her injuries included broken ribs, spine, and collarbone. The most serious injury occurred when a steel handrail pierced her stomach. Frida was not expected to survive, but she was determined to live. Recovery was slow, and she was required to stay in bed. The doctor ordered her to wear a brace, and she was not allowed to sit up. Frida's mother had a special easel built so that she could paint from her prone position.

After her recuperation, Frida took her finished paintings to Diego Rivera, a famous Mexican artist. Diego not only encouraged her in her work, but he eventually married her. She began to take art more seriously and painted pictures that reflected her Mexican heritage. Still, her paintings reflected her sadness. Frida never fully recovered from the accident despite the many operations performed to straighten her spine and repair her foot. Often, she was in pain. Diego, her husband, did not always treat her well. In addition, she could not have children, a circumstance which saddened her most of all. These experiences and feelings were expressed in her paintings.

In her forties, Frida's health gradually failed. She died at the age of 47 on July 13, 1954. About a year before her death, however, she put on a major exhibit of her work. Her four-poster bed was moved into the art gallery and decorated with papier-mâché skeletons and photos of Diego and some of her political heroes. At the show's opening she wore a beautiful Mexican gown and was placed on the bed. Despite her ill health, she was determined to go out with a flourish. Today her paintings live on to tell the story of the tragedies and joys in her life.

The Little Deer

Note: Have students complete the following project after reading the information on page 376.

Focus: Frida Kahlo used art to fight life's obstacles.

Activity: creating a self-portrait to depict a problem or challenge

Vocabulary: Mexican art; self-portrait; surrealist

Materials

✦ drawing paper or construction paper

✦ scissors

✦ glue stick or white household glue

✦ old magazines

✦ pencils

✦ colored pencils or markers

Directions

1. Look closely at the picture *The Little Deer.* Tell the students to explain what the arrows in the deer's body might represent. Discuss the significance of the broken branch and the forest setting.

2. Direct the students to think of problems which they have had to overcome or to think of situations in their lives which have made them sad, angry, or disappointed.

3. Have the students look through the magazines and find a picture of an animal that best suits this feeling. Ask them to cut out the picture and glue it onto the drawing or construction paper.

4. Encourage students to draw an appropriate background scene and add any desired details to the animal.

Music Appreciation Week

Use the following activities to enhance your unit of study on music.

Class Symphony

Gather instruments, such as hardwood blocks, 4-inch (10 cm) triangles, 6-inch (15 cm) triangles, wrist bells, finger castanets, sand blocks, ankle bells, rhythm sticks, and different types of drums. Be sure there are enough instruments for every student to have one. Stress to students that this activity is not a time for them to aimlessly bang on instruments. In addition to music skills, students will be practicing how to listen and follow directions.

Have students sit in a circle with the instruments on the floor in the center of the circle. Ask one student at a time to select an instrument. Have students name the instruments they have chosen. Ask them to play their instruments, one at a time. This will help reinforce students' association of the names of the instruments with their sounds.

Have students sing songs such as "Old McDonald Had a Farm," "Hickory, Dickory, Dock;" or "Pop Goes the Weasel." Ask them to play their instruments as they sing the songs. Remind them to play softly so that the singing can be heard over the instruments. After students have played the instruments for a while, have them pass their instruments to the person sitting on their right. Regularly rotate the instruments in this manner to ensure that all students get to play the different kinds of instruments.

Musical Chairs

Arrange the chairs so that every student will have one to sit on when the music stops. Do not remove any of the chairs as in the traditional game of Musical Chairs. The purpose of this activity is to help students improve their listening skills rather than foster a feeling of competitiveness. Tell students that they must be sure to sit down when they hear the music stop. Remind them that everyone will have a place to sit. Point out that each time the music stops they will probably be sitting in a different chair.

Working Together

We work together when _____

_____

Draw a picture to show how you work together.

Puppet Dialogue

Choose a partner. Create two paper bag puppets (one for each partner). Decorate the puppets however you wish.

Now you are going to create a dialogue for your puppets. *A dialogue is a conversation between two or more people* (or puppets, in this case). Pretend your puppets can talk to each other. What will they say? Write your dialogue below. After you have practiced your complete dialogue, perform it with your puppets for the class!

Name your puppets!

Puppet #1_____　Puppet #2 _____

Place of Dialogue _____

Dialogue

Puppet #1: " _____

_____ "

Puppet #2: " _____

_____ "

Puppet #1: " _____

_____ "

Puppet #2: " _____

_____ "

Puppet #1: " _____

_____ "

Puppet #2: " _____

_____ "

Folk Dancing

In this activity, students will discover that dancing is a popular activity throughout the world. Use this page and page 382 to introduce some simple folk dances to your students.

Israeli Horae

Directions:

Step 1: Have students hold hands in a circle. Tell them that they will be moving to the left. (You might want to check to be sure all students know which way is left.)

Step 2: Have students step to the side with their left feet.

Step 3: Have them cross their right feet behind their left feet.

Step 4: Have students step to the side with their left feet.

Step 5: Have them cross their right feet in front of their left feet.

Step 6: Have students repeat Steps 2-5.

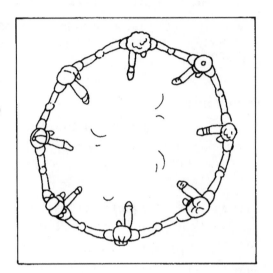

American Bunny Hop

Use music that has a fast beat (4/4).

Directions:

Step 1: Have students form a single line, one behind the other, and hold each other's waists.

Step 2: Have them take four running steps, beginning with the right foot.

Step 3: Have students take hops on their left feet.

Step 4: Have them stamp their feet: right-left-right.

Step 5: Have students kick to their right sides.

Step 6: Have them kick to their left sides.

Step 7: Have students hop backwards three times.

Step 8: Have students repeat Steps 2-7.

Folk Dancing *(cont.)*

Here are some more simple folk dances your students will enjoy learning.

Latin American Rumba

Use lively Latin American folk music that has a fast beat (4/4). The directions below indicate which way the boys should move. The girls' movements should mirror the boys'. If students have difficulty coordinating their dance steps with a partner, have them try the dance by themselves.

Directions:

Step 1: Assign a partner for each student. If possible, have each girl paired with a boy. If this is not possible, assign one student to play the part of the girl and the other student to play the part of the boy.

Step 2: Have the partners stand facing each other. Have the boys step forward with their left feet and push their weight onto them.

Step 3: Have the boys step to the right with their right feet and push their weight onto them.

Step 4: Have the boys move their left feet close to their right feet. Have them push their weight onto their left feet.

Step 5: Have the boys step back with their right feet and push their weight onto them.

Step 6: Have the boys step to the left with their left feet and push their weight onto them.

Step 7: Have the boys move their right feet close to their left feet. Have them push their weight onto the right feet. Then have students repeat Steps 2-7.

Greek Hapapikos

Use fast Greek music.

Directions:

Step 1: Have students form a circle with their hands on one another's shoulders. Have them move their right feet one step to the right side.

Step 2: Have students cross their left feet over their right feet.

Step 3: Have them move their right feet one step to the right.

Step 4: Have students hop on their right feet.

Step 5: Have students move their left feet one step to the left.

Step 6: Have them hop on their left feet. Have students repeat Steps 2-7.

Ways of Seeing

Action Drawing: The way to learn to draw is by drawing. Making art takes more than knowing about it, although you do need to know. A chemist may understand the chemical reactions in foods placed over high heat, but not be able to make a decent soup. He might not be able to sense what makes up a delicious taste, as would a skilled chef.

Drawing takes lots of drawing—sometimes furiously, sometimes by taking great pains—but always drawing.

Use a soft lead pencil (3B or 4B) with a blunt, thick point and lots of 10" by 15" (25 cm x 38 cm) sheets of newsprint. Have a model volunteer to stand in front of the class and move around freely— stretching, practicing moves in football, baseball, or basketball, stooping to pick up something, dancing. As the model moves, you draw NOT WHAT YOU SEE BUT WHAT THE MODEL IS DOING.

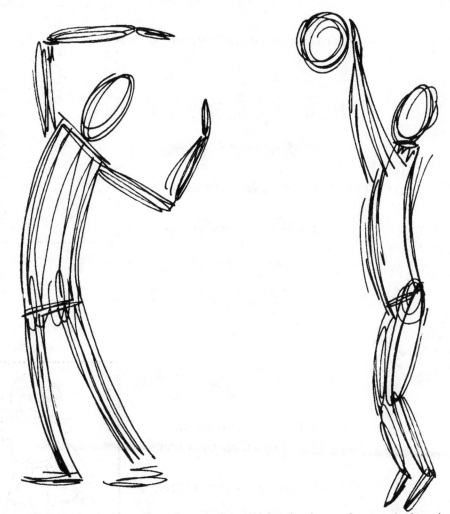

Feel how the model lifts or droops, pushes forward, pulls back, drops down. A drawing of a prize fighter would show the push, from foot to fist, behind his blows.

Yankee Doodle

Although it began as a British song used to make fun of the Americans, "Yankee Doodle" was adopted by the Americans as their own. They sang, whistled, and played it throughout the Revolutionary War. It could be heard as the British retreated from Concord as well as after their surrender at Yorktown.

It did not really matter which words were sung. Americans used the tune freely, composing their own lyrics for whatever the occasion called.

The version most people know is:

Yankee Doodle went to town,

Riding on a pony,

He stuck a feather in his cap

And called it macaroni.

Yankee Doodle keep it up,

Yankee Doodle dandy,

Mind the music and the step

And with the girls be handy.

Directions

As a class or in groups, choose one or more of the following ways to perform Yankee Doodle.

1. **PLAY IT!** Use kazoos, combs with wax paper wrapped around them, or other musical instruments.
2. **WHISTLE IT!** See if your class can whistle together in unison.
3. **SING IT!** Compose your own lyrics to create a funny song about something that happened at your school or in your classroom.

For any of these performance options, select a few students to add drums to create a more authentic sound.

Create a Greek Drama

Challenge your class to perform a short drama in Greek style with a chorus and only three actors.

Preparing for the lesson:

1. Divide the class into drama groups with seven or eight students in each group.

2. Choose appropriate material for the dramas, such as a reenactment of a famous Greek myth, or an original work written by the drama group. Another good source for short Greek plays is *Mythology I, Overhead Transparencies for Creative Dramatics* (Creative Teaching Press).

Teaching the lesson:

1. Tell the groups that they are going to perform a short Greek drama for the class. They will be evaluated on how well they tell the story and perform authentically with a chorus and actors wearing masks.

2. Assign each group a story to reenact. Discuss possible ways to structure the dramas.

   - The chorus enters and introduces the drama by giving necessary background information in unison speaking, chanting, singing, or dancing.

   - The actors enter and proceed with dialogue, wearing appropriate masks and costumes.

   - Each time a costume/mask change is needed, or when the plot changes scenes, the chorus should enter and describe through singing and dancing what is taking place. The chorus can also interject with sound effects or emphasis during the actors' dialogues.

   - Determine what the lesson is, and stage a climax scene depicting this.

   - The chorus ends the drama by explaining the moral and lessons expressed by the play.

3. Allow time for each group to assign three actors and a chorus. The actors will play all of the roles in the drama, so they will need to plan for simple costumes and mask changes. (See the following lesson on making Greek masks.) The chorus will need to plan simple dance/movements and appropriate messages for speaking in unison/singing to help narrate the action of the drama.

4. Have groups plan and practice their dramas. Sometimes it is easiest for the actors of the group to work separately from the chorus once the actual sequence of the drama has been established.

5. Have students perform their dramas for the class. Evaluate their ability to clearly tell the story and effectively use the chorus and actors. (You may wish to do this again during the section called Living History—A Day in Ancient Greece.)

Make a Greek Mask

Every Greek actor wore a mask while on stage. It was usually made from stiffened linen or cut out of cork. The expression was exaggerated so that the entire audience could see. The mouth was made with a large opening so that the actor could project his voice. When the actors changed parts or needed to show a different feeling, they simply changed masks. Have your students create Greek masks for display or to use in a drama of their own.

Preparing for the lesson:

1. Gather for each student a 9" x 12" (23 cm x 30 cm) sheet of stiff construction paper, colored construction paper scraps, scissors, glue, crayons, and markers.

2. Gather a hole puncher, yarn or elastic, and hole reinforcers.

Teaching the lesson:

1. Have student pairs hold construction paper against their partner's face and carefully mark the position of the eyes, nose, mouth, and chin. Tell them to let the paper extend at least two inches below the chin.

2. Have students decide on an expression for their mask. On the chalkboard, draw an example of the expressions and label them with the emotions they depict. Show students how to draw in the angle of the eyes, eyebrows, and mouth to help convey the expressions.

3. Have students cut out the eyes of the mask, make a wedge cut for the nose, and cut an enlarged mouth hole to allow clear speech. Tell them to round the bottom edge of their mask and cut the rest to a desired shape. Ears, hair, and other features and decorations can be added with other scraps of construction paper and crayons or markers.

4. Demonstrate for students how to cut two parallel slits at the chin of the mask about 1 inch (2 cm) apart from each other and overlap them to contour the mask. Then show them how to glue down the flap on top of the overlap.

5. Help students position their masks on their faces and then punch holes on either side, reinforce them, and add yarn or elastic to hold the masks in place.

Surprise

Anger/Evil

Sad

Happy/Love

Leaf Rubbings

Leaf rubbings make beautiful autumn decorations. They have the added advantage of not drying up and crumbling the way real autumn leaves do. Plan to make several because each one will be unique.

To make a leaf rubbing, follow the directions below.

Materials:

- drawing paper (white works the best)
- crayons (old ones without wrappers)
- a variety of leaves and other plant materials such as weeds and dried grasses.

Directions:

1. Lay down a sheet of paper and arrange your leaves and other plant materials on it. Experiment with moving them around until you find an arrangement you like.

2. Carefully place another sheet of paper on top of your leaf arrangement.

3. Hold on to the papers so they don't slip and, using the side of a crayon, rub it across the top paper until the shapes of the leaves start to show. Continue to rub until you get the effect you want.

4. You can vary the effect by changing crayons to a different color and by moving the arrangement around then repeating the coloring process.

Note: Autumn colors such as brown, orange, yellow, and red make effective rubbings. Mount your finished product on a sheet of construction paper in a color that sets the rubbing off to its best advantage.

Create a Colorful Bird

Materials: 1 piece of white construction paper per student; bird patterns; black crayons; watercolors and brushes; containers ¹/₃ full of water

Directions

Do this project after reading at least one book about the rain forest in which tropical birds are discussed. Review the tropical birds mentioned in the books with the class. Discuss their shapes and colors. Reproduce the pattern below onto tagboard. Have students trace the patterns with a pencil onto the white construction paper.

Conduct a vocabulary lesson by directing the students to add other features one by one in pencil. The features should include beaks, wings, tail, feathers, eye, feet, and a place to perch. Encourage creativity and variety within your directions. Have students trace over all lines with black crayon and then use watercolors to fill in the colors of the bird.

Rain Forest

Author: *Helen Cowcher*

Publisher: *Farrar, Straus and Giroux, 1988*

Summary: This is a beautifully illustrated view of the South American rain forest. Its lush vegetation and exotic animals depict a peaceful and ancient world. However, it is being invaded by powerful and threatening machinery run by man. Will it survive? This book poses that question and is a powerful plea to protect the delicate balance of nature.

Geographical Concepts and Vocabulary: map reading; South American rain forest; animal's adaptation to the environment; man's responsibility toward the environment

Getting Started

1. Find the rain forest area of South America on the map and on the globe.
2. Discuss the importance of the rain forests to the global environment.
3. Create a new butterfly. Remind the students that many insects and plants are still waiting to be identified. The rain forest has a wealth of unidentified living things. How sad it would be for a species to disappear from the earth before we even knew it had existed.

Materials: 12" x 18" (30 cm x 46 cm) construction paper; tempera paints and brushes; crayons or markers

Directions:

a. Fold the construction paper in half and open it.
b. Paint a half of a butterfly on one side of the paper only. Paint should be thick, not runny.
c. Add details with other colors.
d. While paint is still wet, fold the paper in half and rub gently with your hand to spread and blend the paint.
e. Let dry. Outline with black marker. Add details with other colors of crayons.
f. Give the butterfly a name.
g. Discuss how you would feel if your butterfly became extinct before anyone ever knew it existed.

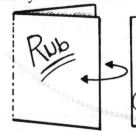
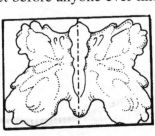

Create an Insect

This is an excellent and easy project that teaches science through art.

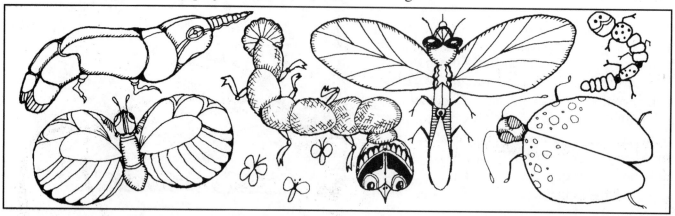

The rain forests of the earth have over 20,000,000 different types of insects. Many are as yet undiscovered and unnamed. Use the following characteristics and your imagination to create an insect. Be sure to give your discovery a name!

All insects have three body parts.

All insects have six legs.

Materials: construction paper scraps (lots of different colors); scissors; glue or paste; materials such as buttons, glitter, wiggle eyes, and chenille sticks to add features to the insect; 12" x 18" (30 cm x 45 cm) story paper

Directions:

1. Give each child three pieces of paper at least 3 inch (7.5 cm) squares. Have them cut out the three main body parts: head, thorax, and abdomen.
2. They should arrange the body parts and glue them onto a piece of writing paper.
3. Give each child paper or chenille sticks for the legs. Have them make six.
4. Have students glue the legs onto the insect.
5. They may then add details: eyes, feelers, wings using scraps of construction paper.
6. Children should write or dictate a story about insects.

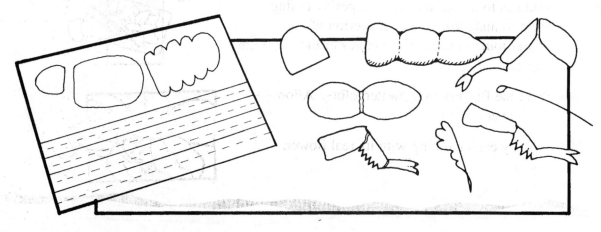

Oriental Poppies

Focus: Georgia O'Keefe's flowers filled up the canvas, giving the viewer an inside look at nature.

Activity: drawing a large picture of a flower

Vocabulary: abstract; Impressionism; avant-garde; landscape

Art Lesson

Materials

✦ watercolors

✦ paintbrushes

✦ fresh flowers

✦ magnifying glasses

✦ pencils

✦ 12" (30 cm) square sheet of drawing paper (can be larger)

Directions

1. Observe the details of an O'Keefe flower. Notice that stems and leaves may be missing, that the inside of the flower is the part that is emphasized.

2. Direct the students to choose a fresh flower for their model and to study it in detail.

3. Have them focus on an area of the flower to study with the magnifying glass.

4. When they are ready, tell the students to lightly pencil an outline of the magnified flower section on their paper. Encourage students to use up all of the paper by telling them to make sure that one section of the flower touches each of the edges of the paper.

5. Paint the flowers using watercolors. Allow the flowers to dry.

6. Display each painting with its real flower.

Beautiful Butterflies

(A Stained Glass Creation)

Materials:

- butterfly pattern on page 393
- 12" x 18" (30 x 46 cm) black construction paper
- old crayons
- plastic knife
- pencil sharpener
- wax paper
- newspaper (plenty to protect iron and work area)
- glue
- an iron
- yarn
- scissors

Directions:

1. Cut out the butterfly pattern on all solid lines. Take a sheet of 12" x 18" (30 cm x 46 cm) black construction paper and fold it in half, putting the short ends together. Trace the butterfly pattern onto the construction paper. Cut out the double paper so that you end up with two identical butterflies.

2. Using either the plastic knife or pencil sharpener, shave crayon bits onto a sheet of wax paper approximately 10 inches (25 cm) long.

3. Cover the shavings with another piece of wax paper the same size.

4. Carefully place wax paper "sandwich" onto a thick layer of newspaper and cover with another two sheets of newspaper.

5. Using an iron (set on the coolest setting), iron the wax paper together so that the shavings melt inside the wax paper.

6. Glue one butterfly cutout to the crayoned wax paper. Trim the excess wax paper.

7. Place the second butterfly directly on top of the first. Glue butterflies together so the wax paper is sandwiched between both halves.

8. Attach a piece of yarn to hang up your beautiful butterfly.

Beautiful Butterflies *(cont.)*

Butterfly Pattern

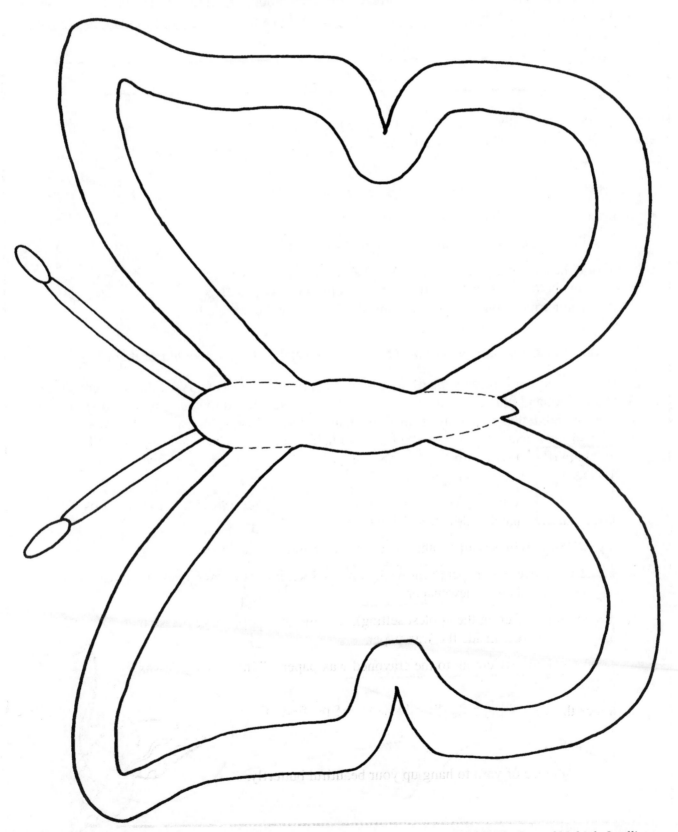

Insect Creations

Insects live nearly everywhere on earth. There are more than 800,000 kinds of insects already named by scientists. It is believed that the rain forests contain millions of types of insects, many of which are undiscovered and unclassified.

Activity

Use the following characteristics and your imagination to create an insect. Name it after the famous scientist who is first bringing it to the world's attention—you!

- All insects have three body parts—head, thorax, and abdomen.

- All insects have six jointed legs.

- The head has eyes, antennae, and a mouth that sucks or chews.

- The thorax has six legs (three on each side) and usually four wings. Some wings help an insect fly, and some wings protect. Wings are always symmetrical—one side is the same size, shape, and color as the other.

- The abdomen has ten or eleven segments. You can usually see five to eight of them.

Use the patterns below (or make some of your own) to create your insect. Trace them on construction paper, cut them out, and glue them together. Be sure your insect has three body parts and six jointed legs. Add color and details with crayon, markers, tissue paper, etc.

Teacher Created Materials
Book Reference Index

Language Arts

Social Sciences

Teacher Created Materials
Book Reference Index *(cont.)*

Mathematics

Science

Teacher Created Materials
Book Reference Index *(cont.)*

The Arts

Summary of the Multiple Intelligences

Verbal/Linguistic

Description: The verbal/linguistic intelligence is used in formal and informal speech and conversation. It is found anytime people put their thoughts on paper, whether in letters to friends or in creative writing. Storytelling and humor involving a play on words or twists of the language are also products of the verbal/linguistic intelligence. Understanding and using analogies, metaphors, similes, good grammar, and syntax are evidence of the verbal/intelligence in practice.

Students who are strong in the verbal/intelligence think in words and are good with language. They enjoy reading, writing, telling stories and jokes, and playing word games. They are effectively taught with books, tapes, writing stations, discussions, debates, and stories.

Logical/Mathematical

Description: In practice, the logical/mathematical intelligence is most evident when a person has to solve a problem. People often think of this intelligence as being scientifically oriented. Actually, we use the logical/mathematical intelligence when we recognize abstract patterns. It is this intelligence that enables us to count by twos and fives or to do the mental math calculations in a restaurant to figure how much of a tip to leave for a waiter or waitress. Recognizing relationships between two seemingly unrelated objects is also a product of the logical/mathematical intelligence. People who make lists, set priorities, or make long-range plans are using their logical/mathematical intelligence.

Students who are strong in the logical/mathematical intelligence area think by reasoning. They enjoy questions, figuring out logical problems, doing calculations, and experimenting. They are effectively taught by being given things to explore and think about, science centers, manipulatives, and by satisfying their curiosities.

Visual/Spatial

Description: The visual/spatial intelligence is at work when children use their imagination to play. The ability to follow written and diagrammed instructions to assemble products is also evidence of this intelligence area. People who can decorate a room of a house to produce a specific atmosphere are using the visual/spatial intelligence. We also use it when we draw, doodle, or express ourselves with pen or color without using words.

Students who are strong in the visual/spatial area think in images and pictures. They enjoy visualizing, drawing, doodling, and designing. They are effectively taught with imagination games, mazes, illustrated books, videos, slides, movies, and trips to see displays of their topics of study.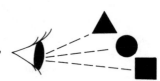

Summary of the Multiple Intelligences *(cont.)*

Bodily/Kinesthetic

Description: The bodily/kinesthetic intelligence is at work even when you are not aware of it. Reflex actions such as catching a falling object are a product of the bodily/kinesthetic intelligence. Driving a car is an activity that relies on the bodily/kinesthetic intelligence. A person does not have to consciously think about changing gears, braking, or turning. Once you have learned these skills, you can do it with relatively little thought. Any activity that requires gestures or bodily movement is also one that falls under this intelligence area. Athletes and dancers are professional people who use their bodily/kinesthetic intelligence to a great extent.

Students who are strong in the bodily/kinesthetic intelligence area think through somatic sensations. They enjoy running, moving, building, touching, and gesturing. They learn effectively through role play, drama, sports, and physical games, tactile experiences, and hands-on learning.

Musical/Rhythmic

Description : The musical/rhythmic intelligence is at work when we listen to music to help us relax or hurry up. Music is used for exercise routines, for marching, and sleeping (lullabies). Our ability to remember advertisement jingles is a product of the musical/ rhythmic intelligence. When a person uses music to communicate feelings and beliefs or to express patriotism or reverence, it is also a use of this intelligence. Composers and performers are professional people who use their musical/rhythmic intelligence at high levels.

Students who are strong in the musical/rhythmic intelligence think in rhythms and melodies. They enjoy singing, whistling, humming, tapping their feet and hands, and listening. They learn most effectively through sing-along time, musical experiences at school and home, and by being involved in music programs (choir, band, instruments, etc.).

Interpersonal

Description: The interpersonal intelligence is at work when we discern and understand differences in other people's actions, moods, and feelings. This includes accurately interpreting facial expressions, voices, and physical gestures. We are also using the interpersonal intelligence anytime we are part of a team. Our ability to effectively communicate verbally and nonverbally with others is a product of our interpersonal intelligence. When we are able to influence a person or group of people by what we say or do, it is a direct use of this intelligence. People who use their interpersonal intelligence to a high degree are political leaders, teachers, and counselors.

Students who are strong in the interpersonal intelligence think by proposing ideas to other people. They enjoy leading, organizing, relating, mediating, and socializing. They learn effectively through working with friends, groups, games, social gatherings, clubs, apprenticeships, and community events.

Summary of the Multiple Intelligences *(cont.)*

Intrapersonal

Description: We use our intrapersonal intelligence when we step back and watch ourselves, almost like outside observers. Our ability to understand ourselves, our feelings, thoughts, ideas, and perceptions, all involve the intrapersonal intelligence. Goal setting, planning for the future, recognizing our position in a larger order of things, and dealing with higher states of consciousness are all products of our intrapersonal intelligence. This is probably the area in which we recognize and practice spirituality, although Howard Gardner suggest that this (spirituality) might, at some time, be added as an eighth intelligence.

Students who are strong in the intrapersonal intelligence area think deeply inside themselves. They enjoy setting goals, dreaming, being quite, and planning. They learn most effectively in secret places by having time alone, by working on self-paced projects, and by having choices.

Naturalist

Description: The Naturalist Intelligence can be illustrated in the work of the world's great biologists. It is the intellectual home to those who seem to have not only ability but also a driving need to master taxonomy.

Some see trees...those possessed with a high degree of Naturalist Intelligence see elms and birches...and not only birches, but particular kinds of birches. These individuals seem to understand similarities and differences between species of flora and fauna and can easily recognize patterns in nature.

Asked to explain such intellect, Gardner was left to either piece together bits of several intelligences or test whether this intelligence met the tests designed for the original seven. His most recent work and judgment is that the most comfortable explanation is to view this intelligence as a full partner with the original seven.

Not only do those particularly gifted in this intelligence seem able to classify and categorize, to note and make distinctions in the natural world, but such folk also seek to use this intelligence productively in our world. This intelligence not only has value today, but was demonstrated in our evolutionary past by hunters and gatherers, farmers and environmentalists who sought not only intellectual knowledge, but also the knowledge required for survival.

Like all other intelligences, we all possess these abilities, with uneven depth and intensity, even from a very early age; and like all other intelligences we can grow in our ability to develop more sopistication and depth.